EXPLORING SCIENCE
INTERNATIONAL 11-14
PHYSICS

Penny Johnson, Mark Levesley

Pearson

CONTENTS

HOW TO USE THIS BOOK

You should be able to answer the question at the top of the page by the time you have finished the page.

Fact boxes contain fascinating facts for you to think about.

The **Key words** for the page are in bold. You can look up the meaning of these words in the **Glossary**, on pages 185–190.

Questions are spread throughout the page so you can answer them as you go along.

If you are having trouble finding information about something, use the **Index**, on pages 193–194.

I can ... boxes help you to reflect on what you have learned. Consider each statement carefully and think about how well this applies to you.

7Ic FUELS

WHERE DO FUELS COME FROM?

A **fuel** is a substance that contains a store of chemical or nuclear energy that can easily be transferred. Most fuels are burnt to release the energy they store, and the energy is transferred to the surroundings by heating. Burning a fuel does not make energy, it only transfers it. **Nuclear fuels**, such as **uranium**, release energy in a different way.

Energy from the fuels used in power stations is transferred to homes, schools, factories and offices using electricity. We say that the electricity is **generated** in power stations.

1 a| What is a fuel? b| Name three fuels.

2 Write down three things humans use fuels for.

A | The energy for lighting is transferred by electricity from power stations.

FACT
1 kg of nuclear fuel stores around 3 500 000 times as much energy as 1 kg of coal.

Fossil fuels

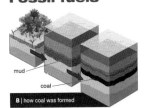

mud
coal

B | how coal was formed

Fossil fuels are made from the remains of **organisms** that died millions of years ago. **Coal** was formed many millions of years ago from plants. When the plants died they became buried in mud, which stopped them from rotting away. More layers of the mud squashed the plant remains. This squashing, together with heat from inside the Earth, turned the mud into rock and the plant remains into coal.

C | The food van uses energy stored in the chemicals in the bottled **gas**. The gas is made from oil.

Oil and **natural gas** formed from tiny animals and plants that lived in the sea millions of years ago. These fell to the sea bed when they died and got buried in mud and sand. More layers of mud and sand fell on top of them and squashed them, turning them into crude oil and natural gas. Fuels such as petrol and diesel are made from oil.

12

Coal, oil and natural gas are **non-renewable** fuels because they cannot be replaced at the rate that humans use them up. It takes many millions of years for them to form and so our supplies will eventually run out.

3 Look at graph D.
a| Which fossil fuel will run out first?
b| Why do you think the bars on the graph have no definite end?

4 a| Write down two similarities between the formation of coal and oil.
b| Write down one difference.

How the time left varies for different fuels

oil
gas
coal

0   50   100   150   200
Years until the fuel runs out

D | Scientists are not certain how long the different non-renewable fuels will last. It depends on how fast we use them, and whether more sources are discovered.

Other fuels

Biofuels are made from plants or the wastes from animals. They are **renewable** fuels, because more plants can be grown to make more fuel.

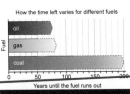
F | In some countries, animal wastes are dried to be used as a **solid** fuel. Animal and plant wastes can also be turned into methane, the main substance in natural gas.

E | Crops can be grown to make biofuel. Some biofuels are made out of waste cooking oil, which originally came from plants.

G | This car has an electric motor. A fuel cell in the car combines hydrogen with **oxygen** from the air to produce electricity.

Gases such as **hydrogen** can also be used as fuel. At the moment, most hydrogen is made from natural gas, but scientists are trying to find ways of making it cheaply from water.

5 A friend of yours says, 'Electricity is a fuel'. Explain why your friend is wrong.

6 Fossil fuels are being formed slowly in the Earth today, so why are fossil fuels called non-renewable fuels?

I can ...
- describe what fossil fuels are and how they were made
- explain why fossil fuels are described as non-renewable
- name some renewable fuels

13

7|a ENERGY AND CHANGES

A

There are a lot of things happening in a theme park. Almost everything that happens involves **energy** in some way. For example, your body needs energy to stay alive, and to allow you to move around. Energy is needed to make all the rides in the theme park work. The energy needed is stored in food and in fuels, such as petrol.

B | Food is a store of energy.

1. Which of the rides shown in photo A needs the most energy and which the least energy? Explain your answers.

2. a| Write down five different things that are happening in photos A and B that need energy.

   b| How is energy provided for these things to happen?

3. a| Write down five things you did yesterday that needed energy.

   b| Which of these things do you think needed the most energy, and which needed the least energy? How do you know?

7la ENERGY FROM FOOD

HOW DO OUR BODIES USE ENERGY?

Humans and other animals need energy to live. We need energy to help us to grow and repair our bodies, and to move and keep warm. Our bodies use food as a source of energy.

The unit for measuring energy is the **joule (J)**. The amount of energy needed to lift an apple from the floor onto a table is about 1 J. Most foods contain a lot more energy than this, so we usually measure the energy in foods using **kilojoules (kJ)**. 1 kJ = 1000 J.

Nutrition Information		
Typical values	Per bun (65g)	Per 100g
Energy	544 kJ/130 kcal	837 kJ/200 kcal
Protein	6 g	9.2 g
Carbohydrate (of which sugar)	21 g (4 g)	32.3 g (6.2 g)
Fat (of which saturates)	2.5 g (0 g)	3.85 g (0 g)
Fibre	1.2 g	1.8 g
Sodium	0.2 g	0.3 g

Nutrition Information		
Typical values	Per falafel burger (125 g)	Per 100g
Energy	1990 kJ/476 kcal	1592 kJ/381 kcal
Protein	17 g	13.6 g
Carbohydrate (of which sugar)	63 g (5 g)	50 g (4 g)
Fat (of which saturates)	15 g (2 g)	12 g (1.6 g)
Fibre	7 g	5.6 g
Sodium	2 g	1.6 g

A | Nutrition information labels show how much energy is stored in food.

1 Why does your body need food?

2 a| How much energy does 100 g of falafel burger contain? Give your answer in kilojoules.

b| Mark eats two burgers (each burger is one falafel burger in a bun). How much energy is in the food he eats?

B

Different people need different amounts of energy. Your body needs energy to help it to grow. You also need energy to move around. If you do a lot of exercise, you need more energy than if you spend most of your time watching television.

A good **diet** should provide only the amount of energy that a person's body needs. If the diet contains more energy than the person needs, the body will store the energy in fat and the person will gain **weight**. If the diet does not contain enough energy the person will lose weight and become thinner. A good **balanced diet** also provides all the **nutrients** that the body needs for health, and includes a **mixture** of different foods.

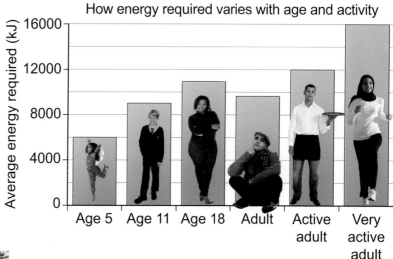

How energy required varies with age and activity

C | Different people have different daily energy needs.

D | Mountain climbers need to take their food with them. They need to take food that will give them about 19 000 kJ per day.

FACT

E

Koalas live in Australia, and feed on eucalyptus leaves. The leaves do not provide much energy, so koalas sleep for around 20 hours every day.

3 a| Suggest why a teenager needs more energy than a 5-year-old child.

b| Why do you think a pregnant woman needs more energy from food than a woman who is not pregnant?

4 a| Write down these people in order of the energy they need, starting with the one who needs the least energy: baby, fire-fighter, secretary, 11-year-old child.

b| Explain your answer to part a.

5 a| A 5-year-old only eats buns. How much would he have to eat each day to get the energy he needs?

b| If he only ate falafel burgers, how much would he have to eat each day?

c| Why shouldn't you always eat only one type of food?

6 Explain the link between the amount of food someone eats, the amount of activity they carry out and the amount of weight they gain.

7 Look at photo E. How will the amount of time koalas spend asleep affect the amount of food they need to find?

8 Scientists can measure the amount of energy stored in different foods. How can this knowledge help mountain climbers and explorers?

I can ...

- recall that our bodies need energy, which we get from food
- explain why different people need different amounts of energy from food
- recall that the units for measuring energy are joules (J) or kilojoules (kJ). 1 kJ = 1000 J.

7

FAIR COMPARISONS 71a AND RATIOS

HOW CAN YOU COMPARE THE ENERGY STORED IN DIFFERENT FOODS?

You can compare the amount of energy stored in different foods by burning them. Photo B shows the kind of **apparatus** you need. The energy released by the burning food heats the water in the boiling tube. The higher the temperature of the water, the more energy the food released when it was burnt.

A | Different foods contain different amounts of energy.

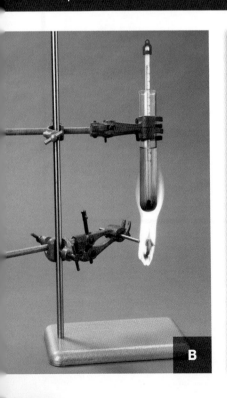

B

Method

A | Find the mass of a piece of food.

B | Carefully put the food on a pin (which has its other end in a piece of cork).

C | Put 10 cm³ of water into a boiling tube. Record its temperature.

D | Light the food using a Bunsen burner, and hold the burning food under the boiling tube. Make sure the flame is touching the boiling tube.

E | When the food has finished burning, record the temperature of the water again.

F | Let the food cool down, then carefully push what is left off the pin and find its mass. If there is no food left on the pin, write down 0 g for its mass.

G | Repeat steps A to F for other foods.

 Wear eye protection.
Do not eat any of the foods.
Do not use nuts.

Table C shows the results of an investigation. The student has used the masses of food at the beginning and end to work out the **mass** of each food burnt, and has also calculated the change in temperature.

C	Food used	Mass of food burnt (g)	Temperature rise (°C)
	bread	2.0	4.0
	cheese	4.0	16.0
	cornflakes	4.0	14.0
	crackers	1.0	4.5

Burning 4 g of cheese made the temperature of the water rise by 16 °C. What would be the temperature rise if only 1 g of cheese had been burnt?

1
a| Look at tables C and D. Write down the foods in order of the temperature rise, starting with the lowest (bread).

b| Now write down the foods in order of the temperature rise per gram of food.

c| Which list is the best comparison of the amounts of energy stored in the different foods? Explain your answer.

Ratios

Ratios can help us to compare the energy stored by different foods. The investigation shows that 1 g of bread raises the temperature of the water by 2 °C, and 1 g of cheese raises it by 4 °C. We can write these numbers as a ratio like this:

	temperature rise for 1 g bread (°C)		temperature rise for 1 g cheese (°C)
	2	:	4
E	1	:	2

It is easier to understand the ratio if one number is a 1. Simplify the ratio by dividing *both* sides by the smallest number needed to make one side become 1.

So we can write the ratio as 1:2. This shows that cheese raises the temperature of the water by twice as many degrees as bread.

Comparing results

Table C shows that burning the cheese produced the greatest change in water temperature. However, it is not a fair test because different masses of each food were burnt.

We can make a fair comparison of the results by working out the temperature rise for each **gram (g)** of food burnt. We do this by dividing the temperature difference by the mass of food. Table D shows the results of this calculation.

D	Food used	Temperature rise per gram of food (°C/g)
	bread	2.0
	cheese	4.0
	cornflakes	3.5
	crackers	4.5

2 The student also tested diet crispbreads in the investigation. The temperature rise per gram was 1.0 °C. What is the ratio of the temperature rise caused by the crispbreads compared with:

a| the bread   b| the cheese?

3 A student says 'I would get the same energy from eating 50 g of bread or 25 g of cheese.' Is the student correct? Explain your answer.

4 Pears store 175 kJ of energy per 100 g of fruit, and bananas store 350 kJ per 100 g. Calculate the ratio of the energy stored in the two kinds of fruit.

I can ...

- make a fair comparison of results
- calculate ratios

ENERGY TRANSFERS
71b AND STORES

HOW IS ENERGY STORED AND MOVED?

Energy can be stored. For example, energy is stored in the chemical substances in food, petrol and **cells** (batteries). We call this **chemical energy**. Things happen when energy *moves* from a store. We say that the energy is **transferred**.

This can happen by:

- heating - light - sound - **electricity** - **forces**.

> **1** Write down three things that:
>
> a| transfer energy by heating or light
>
> b| transfer energy by sound
>
> c| use energy transferred by electricity.

Many machines allow energy stores to be transferred into energy stored in other ways. For example, moving objects store energy. We call this **kinetic energy**.

| energy stored in the chemical substances in diesel fuel | → | fairground ride transfers energy by electricity and forces | → | energy stored in the moving people and ride ('kinetic energy') |

B | Many fairground rides are powered by diesel generators. Energy is stored in the substances that make up the diesel fuel. Energy from the burning fuel is transferred by electricity and forces to the ride. The flow diagram represents the energy transfers.

A | The chemical substances inside the firework rocket store energy. When the firework goes off, energy is transferred by light, sound and heating.

When energy is transferred, it is not used up. Energy cannot be created or destroyed; it can only be transferred and stored in different ways. This is called the **law of conservation of energy**.

> **2** Diesel fuel is a store of energy in chemicals. Write down three other things that store energy in chemicals.

Energy can be stored in other ways. A hot object can be a store of **thermal energy**.

Energy is stored whenever something springy is squashed, stretched, bent or twisted. We call this **strain energy**, or **elastic potential energy**. A stretched elastic band is storing energy in this way.

Anything in a high position stores energy. We call this **gravitational potential energy**. It took energy to move the object up to its high position, and this energy can be transferred again when the object falls.

Energy is stored inside all materials. Some materials can transfer this energy in nuclear power stations. We call this **nuclear energy** (or **atomic energy**). This energy store cannot be transferred by burning. Nuclear power stations use this energy to produce electricity. The Sun also contains a store of nuclear energy, some of which is transferred to the Earth by heating and light.

D | The carriage is storing gravitational potential energy when it is at the top of the track.

C | The passenger car is attached to two bungee (elastic) cords. The car is pulled down so that energy is stored in the stretched bungees. This energy is transferred by forces to a store of movement (kinetic) energy when the bungee cords are released.

3 Write down three different ways in which energy can be stored as strain energy.

4 Look at photo C. Copy and complete the flow diagram below to show the energy transfers.

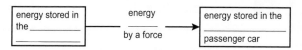

| energy stored in the _____ _____ | energy _____ by a force → | energy stored in the _____ passenger car |

5 The flow diagram below shows the energy changes and transfers for a room being heated by an electric fire. The electricity comes from a nuclear power station.

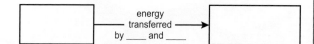

energy transferred by ____ and ____

a| Copy the diagram and label the two energy stores (in the squares) and the energy transfers (on the arrow).

b| 2000 J of energy goes into the electric fire every second. How much energy is transferred out of it? Explain your answer.

c| Draw a similar diagram for a car travelling along a road.

I can ...

- describe the different ways in which energy is transferred
- describe different ways in which energy is stored
- recall the law of conservation of energy.

7Ic FUELS

WHERE DO FUELS COME FROM?

A **fuel** is a substance that contains a store of chemical or nuclear energy that can easily be transferred. Most fuels are burnt to release the energy they store, and the energy is transferred to the surroundings by heating. Burning a fuel does not make energy, it only transfers it. **Nuclear fuels**, such as **uranium**, release energy in a different way.

Energy from the fuels used in power stations is transferred to homes, schools, factories and offices using electricity. We say that the electricity is **generated** in power stations.

A | The energy for lighting is transferred by electricity from power stations.

> **1** a| What is a fuel? b| Name three fuels.
>
> **2** Write down three things humans use fuels for.

Fossil fuels

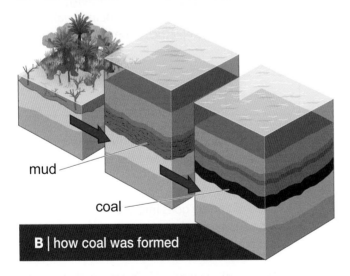

mud

coal

B | how coal was formed

Oil and **natural gas** formed from tiny animals and plants that lived in the sea millions of years ago. These fell to the sea bed when they died and got buried in mud and sand. More layers of mud and sand fell on top of them and squashed them, turning them into crude oil and natural gas. Fuels such as petrol and diesel are made from oil.

FACT

1 kg of nuclear fuel stores around 3 500 000 times as much energy as 1 kg of coal.

Fossil fuels are made from the remains of **organisms** that died millions of years ago. **Coal** was formed many millions of years ago from plants. When the plants died they became buried in mud, which stopped them from rotting away. More layers of the mud squashed the plant remains. This squashing, together with heat from inside the Earth, turned the mud into rock and the plant remains into coal.

C | The food van uses energy stored in the chemicals in the bottled **gas**. The gas is made from oil.

Coal, oil and natural gas are **non-renewable** fuels because they cannot be replaced at the rate that humans use them up. It takes many millions of years for them to form and so our supplies will eventually run out.

> **3** Look at graph D.
>
> a| Which fossil fuel will run out first?
>
> b| Why do you think the bars on the graph have no definite end?
>
> **4** a| Write down two similarities between the formation of coal and oil.
>
> b| Write down one difference.

How the time left varies for different fuels

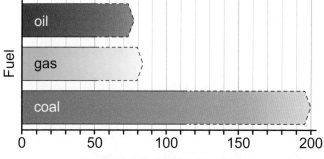

D | Scientists are not certain how long the different non-renewable fuels will last. It depends on how fast we use them, and whether more sources are discovered.

Other fuels

Biofuels are made from plants or the wastes from animals. They are **renewable** fuels, because more plants can be grown to make more fuel.

F | In some countries, animal wastes are dried to be used as a **solid** fuel. Animal and plant wastes can also be turned into methane, the main substance in natural gas.

Gases such as **hydrogen** can also be used as fuel. At the moment, most hydrogen is made from natural gas, but scientists are trying to find ways of making it cheaply from water.

> **5** A friend of yours says, 'Electricity is a fuel'. Explain why your friend is wrong.
>
> **6** Fossil fuels are being formed slowly in the Earth today, so why are fossil fuels called non-renewable fuels?

E | Crops can be grown to make biofuel. Some biofuels are made out of waste cooking oil, which originally came from plants.

G | This car has an electric motor. A fuel cell in the car combines hydrogen with **oxygen** from the air to produce electricity.

I can ...

- describe what fossil fuels are and how they were made
- explain why fossil fuels are described as non-renewable
- name some renewable fuels.

HOW DO TRANSPORT MANAGERS WORK?

Goods in a supermarket come from many places. The companies who make the goods employ transport managers to make sure their products get to the shops on time. Goods that need to be moved a very long way are often transported by aeroplane or ship. Goods that only need to be carried a short distance are moved by rail or road.

Almost every kind of business uses goods or materials that have to be transported.

A | Transport managers help to make sure the shelves are always full.

B | Many goods are delivered to shops using trucks or vans.

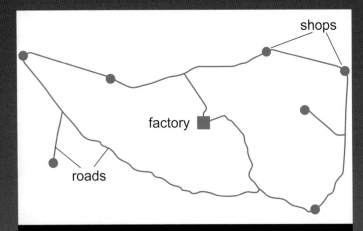

C | a map showing a factory and seven shops that sell goods made in the factory

> **1**
> a | Write down three different businesses in your town. These can be shops or factories.
> b | Write down three different things that need to be taken to or from each of these places.

Transporting goods cheaply

Businesses need to make a profit. They do this by selling their goods for more money than it costs to make and deliver them. A transport manager has to work out how to keep the cost of moving things around as low as possible.

Transport managers decide the number of trucks needed to deliver the goods, what kind of trucks to buy, and what type of fuel they should use. They also work out the best routes, so the trucks use as little fuel as possible. One way of solving problems like this is to think of several different solutions, then compare the advantages and disadvantages of each one.

2 Look at map C. A transport manager is deciding whether she should buy one or two trucks to make deliveries to the shops. She needs to compare the costs of the two options. Write down three things she needs to take into account to make this comparison.

3 A food company delivers fresh vegetables to 40 shops in four different towns. It costs more to buy four small vans than to buy one big truck. Suggest why the transport manager decides to buy four vans.

It is difficult to work out the best routes when trucks have to make deliveries to a lot of places. Transport companies use computer models to work this out.

Careers in transport

Transport managers usually have a university degree in a technical or mathematical subject. They need to be good at solving problems and using reasoning and mathematics to work out the best ways of delivering goods. They need to communicate their decisions clearly to other workers, such as drivers and warehouse staff.

D | GPS navigation systems use computer models to compare different routes and choose the fastest one.

4 Suggest what information a computer model uses to work out a route.

ACTIVITY

1 Lorries can run on fuels including petrol, hydrogen and biofuel. Fuels release their energy when they burn.

You could investigate the amount of energy released by each fuel by:

- carrying out your own experiment to get primary data

- using the results of other people's experiments (secondary data).

a Make a list of the advantages and disadvantages for each approach.

b Explain which approach you would use.

2 Map E shows five different locations (A to E), and the distances between them in kilometres. Work out the shortest route from A to D.

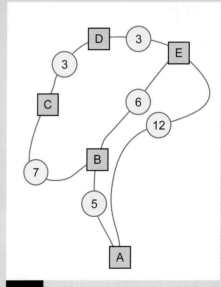

E

7Id OTHER ENERGY RESOURCES

WHAT OTHER ENERGY RESOURCES ARE AVAILABLE?

Biofuels are a renewable energy **resource**. Some biofuels are used in cars and other vehicles, and some are used for heating, cooking or generating electricity.

1 Why can biofuels be described as renewable resources?

Other renewable energy resources can be used for heating, but most are used to generate electricity.

Solar power uses energy transferred from the Sun. **Solar panels** consist of tubes full of water, which heat up. These can be placed on roofs and the hot water used to heat the building or to provide hot water for washing. **Solar cells** use energy transferred by light to produce electricity directly. Electricity can also be produced using solar energy by using mirrors in a **solar power station**.

A | This ride runs on biodiesel.

B | These solar cells are being used to provide electricity for Europa-Park in Rust, Germany.

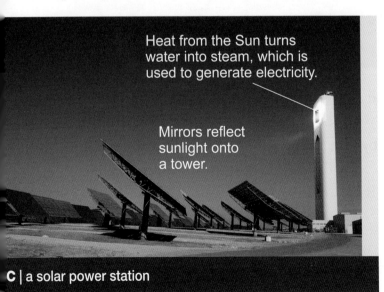

Heat from the Sun turns water into steam, which is used to generate electricity.

Mirrors reflect sunlight onto a tower.

C | a solar power station

FACT

Wind turbines would need to cover an area the size of 53 000 soccer pitches to produce the same energy as one nuclear power station.

Wind turbines use the wind to turn large blades, and the blades turn a generator. Moving water can be used to generate electricity in a **hydroelectric power** station. Waves and tides can also be used to generate electricity.

In some places, rocks under the ground are hot. Water can be heated by pumping it through the rocks. This is called **geothermal power**.

Most renewable resources are not available all of the time, because they depend on the weather. Only hydroelectricity and geothermal power are available at any time; however, these resources can only be used in locations with a suitable place for a reservoir or hot rocks underground.

2 Write down three ways in which solar power can be used.

3 Write down three examples of using water to generate electricity.

Nuclear energy from the Sun

Nearly all the energy stored in our energy resources originally came from the Sun. The Sun is a store of nuclear energy, and some of this is transferred by light and heating. We use some of this energy directly in solar panels and solar cells.

Sunlight also provides the energy for plants to grow. The energy is needed for **photosynthesis**. This is the process by which plants make their own food using **carbon dioxide** from the atmosphere.

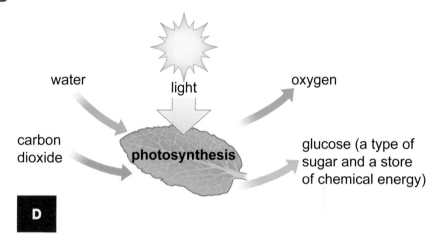

water — light — oxygen

carbon dioxide — **photosynthesis** — glucose (a type of sugar and a store of chemical energy)

D

The energy in fossil fuels came from the bodies of the plants and animals from which the fuels were formed. The animals got their energy from the plants that they ate, and the plants got their energy from the Sun.

Clouds form from water evaporated by the heat of the Sun. Eventually the water falls back to Earth as rain. Hydroelectric power therefore depends on the Sun. Energy from the Sun also causes the wind and waves. The only energy resources we use that do not depend on the Sun are nuclear fuels, tidal power and geothermal power.

FACT

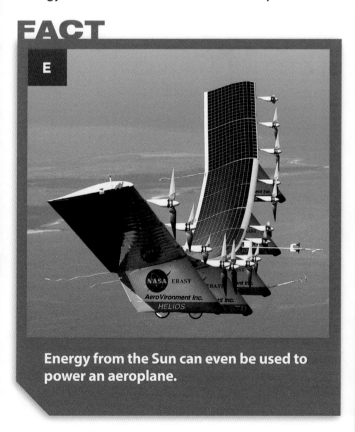

E

Energy from the Sun can even be used to power an aeroplane.

4 The energy stored in a bowl of cornflakes and milk originally came from the Sun. Explain how the energy got into the cornflakes and milk.

5 Bunsen burners use energy stored in natural gas. Explain where this energy came from originally, and how it came to be stored in the gas.

6 Most renewable energy resources are not available all of the time. Write down the renewable resources that:

a| depend on the weather

b| are available at any time

c| are only available at certain times of the day or night.

I can ...

- give some examples of renewable energy resources
- explain how the Sun is the original source of energy for most of our energy resources
- recall which energy resources do not depend on the Sun.

7Ie USING RESOURCES

WHICH ENERGY RESOURCES SHOULD WE USE?

Energy resources are stores of energy that we can use. There are advantages and disadvantages to renewable and non-renewable resources.

Energy resource	Advantages	Disadvantages
fossil fuels (used to generate electricity, to power transport and for heating)	■ cheap compared with other resources ■ convenient to use in cars and other vehicles	■ release polluting gases when they burn ■ non-renewable
nuclear (used to generate electricity)	■ no polluting gases	■ power stations are very expensive ■ produces dangerous waste materials ■ non-renewable
renewable resources (mainly used to generate electricity)	■ no polluting gases ■ renewable	■ most are not available all of the time

A | some advantages and disadvantages of different kinds of energy resource

1 What does non-renewable mean?

2 a| Name two renewable energy resources that are not available all the time.

b| Explain why they are not available all the time.

Climate change

Most of the energy we use comes from burning fossil fuels. Most scientists who study the climate think that fossil fuels are helping to make the Earth warmer because a gas called carbon dioxide is produced when they burn. Extra carbon dioxide in the atmosphere makes the Earth warmer.

We can reduce the amount of carbon dioxide we add to the atmosphere by using less fossil fuel. This will also help to make our supplies of fossil fuels last longer.

B | Some people object to wind farms because they say they kill a lot of birds.

Wear a jumper instead of keeping the house very warm in winter.

Using less ...

Walk, cycle or use public transport instead of using a car.

Use efficient appliances when you can. Labels on appliances show you how efficient they are.

Insulate homes so that less energy escapes by heating, or is needed for cooling.

3 a| Describe three ways in which we could use less fossil fuel.
b| Give two reasons why it is important to use less fossil fuel.

Efficiency

Energy cannot be created or destroyed, but not all the energy transferred by a machine ends up as useful stores of energy. Some of it is wasted. The carriages in photo D are being moved to the top of the ride using an electric motor. Flow diagram E shows the energy transferred.

Energy cannot be created or destroyed, so all the energy transferred by the electricity is still there. The wasted energy is spread out in the surroundings.

Efficiency is a way of saying how much of the energy transferred by a machine is useful. An efficient machine does not waste much energy. If you use a more efficient machine there will be less wasted energy. This means that less fossil fuel will be burnt to produce the electricity to run it, and your electricity bills will also be cheaper.

D

energy transferred to the ride by electricity

→ energy stored in the carriages as they get higher (gravitational potential energy) — useful energy transferred

→ energy stored in the motor and surroundings, which get warmer (thermal energy) — wasted energy transferred

E

4 Mr Smith buys some solar panels to heat the water for his house. Explain how this will:
a| help to reduce his gas bills   b| help the environment.

5 Two light bulbs receive 20 J of energy every second. Bulb A transfers 18 J of energy by light every second, and bulb B transfers 4 J by light every second. Which bulb is more efficient? Explain why.

I can ...

- describe advantages and disadvantages of different energy resources
- describe some ways of using less fossil fuel
- explain what efficiency means.

MAKING CHANGES

HOW CAN WE USE LESS FOSSIL FUEL?

The way we live needs a lot of energy – for heating, transport and generating electricity. Almost all of the vehicles on our roads use fuels obtained from oil, and over 75 per cent of our electricity is generated using fossil fuels.

We need to burn less fossil fuel, because this is a non-renewable resource, and because burning fossil fuels is harming the **environment**. But how can we change?

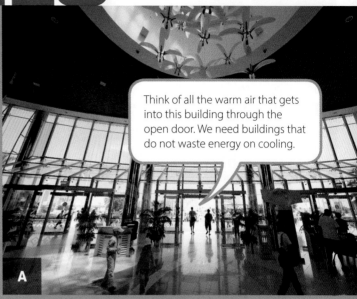

Think of all the warm air that gets into this building through the open door. We need buildings that do not waste energy on cooling.

A

I always use efficient appliances because they use up less of our country's store of electricity.

B

Anything I change will not make any difference. It is up to the government to change the way the country runs.

C

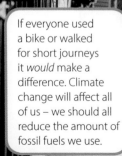

If everyone used a bike or walked for short journeys it *would* make a difference. Climate change will affect all of us – we should all reduce the amount of fossil fuels we use.

D

1. Look at photo A. Describe the energy stores shown in the photo, and the ways in which energy is being transferred.

2. Look at photo B. In what way is the person:
   a| correct   b| wrong?

3. Why do you think that most of the electricity we use in the world is generated from non-renewable resources? Give as many reasons as you can.

4. a| Explain why we should use less fossil fuel.
   b| Look at photo C. Suggest five ways in which the person in the photo *could* make changes.

5. A kettle uses electricity. Starting with the Sun, draw a flow chart to show the energy stores and transfers when you boil the kettle, if the electricity comes from:
   a| a coal-fired power station
   b| a hydroelectric power station.

HAVE YOUR SAY

Who should be responsible for developing renewable energy sources – individuals, businesses or the government?

7Ja DISCOVERING ELECTRICITY

People have known about the effects of **static electricity** for thousands of years. The ancient Greeks knew that you could charge certain materials by rubbing them. They also used electric shocks from catfish and other animals to try to stop headaches and some other illnesses.

Early scientists carried out some experiments with **electricity** using lightning, but this was very dangerous. In the 1600s, scientists invented machines that could produce static electricity. Some of these machines were used for scientific research, but some were used for entertainment or for medical treatments. It was not until Alessandro Volta invented the electrical **cell** in 1800 that scientists had a constant supply of electricity to experiment with.

Today almost everything we do depends on electricity in some way. You can investigate electricity at school by making circuits and using cells or **power packs** to provide the electricity.

A | Static electricity is making this child's hair stand up. This happened as his clothes rubbed against the slide.

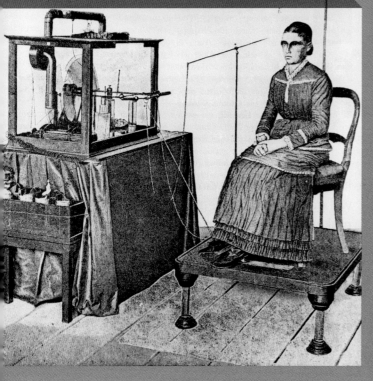

B | This illustrates electricity being used to treat a patient with a nervous disorder in 1882.

1 The wires used in electric circuits are made of metal, with a coating of plastic on the outside. Explain why these materials are used.

2 Photo C shows a circuit that can be used to turn a bulb on and off.

C

a| Write a list of the apparatus used to make the circuit.

b| Use standard symbols to draw a diagram of the circuit.

7Ja SWITCHES AND CURRENT

HOW DO WE MEASURE ELECTRICITY?

The **current** is the amount of electricity that is flowing around a circuit. The current carries **energy** to bulbs or other **components**. In electricity experiments the current in a circuit is provided by a cell or power pack. There must be a complete circuit or the current will not flow.

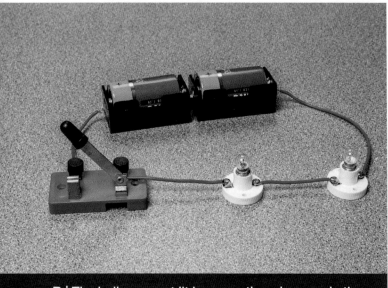

B | The bulbs are not lit because there is a gap in the circuit.

A

FACT

The original cell was invented by Alessandro Volta in 1800.

If one of the bulbs in circuit C breaks, the other bulb will go out. This happens because the broken bulb makes a gap in the circuit.

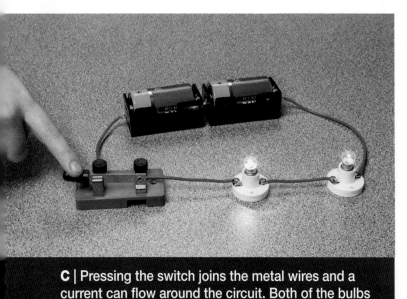

C | Pressing the switch joins the metal wires and a current can flow around the circuit. Both of the bulbs come on.

1 Look at circuit B. Explain how the switch works to turn the bulbs on and off.

2 Look at circuit C. What will happen if you take one of the bulbs out of its holder and then press the switch?

Many bulbs light up because the electricity flowing through them makes a **filament** glow. If you add more bulbs to the circuit, all the bulbs in the circuit will give out less light.

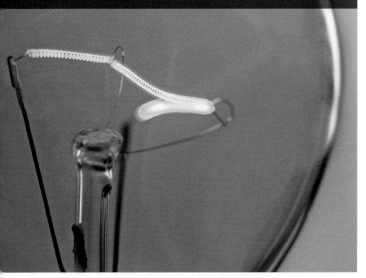

D | The current in this bulb has to flow through a very thin piece of wire called the filament.

Measuring current

We measure the current using an **ammeter**. The units for current are **amperes (A)**. It does not matter where the ammeter goes in the circuit. Current is not used up as it goes around the circuit, so the current is the same everywhere.

5 a| What does an ammeter measure?

b| Draw the symbol for an ammeter.

6 Look at circuit F.

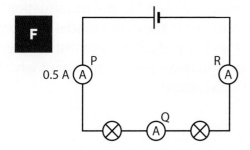

a| What current will ammeter Q show?

b| What current will ammeter R show?

7 A torch is not working. Write down all the things that could be wrong with it.

3 Describe how you could carry out an investigation to show how the brightness of bulbs changes when you add more bulbs to a circuit. Include a list of the apparatus you need.

4 Look at circuit C. Another circuit (circuit X) is identical but has one fewer bulb.

a| How will the brightness of the bulbs compare in the two circuits?

b| What will happen to the brightness of the bulbs in circuit C if another bulb is added to it?

c| One of the bulbs in circuit C breaks. Explain what happens to the other bulb.

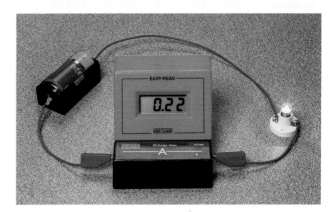

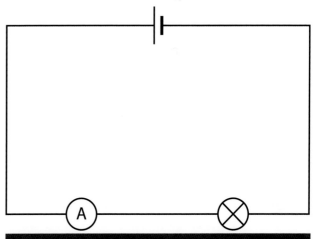

E | An ammeter in a circuit. The diagram shows the symbol for an ammeter.

I can ...

- explain how switches work
- describe what happens when the number of bulbs in a circuit is changed
- describe what a current is and how it is measured.

7Jb MODELS IN SCIENCE

HOW ARE MODELS USED IN SCIENCE?

If someone asks you to explain what a **model** is, you may think of a model aeroplane. There are many other kinds of model. A model is a way of showing or representing something. In science we use models to help us to think about complicated ideas.

We can use models to help us to think about what happens in electric circuits. The drawing shows two models that students want to build to help them to think about electrical current. The different parts represent different parts of an electrical circuit.

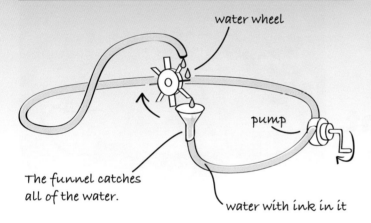

A | Sam's model

water wheel

The funnel catches all of the water.

pump

water with ink in it

B | Nat's model

The marbles represent the current going around the circuit.

Some marbles fall through the hole.

This represents the cell.

'ting'

Some of the 'current' is used to make the bell ring.

---

1. Look at drawing A. Which part of Sam's model represents:

   a| the cell

   b| the current

   c| a bulb or motor?

2. Explain your answers to question 1.

3. Describe what happens to the size of the 'current' as it goes around:

   a| in Sam's model (drawing A)

   b| in Nat's model (drawing B).

A good model behaves like the real situation. In this case, the 'current' in the better model will do what current does in a real circuit. Scientists can use a good model to make predictions about what they will find in investigations.

Testing models

Sam and Nat need to check what happens in a real circuit to find out which model is better.

> **4** Describe an investigation that Sam and Nat could carry out to find out which model is better.
>
> a| Write a list of the apparatus they need.
>
> b| Draw a circuit diagram to show how they should set up their apparatus.
>
> c| Describe the method they should use. Write a separate instruction for each step in the method.
>
> **5** Predict the results that Sam and Nat should get in their investigation:
>
> a| if Sam's model is the better one
>
> b| if Nat's model is the better one.
>
> **6** Use what you know about current in circuits to explain which model is the better one.

Physical and abstract models

The model circuits that Sam and Nat want to build are **physical models**, because you could build them and touch them. Photo D shows a physical model of the Solar System. It helps people understand how the planets move around the Sun.

Models that cannot be touched and only exist inside people's minds or on computer screens are **abstract models**. Photo E shows an abstract model of the Solar System.

E | This is an abstract model of the Solar System.

C | Sam and Nat could use some of this apparatus.

An **analogy** is a model in which you compare something complicated with an everyday thing that is easier to understand. These models for circuits are both analogies. When young children investigate the attraction between two magnets they often use the analogy that the magnets 'like' each other. It is important to remember that analogies are only a way of thinking about things. Magnets do not have feelings, so they cannot like each other!

D | This type of physical model of the Solar System is called an orrery.

> **7** Dan uses balls of different sizes to model the Earth and the Moon. Explain whether this is a physical or an abstract model.

I can ...

- identify when physical or abstract models are being used
- identify what the parts of a physical model represent
- plan an investigation to help to evaluate a model.

7Jb MODELS FOR CIRCUITS

HOW CAN WE USE MODELS TO HELP US TO THINK ABOUT ELECTRICITY?

Until just over 100 years ago, scientists thought of electricity as a **liquid** that flowed through wires, although they did not know what that liquid was. This model changed in 1897 when a British physicist called J.J. Thomson discovered that electricity was tiny **charges** moving through metals.

An electric current is a flow of charges, and carries energy from the cells (or electricity supply) to the components.

Metals are **conductors** because the charges can move around easily inside them. Charges cannot move around easily inside **insulating** materials.

It is difficult to think about these charges because they are too small to see, even with a very powerful microscope. We can use models to help us to think about electricity. One of the models we can use is very similar to the one used by scientists before the charges were discovered (diagram A).

FACT

A current of 1 ampere means there are 6 250 000 000 000 000 000 charges going past every second.

1	What is an electric current?
2	Why can metals conduct electricity?

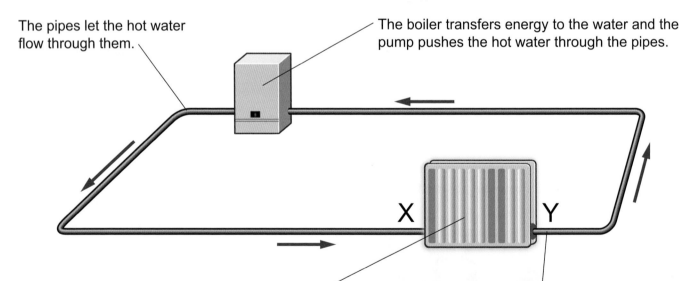

The pipes let the hot water flow through them.

The boiler transfers energy to the water and the pump pushes the hot water through the pipes.

In the radiator, energy is transferred from the hot water to the room. The room warms up.

All the water stays in the pipes. If you measure the amount of water flowing, you will get the same reading at X and Y, but the water at Y would be storing less energy than the water at X (the water at Y will be cooler than the water at X).

A | A central heating system is used in cold countries to keep homes warm. This is a physical model of the electric circuit in diagram B.

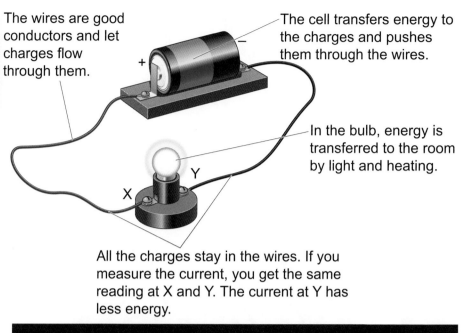

The wires are good conductors and let charges flow through them.

The cell transfers energy to the charges and pushes them through the wires.

In the bulb, energy is transferred to the room by light and heating.

All the charges stay in the wires. If you measure the current, you get the same reading at X and Y. The current at Y has less energy.

B | This circuit transfers energy to its surroundings.

3	Why do we need to use models to help us to think about electricity?
4	Use the central heating model to help you to explain:

a| why a central heating boiler (with a pump) is like a cell

b| why a radiator is like a light bulb.

| 5 | How is the central heading model *not* like an electric circuit? |

Diagram C shows a different model for helping you to think about electricity.

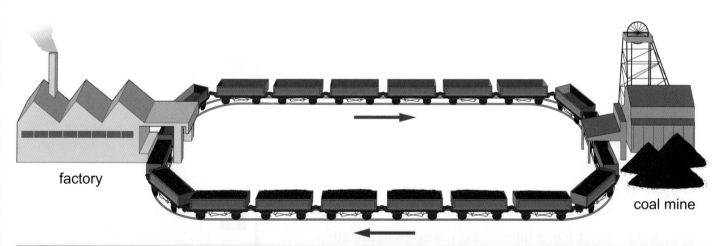

factory

coal mine

C | This is a model for thinking about a circuit in terms of a train, coal and a factory.

6	Look at drawing C. What do you think these things represent:

a| the coal mine   b| the factory

c| the train   d| the coal?

7	How is the model *not* like an electric circuit?
8	Which of the models on these pages is the best to help you to think about electricity in a circuit? Explain why you think the model you have chosen is best.

I can ...

- explain why models are used
- identify what the parts of a physical model represent
- use a physical model to help explain electric circuits
- evaluate a physical model
- state what is meant by current.

7JC SERIES AND PARALLEL CIRCUITS

WHAT ARE THE DIFFERENCES BETWEEN SERIES AND PARALLEL CIRCUITS?

A circuit like circuit A, with all the bulbs in one loop, is called a **series circuit**.

If the bulbs are on separate branches of a circuit, it is a **parallel circuit** (circuit B). A parallel circuit can have lots of branches. Each branch can have more than one component in it.

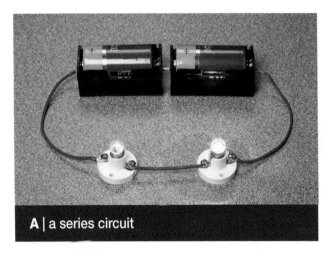

A | a series circuit

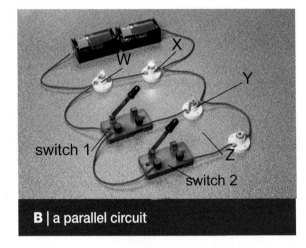

B | a parallel circuit

Parallel circuits are useful because each light can be switched on and off separately from the others.

In circuit A, both bulbs are on all the time. In circuit B, bulbs W and X are on all the time. Bulb Y only comes on if you press switch 1. If you want all the bulbs to come on you have to press both switches.

The two types of circuit behave in different ways.

- In a series circuit, if one bulb breaks all the others go out, because the broken bulb makes a gap in the circuit.

- In a parallel circuit, if one bulb breaks the bulbs in the other branches stay on.

- The current is the same everywhere in a series circuit, but in a parallel circuit the current from the cell divides when it comes to a branch. The currents in all the branches add up to the current in the main part of the circuit (see circuit C).

- If you add more bulbs to a series circuit the current gets smaller and the bulbs give out less light. In a parallel circuit, if you add more branches with bulbs in, the bulbs stay bright. It is easier for the current to flow with more branches, because there are more ways for the charges to go. The current in the main part of the parallel circuit increases.

1 What is the difference between a series circuit and a parallel circuit?

2 Do you think the lights in your house are on a series or a parallel circuit? Explain your answer.

3 Write a plan to show how you could investigate what happens to the brightness of bulbs if you put more of them into a parallel circuit.

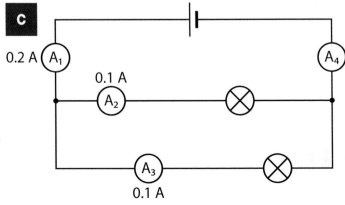

C

0.2 A A_1

0.1 A A_2

A_4

A_3

0.1 A

Some of the world's first streetlights were installed in 1878 in London, along the River Thames.

D

Combinations of switches can be used to make **AND** and **OR** circuits. Look at circuit E. The bulb will only come on if both switch W and switch X are closed. In circuit F, the bulb will come on if switch Y or switch Z are closed.

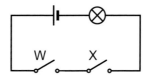 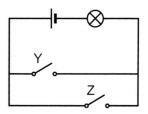

E | an AND circuit   **F** | an OR circuit

We can show what happens in AND and OR circuits using truth tables. Table G shows what happens in circuit E.

Switch W	Switch X	Bulb
open	open	off
closed	open	off
open	closed	off
closed	closed	on

G | a **truth table** for circuit D

4   Look at circuit H.

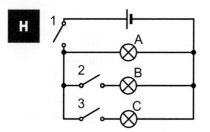

H

a| Which switches have to be closed for bulb A to come on?

b| Which bulbs will come on if you press switches 1 and 3?

5   Look at circuit C.

a| What will be the reading on ammeter 4?

b| How will the brightness of the bulbs change if you add another branch with a bulb in it?

6   All the streetlights in a town need to be on or off at the same times. Explain which type of circuit should be used to connect them.

7   Look at circuit F. Will the bulb be on or off when:

a| switch Y is open and switch Z is closed

b| switch Y and switch Z are open?

8   Draw a truth table similar to table G to show what happens in circuit F.

I can ...

- state what is meant by a series circuit and a parallel circuit
- explain how switches can control different kinds of circuit
- describe how changing the number or type of components in a circuit affects the current
- describe the differences in how current behaves in series and parallel circuits.

7Jd CHANGING THE CURRENT

HOW CAN WE CHANGE THE CURRENT IN A CIRCUIT?

The size of the current in a circuit depends on the **voltage** of the cells or power pack, and on the components in the circuit.

The voltage provided by a cell or power pack helps to push the charges around the circuit. The higher the voltage of the cells in a circuit, the more charges it can push around. This means that increasing the voltage of cells or power packs increases the current.

We measure the voltage using a **voltmeter**, and the units are **volts (V)**. The voltmeter is connected *across* a component (e.g. a cell or a bulb), as shown in diagram A.

The current transfers energy to components in the circuit. The voltage across a component is a way of measuring how much energy is being transferred by the current.

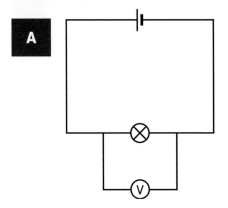
A

---

1   a| What does a voltmeter measure?

b| Describe the difference between the ways ammeters and voltmeters are put into circuits.

2   Look at circuit B. Explain how the current in this circuit will change if you change the cell to a 3 V cell.

If you add more bulbs to a series circuit, the bulbs give out less light. It is difficult for the current to flow through the thin wire in the filaments of the bulbs. The more bulbs there are, the harder it is for the current to flow and so the current gets smaller.

FACT

Air is normally an **insulator**, but at very high voltages electricity can jump across an air gap. The voltage between a cloud and the ground in a thunderstorm can be up to 100 000 000 volts!

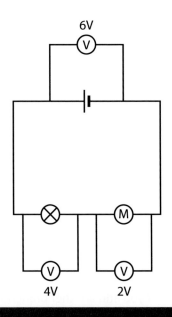

B | The current is transferring more energy to the bulb than to the motor (M).

Components (including bulbs) that make it more difficult for a current to flow around a circuit have a high **resistance**. Components that do not make it difficult for the current to flow have a low resistance. Connecting wires have a low resistance.

Sometimes we only need a very small current in a circuit. We can make the current smaller by using a **resistor** in the circuit. A resistor has a high resistance and makes it harder for electricity to flow.

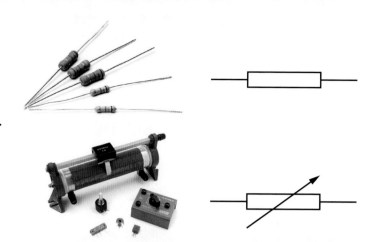

| 3 | What happens to the current in a circuit if the resistance of the components in the circuit is increased? |

C | This shows resistors and their symbols. The resistance of a **variable resistor** (bottom) is changed by moving the slider.

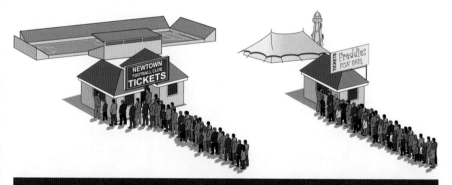

D | queues of people waiting to get into a fairground and a soccer match

When you add bulbs to a circuit in parallel, the brightness of the other bulbs does not change. As you add more branches, the current flowing from the cell increases. It is easier for the current to flow when there are more branches because there are more ways for the current to go. The overall resistance of the circuit is less. Drawing D shows a model to help you to think about this.

| 4 | Look at drawing D. |

a| Which queue will move faster? Explain your answer.

b| What do the people represent in this model of a circuit?

c| What do the entrances represent?

d| How does this model help you to think about resistance in a parallel circuit?

| 5 | Look at circuits E and F. The bulbs in the circuits all have the same resistance. |

a| Explain which circuit will have the higher current.

b| Explain what will happen to the current in circuit E if you add another bulb in series.

c| Explain what will happen to the current in circuit F if you add another bulb in parallel.

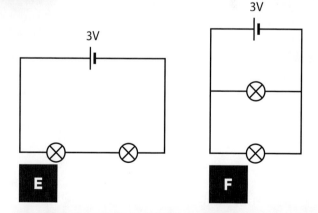

E

F

I can ...

- describe how changing the number or type of components in a circuit affects the current
- describe how a voltmeter is used
- explain why the current increases when the voltage of the supply is increased
- describe the relationship between resistance and current.

WHAT DO ROBOT ENGINEERS DO?

A robot is any machine that performs complicated tasks automatically. Robots are controlled by computers. Many factories use robots to assemble cars and other machines. They are also used for jobs that are too difficult or dangerous for humans.

A | Robots are used to help sick and elderly people who cannot move around easily.

B | This robot is exploring Mars. It is very difficult, dangerous and expensive to send humans to Mars.

1 Suggest two tasks robots could perform:
a | in your home
b | in your town.

2 Suggest two parts of the Earth where robot explorers should be used instead of humans.

Controlling robots

Self-driving cars are robots. They must be designed to drive to the correct place without bumping into anything. Diagram C shows a flowchart model for what a human driver does when seeing an obstacle ahead.

A self-driving car needs sensors to detect what is around the car. It also needs motors to control the steering and speed, and a computer control system to decide what to do.

The sensors and motors are all in circuits that are controlled by switches and variable resistors. The control system receives electrical signals from sensors such as cameras. It then switches on motors or other devices to control the car. The engineers who design the control system have to think of all the possible tasks the car needs to do, and program the computer to make the correct response each time. The same ideas apply to designing any kind of robot.

1 Sees an obstacle ahead

↓

2 Decides to slow

↓

3 Presses brake pedal

C | a model for how a human driver controls a car

3 Look at flow diagram C.

a| Which parts of a human carry out tasks 1, 2 and 3?

b| Suggest what a self-driving car could use to carry out tasks 1 and 2.

Careers in robotics

Robotics engineers need a degree in a subject such as electronics, computer science or mechanical engineering. A robot is designed to do particular tasks, so engineers also need to communicate with the people who will use it, so they understand what those tasks are.

The engineers in photo D need to understand the conditions on Mars so they can make sure the robot will work when it gets there.

There are lots of things to think about when designing a robot space explorer, such as how the robot moves, how it examines rocks, and how to keep it powered. Each task can be broken down into smaller problems to be solved. For example, if scientists want to receive photos of rocks with a particular colour:

- Which sensor should the robot use?

- How can it decide if the rock is the right colour?

- How will the pictures be sent back to the scientists on Earth?

D | These engineers are developing a new robot to explore Mars.

4 Look at the list of problems to be solved for a robot Mars explorer. Suggest one solution for each problem.

ACTIVITY

Photo E shows *Robear*. This robot is designed to lift patients in hospitals or care homes. Engineers have to work out how it can do tasks such as:

- understand what the patient wants

- find the patient

- lift the patient safely

- put the patient down safely in the correct place.

Work in a group and choose one of these tasks to discuss. Break the task down into three or four parts and suggest a solution for each part. Summarise your conclusions in a report or presentation.

E | *Robear* being tested

7Je USING ELECTRICITY

HOW DO WE USE ELECTRICITY SAFELY?

The world's first coal-fired public power station was opened in London in 1882. Today, there are many thousands of power stations around the world, providing a 'mains supply' of electricity to homes, offices and factories. Although electricity is very useful, it is also a **hazard** (it can cause harm). Mains electricity has a higher voltage than cells, so there is a greater **risk** that it will cause harm.

Electricity flowing through a wire can cause the wire to heat up. This is useful in electric heaters and cookers, but if other components or wires become too hot they may cause fires. Electricity can also be harmful if it flows through the body, causing burns or even causing the heart to stop working.

Reducing risks

If people follow some simple safety rules, the risks of harming themselves are reduced.

- Never touch the bare metal parts of plugs.
- Never push things into sockets.
- Keep electricity away from water, and do not use switches with wet hands.
- Do not plug too many things into one socket.
- Never use something that has a damaged wire.

1	Describe three ways in which electricity can be a hazard.
2	Explain why you should never poke things into sockets.

A | an electrical fire caused by faulty wiring

FACT

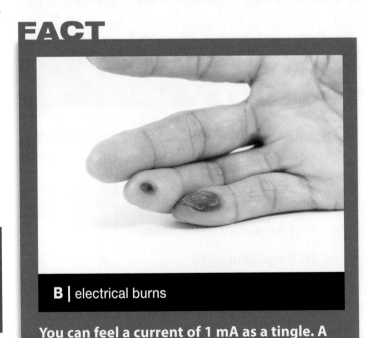

B | electrical burns

You can feel a current of 1 mA as a tingle. A current of 1 A flowing through your body is likely to kill you.

Electrical equipment is designed with safety in mind. Plugs on appliances are fitted with a **fuse**, which is designed to melt and break the circuit if the current is higher than it should be. Fuses have different **ratings**, depending on how much current they are designed to carry without melting.

Many appliances need a cable with three wires inside it. The **live** and **neutral wires** are part of the circuit that makes the appliance work. The **earth wire** is there for safety.

A **circuit breaker** is another safety device that cuts off the current if too much current flows. Circuit breakers work in a different way from fuses, and they are used to protect 'rings' of sockets in a house (often called a **ring main**).

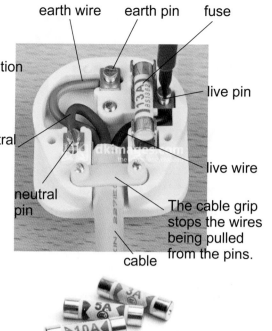

earth wire   earth pin   fuse

live pin

neutral wire

live wire

neutral pin

The cable grip stops the wires being pulled from the pins.

cable

metal conductor   plastic insulation

neutral wire

live wire

earth wire

plastic outer casing

C | The insulation colours are used in many countries around the world, in three-core electrical cables.

D | The photo shows different fuses used in the UK.

E | The wire at the bottom of this box is where electricity is coming into the house. The different circuits in the house are protected by circuit breakers.

3 a| Make a table to show the names and the colours of the coatings of the three wires inside a cable.

b| Suggest why the wires need to have standard colours.

4 What could happen if the current in an appliance was too high?

5 Photo D shows four standard types of fuse. Explain which one should be used for an appliance that has a current of 6 A.

6 How could you find out how much current can flow through a piece of fuse wire before it melts? Write a plan for your investigation, including the apparatus you will need and a circuit diagram.

7 Sometimes the wire to an appliance may become damaged.

a| Suggest what could happen if the appliance is used with a damaged wire.

b| Explain how electrical equipment is designed to stop this happening.

I can ...

- explain some safety precautions to be followed when using electricity
- describe the job that fuses and circuit breakers do
- explain how a fuse works
- recall how the different wires are connected in a plug.

A WORLD WITHOUT ELECTRICITY

HOW HAVE IDEAS ABOUT ELECTRICITY CHANGED THE WAY WE LIVE?

The first power stations were built near the end of the 1800s. The electricity they produced was originally used for lighting. Later, scientists and engineers developed motors and electronic components. Today, we use electricity for many different things in everyday life.

Many of the things we do today could be done without electricity, but there are some things we do that are only possible using electrical equipment.

A | A few steam powered robots were built before electricity. Today, robots are powered by battery packs and can do many more things.

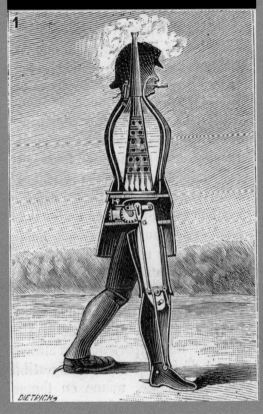

B | entertainment in a living room before electricity

C | Before gas and electricity, candles or oil lamps were the only sources of light.

1 Describe the advantages and disadvantages of using electricity for:

a| making tea and toast

b| washing and drying clothes.

2 We use electricity for many different things. Suggest how our use of electricity would be different if all circuits had to be series circuits. Use as many ideas from this unit as you can in your answer.

HAVE YOUR SAY

Are people's lives better since electricity was developed?

Our life is full of **forces**. We cannot see them but we can see how they affect things. All sports involve forces. You use a force when you kick a football, when you ride a bike and when you run.

When you take part in certain sports you need special equipment to protect you from some forces or to help you to produce bigger forces. Many sports would not be possible without modern technology.

Some sports appear to be dangerous but people doing these sports wear helmets or special clothing to protect them if there is an accident. All the equipment they use for the sport must be designed so that it does not break when it is used.

Engineers who design sports equipment must know about all the different forces involved in the sport. This helps them to make sure the equipment can be used safely.

A | This climber is using ice axes and spikes on his boots to help him climb the ice. He is wearing a helmet and using a rope to reduce the risk of harm.

B | This sport is called fourcross.

1
a| Write down five sports that you can play using only simple equipment such as a ball.
b| Write down five sports that need more specialised equipment.

2
a| What is the force pulling the climber downwards in photo A?
b| The fourcross bike in photo B has brakes to help slow it down. What force is produced in the brakes?

3
The climber is pulling on the ice in order to move upwards. This is a contact force.
a| Name one other contact force.
b| Name two non-contact forces.

4
Climbers can now climb much steeper ice and rock than they could 50 years ago. Suggest why this is.

7Ka DIFFERENT FORCES

WHAT CAN FORCES DO?

A force is a push or a pull. Forces can change the shape of something, its speed, or the direction that it is moving in.

For many forces, the thing providing the force needs to touch an object before the force can affect it. These are called **contact forces**. For example, when you throw a ball, you need to touch the ball to exert a force on it. When you go down a steep hill on a bicycle, the brakes need to touch the wheel to produce **friction** to slow you down. Contact forces include friction, **air resistance**, **water resistance** and **upthrust** (the force that makes things float).

Some forces can affect an object from a distance. These are called **non-contact forces**. **Gravity** is a force that pulls objects downwards (photo A). **Static electricity** can attract

things (photo B). In photo C, the man is climbing the side of a ship using magnets. Magnets have **magnetism**, which attracts objects made of iron and some other metals. Magnets can also repel other magnets.

A

B

C

Forces can be big or small. The unit for measuring force is the **newton (N)**. The direction in which the force is acting is important so we use arrows to show forces. The direction of the arrow shows the direction of the force; a bigger arrow shows a bigger force.

1 Write down three ways in which a force can affect a soccer ball.

2 Write down the names of three:
   a| contact forces   b| non-contact forces.

3 What are the units for measuring forces?

4 Look at photo D.
   a| Which bike has the biggest force on it?
   b| How do you know this from the photo?
   c| What will happen to the two bikes as a result of these forces?

D

Sometimes there are a lot of forces acting on something. There are four forces acting on the diver in photo E.

Weight and mass

Your **weight** is the force of gravity pulling on you. Weight is a force so its units are newtons (N). If you talk about something being '10 kilograms' you are talking about its **mass**. Weight and mass are two different things.

Mass is the amount of matter that makes up an object. The units for measuring mass are **grams (g)** and **kilograms (kg)**.

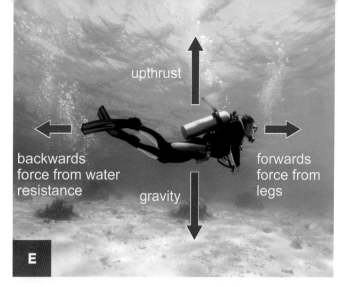

upthrust

backwards force from water resistance

gravity

forwards force from legs

E

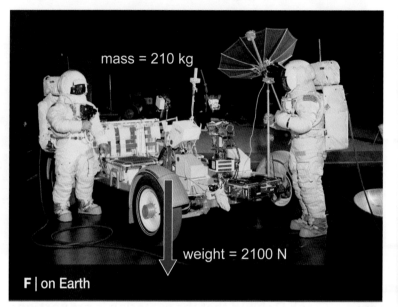

mass = 210 kg

weight = 2100 N

F | on Earth

mass = 210 kg

weight = 344 N

G | on the Moon

The force of gravity is greater on the Earth than it is on the Moon. The lunar buggy in photo F has the same mass wherever it is but it has a greater weight on the Earth than on the Moon. The Earth's gravity pulls on every kilogram with a force of about 10 N, so something that has a mass of 2 kg has a weight of 20 N.

FACT

From 1889 until 2019, all other kilogram masses were measured against this one, in Paris. Today, the kilogram is defined using a special balance.

H

> **5**
> a| What is weight?
> b| What are the units for weight?
> c| What is mass?
> d| What are the units for mass?
>
> **6** Why would you weigh less on the Moon than you do on the Earth?
>
> **7** Why do you think it is important that scientists in different countries all check their ways of measuring a kilogram against the same standard mass?

I can ...

- recall the effects of forces on an object
- name forces and classify them as contact or non-contact forces
- recall how to measure forces and masses and their units.

7Kb SPRINGS

HOW CAN SPRINGS HELP US TO MEASURE FORCES?

Materials and objects can be **stretched** (made longer) or **compressed** (made shorter). The amount of stretch or compression in the material depends on the type of material and the size of the force. It takes a very big force to change the size of some materials.

Most **springs** are made from coils of wire. The **extension** of a spring is the difference between its original length and its stretched length. The spring is **elastic** because it will return to its original length when the force is removed.

> **1** What does elastic mean?
>
> **2** Look at diagram B. Which arrow shows the extension of the stretched spring? Explain your answer.

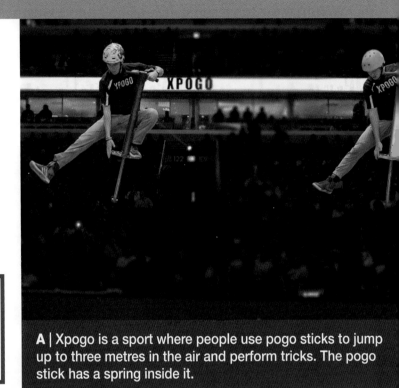

A | Xpogo is a sport where people use pogo sticks to jump up to three metres in the air and perform tricks. The pogo stick has a spring inside it.

The **apparatus** shown in photo C is being used to investigate the extension of a spring. Graph D shows that the extension is **proportional** to the force up to a certain point, called the **limit of proportionality**. This means that for every 1 N increase in the force, the spring stretches by the same amount. The idea that the extension is proportional to the force is **Hooke's Law**. Hooke's Law does not apply to all elastic materials.

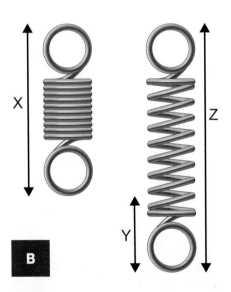

B

> **3** Look at photo C. Explain how you would use this apparatus to find out how much the spring stretches with different forces on it.

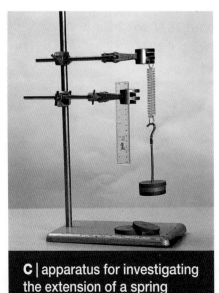

C | apparatus for investigating the extension of a spring

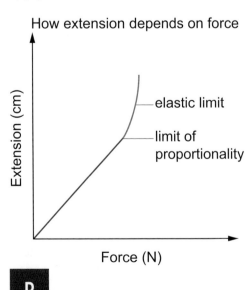

D

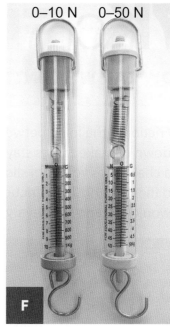

E | It is not just springs that are elastic. A bungee cord will stretch and then pull the jumper upwards again. However, bungee cords do not follow Hooke's Law.

F

If enough force is applied to a spring, it will pass its **elastic limit**. The spring will then no longer return to its original length. Materials that do not return to their original shape when a force is removed are **plastic** materials.

> **4** A spring stretches 2 cm when a 10 N weight hangs on it. How far will it stretch with a weight of 20 N?
>
> **5** a| What is the difference between an elastic and a plastic material?
>   b| Name one plastic material.

Springs are used inside **force meters** (photo F). If the meter is measuring a small force, the spring inside only stretches a little way. If it is measuring a bigger force, the spring stretches further and the pointer moves further along the scale.

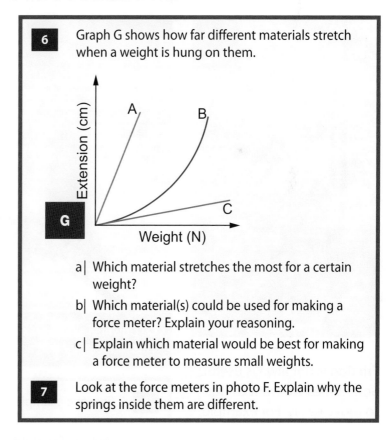

6 Graph G shows how far different materials stretch when a weight is hung on them.

G

a| Which material stretches the most for a certain weight?

b| Which material(s) could be used for making a force meter? Explain your reasoning.

c| Explain which material would be best for making a force meter to measure small weights.

7 Look at the force meters in photo F. Explain why the springs inside them are different.

FACT

Hooke's Law is named after Robert Hooke (1635–1703) who studied how metals behave when they stretch. His work led to the invention of the force meter. However, the units for measuring forces were named after his competitor and enemy, Isaac Newton!

I can ...

- describe how the extension of a spring depends on the force applied.

7Kc FRICTION

HOW CAN WE CONTROL FRICTION?

Friction is the force between two touching objects. It can slow things down or make things stay still. The friction between your clothes and a chair stops you from sliding off the chair. Walking would be very difficult without the friction between your feet and the floor – you would slip and slide everywhere.

A | Rock climbing shoes are made from special rubber that increases friction to give a good grip.

B | This woman is abseiling. She is using friction to control how fast she goes down the cliff.

Friction helps the abseiler to control the rope.

We can increase friction by using certain materials. For example, rubber produces a lot of friction. The rubber tyres of a Formula One racing car stop the car from sliding off the road as it speeds round sharp corners.

C | Downhill skiers wax the bottom of their skis to make them very smooth. This reduces friction and allows them to ski faster.

Friction is not always useful. Sometimes we want things to move easily. For example, a bicycle is very difficult to ride if there is too much friction in the axles. We can reduce friction by making surfaces smooth or by using **lubricants** such as oil or grease. Adding a lubricant is called **lubrication**.

---

1 Give one example of friction making something stay still.

2 Explain why rubber bath mats are useful.

3 a| Why should you oil the axles of a bicycle?
b| Why must you never put oil on the brake blocks of a bicycle?
c| Explain why bicycle brakes do not work well in the rain.

4 The tread on bicycle and car tyres is designed to allow water to escape from under the tyre on wet roads. Explain why this is important.

Friction can wear things away. The brake pads on a bicycle eventually wear away and so do car tyres. Parts of your clothes get thinner as friction wears them away. Friction also produces heat and noise. If a car engine runs without any oil in it, the large amount of friction between the moving parts causes it to overheat and stop working. Rusty door hinges squeak and make a door difficult to open.

Friction due to **gases** and **liquids** can also cause things to slow down. Air resistance and water resistance can be reduced by having smooth surfaces and smooth shapes.

FACT

The tyres used on racing cars wear out during each race and have to be replaced. The average Formula One tyre only lasts for about 120 km and costs over £1000. The racing team choose different tyres depending on the conditions on the track.

E

brake

axle

D | Some parts of a bike are designed to increase friction and some parts are designed to reduce friction.

F | This drag racer has a smooth shape so it can move easily through the air while it is racing. The parachutes are released at the end of the race to increase air resistance to help to slow the car down.

5 a| Why do car owners have to replace their car tyres regularly?

b| Suggest why racing car tyres do not last as long as the tyres on normal cars.

6 How could you stop a door hinge squeaking?

7 Write down three effects of friction between moving objects.

8 Describe as many ways as you can in which friction is useful to you in your everyday life.

9 In a science fiction story, a lubricating mist moves towards a town. Think of three effects this would have on life in the town and write a paragraph of the story in 150 words.

I can ...

- recall the effects of friction
- explain some ways in which friction can be changed
- identify situations in which friction is helpful or not helpful.

7Kd PRESSURE

HOW IS PRESSURE USED IN SPORTS?

Pressure is the amount of force pushing on a certain area. Pressure is important in many sports.

If there is a high pressure beneath a person's feet, or beneath a vehicle, it is more likely to sink into snow, mud or sand. The size of the pressure depends on the size of the force and the size of the area it is pushing on.

If you keep the size of the force the same:

- for a larger area, the pressure will be lower
- for a smaller area, the pressure will be higher.

If you keep the area the same:

- for a larger force, the pressure will be higher
- for a smaller force, the pressure will be lower.

Pressure affects everyday things as well. It is easier to cut something with a sharp knife than with a blunt one. The sharp knife has a smaller edge, so the force you put on the knife is more concentrated over a smaller area on the object you are cutting.

A | The runner is wearing snowshoes to spread her weight. The snowshoes reduce the pressure under her feet, to stop them sinking into the soft snow.

1 Look at the vehicle in photo C.

Should a car like this have wide or narrow tyres? Explain your answer.

C

2 The person in photo A puts on a larger pair of snowshoes. Explain how the pressure under her feet will change.

3 a| Explain why a drawing pin is easier to push into the wall if the point is sharp.

b| Explain why the drawing pin has a large head for you to push on.

B | This mountaineer is walking on hard, slippery ice. The crampons on her boots have spikes to concentrate her weight. The points stick into the ice and stop her slipping. The crampons increase the pressure of her feet on the ice.

We use this formula to calculate pressure:

$$\text{pressure} = \frac{\text{force}}{\text{area}}$$

Force is measured in newtons (N) and area is measured in square metres (m²), so the units for pressure are newtons per square metre (N/m²). This unit is also called a **pascal (Pa)**. 1 Pa = 1 N/m².

If the area being measured is small, you can measure it in square centimetres (cm²). The unit of pressure will then be N/cm².

The points on Alex's crampons have a total area of 0.2 cm². To calculate the pressure under the points:

$$\begin{aligned} \text{pressure} &= \frac{\text{force}}{\text{area}} \\ &= \frac{800\,\text{N}}{0.2\,\text{cm}^2} \\ &= 4000\,\text{N/cm}^2 \end{aligned}$$

Alex   **Sam**

800 N   800 N

D   total area of spike tips = 0.2 cm²   total area of snowshoes = 2400 cm²

FACT

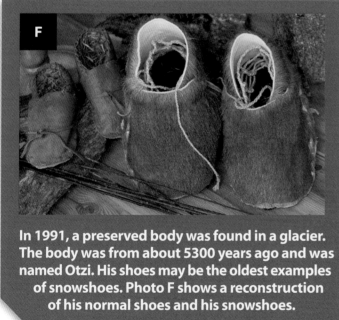

In 1991, a preserved body was found in a glacier. The body was from about 5300 years ago and was named Otzi. His shoes may be the oldest examples of snowshoes. Photo F shows a reconstruction of his normal shoes and his snowshoes.

E | The wide tracks and the skis stop the snowmobile from sinking into the snow. The spikes that stick out of the tracks dig into snow or ice to give grip.

4   How could you find the pressure under your shoes when you are standing up? List the apparatus you will need and explain how you would use it.

5   Look at photo D. Calculate the pressure under Sam's snowshoes.

6   Look at photo E. Explain how the tracks and the spikes work. Use ideas about pressure in your answer.

I can ...

- calculate pressure and recall its units
- describe the effects of high and low pressure in simple situations.

7Kd SI UNITS

WHAT ARE THE STANDARD UNITS USED IN SCIENCE?

The road sign in photo A shows the speed limit on a road. In most of the world, a sign like this means you should not travel faster than 50 kilometres per hour (km/h). If you are driving in the UK, it means you must not go faster than 50 miles per hour (mph) – which is about 80 km/h.

A

Sometimes using different units can have very serious consequences. Figure B is an artist's impression of the Mars Climate Orbiter. This spacecraft crashed when it reached Mars. It went wrong and disintegrated in the atmosphere of Mars because two teams of engineers designing it used different sets of units.

Scientists from all over the world often work together, so it is important that they all use the same units. **SI units** are used by scientists all over the world.

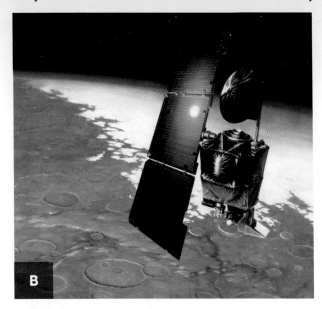

B

Table C shows some of the standard units in the SI system.

Quantity	Unit name	Symbol
length	metre	m
area	metre squared	m^2
volume	metre cubed	m^3
mass	kilogram	kg
time	second	s
force	newton	N
pressure	pascal	Pa (1 Pa = 1 N/m^2)
energy	joule	J
speed	metres per second	m/s

C | some of the units in the SI system

Sometimes these units are not a convenient size. For example, the amount of energy the average teenager needs per day is around 10 000 000 **joules (J)**. It is easier to understand this number if it is written as 10 000 **kilojoules (kJ)**. 1 kJ = 1000 J. 'Kilo' is a **prefix** that tells us when a larger or smaller version of the unit is being used.

Prefix	Symbol	Meaning	Example
mega-	M	1 000 000	1 megajoule (MJ) = 1 000 000 J
kilo-	k	1000	1 kilogram (kg) = 1000 g
deci-	d	$\frac{1}{10}$ (one tenth)	1 cubic decimetre (dm^3) = $\frac{1}{1000}$ m^3 ($\frac{1}{10}$ m × $\frac{1}{10}$ m × $\frac{1}{10}$ m)
centi-	c	$\frac{1}{100}$ (one hundredth)	100 centimetres (cm) = 1 m
milli-	m	$\frac{1}{1000}$ (one thousandth)	1000 milligrams (mg) = 1 g
micro-	μ	$\frac{1}{1000000}$ (one millionth)	1 000 000 micrometres (μm) = 1 m
nano-	n	$\frac{1}{1000000000}$	1 000 000 000 nanometres (nm) = 1 m

D | prefixes used in the SI system

Other units

There are some units that are still commonly used but do not fit the standard pattern.

E	Quantity	Standard unit	Other units still used
	time	seconds	minutes, hours, days, years
	length	metres	miles
	pressure	Pa	newtons per square centimetre (N/cm^2)
	speed	m/s	kilometres per hour (km/h), miles per hour (mph)
	volume	m^3	litres (1 litre = $1000\,cm^3$ = $1\,dm^3$), millilitres (1 ml = $1\,cm^3$)

F | Champion snail racers can move at speeds of up to 0.003 m/s or 3 mm/s. Millimetres per second is not a standard unit for measuring speed but it helps to give us a better idea of how fast snails can move.

1 Which unit would you use for the following measurements? Choose your answers from table C.

a| The distance across a school playground.

b| The amount of ground that a soccer pitch covers.

c| How long it takes you to eat a chocolate.

2 Which unit would you use for the following measurements? Give the best prefix as well as the unit.

a| The thickness of a leaf.

b| The energy stored in your food.

c| The distance between London and Dubai.

3 a| Explain why it is important that all scientists use the same set of units.

b| People in different countries use different units of mass or length when buying food or other goods. Explain why this does not usually cause problems.

I can ...

- explain why scientists use SI units
- record numbers using suitable units.

7Ke BALANCED AND UNBALANCED

WHAT HAPPENS WHEN FORCES ARE BALANCED?

Forces can add together. It is difficult for one person to push a broken-down car. If another person helps, it is easier to push the car because their forces are added together.

Two forces acting on an object can also work against each other if they are in opposite directions. If the two forces are the same size, nothing will change. The forces are **balanced**.

If one of the forces is stronger than the other, something will start to move. The forces are **unbalanced**. If the unbalanced forces are acting on a moving object, the object will *change* its speed.

> **1** Look at photo A.
> a| Why isn't the rope moving?
> b| What will happen if the mule pulls harder?

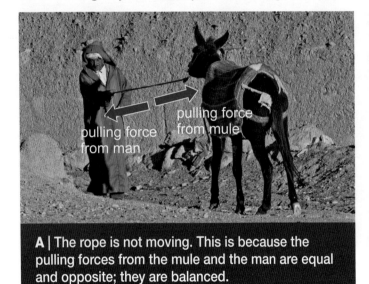

pulling force from mule

pulling force from man

A | The rope is not moving. This is because the pulling forces from the mule and the man are equal and opposite; they are balanced.

B | The pulling forces of all the dogs add together. When the sled is moving at a steady speed, the pulling force from all the dogs is balanced by friction forces trying to slow the sled down.

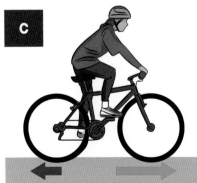

c

friction   force from pedals
speeding up

steady speed

slowing down

1| The forwards force is bigger than the backwards force. The bike speeds up.

2| The forces are equal. Because the bike is already moving, it continues to move at the same speed.

3| The girl has stopped pedalling so there is no forwards force. The bike will slow down until it stops.

All **stationary** (still) objects have balanced forces acting on them. Moving objects can also have balanced forces acting on them. If the forces are balanced, the object carries on moving at the same speed. The speed only changes when the forces are unbalanced.

You can use the idea of balanced forces to explain how a force meter works. When you stretch a spring it gets harder and harder to pull it because the spring 'pulls back'.

There is a similar explanation for why you do not fall through a chair when you sit down. Every object changes shape when a force acts on it but in most cases the movement is too small to see. When you sit on a chair, you squash it slightly and, just as with a spring, the chair pushes back.

2 Look at cartoon C.

a| How could the girl increase the size of the friction forces on the bike?

b| How would increasing the size of this force affect her speed?

3 Look at photo B. What will happen when the dogs get tired and cannot pull as strongly?

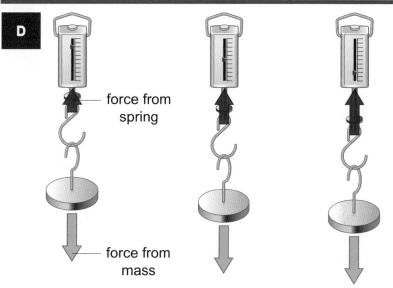

force from spring

force from mass

When you first hang something on a force meter, the forces are not balanced, so the spring begins to stretch.

As the spring stretches, it produces a bigger force.

Eventually the forces are balanced. The force meter is showing the weight of the object.

4 Look at diagram D. Explain what will happen if a larger mass is put on the force meter.

5 Look at photo E.

a| Why is the man not moving?

b| How will the forces be different if a lighter man uses the tightrope?

6 To investigate the friction between different surfaces, you measure the force needed to pull an object at a steady speed. Explain why you need to use a steady speed to find out the size of the friction force.

E | The tightrope stretches a little when the man stands on it. The rope pulls back and provides a force that balances the weight of the man.

I can ...

- identify balanced and unbalanced forces
- explain the effects of balanced and unbalanced forces.

HOW DO ARCHITECTS AND CIVIL ENGINEERS WORK TOGETHER?

Architects and civil engineers work together to design bridges, buildings, shopping malls and housing.

Architects design structures for the way people will use them. For example, for an office block, they need to know things like the number of people who will work in the building, and how many offices, meeting rooms and washrooms are needed. Surveys are used to find out this information, which is used to help make the design.

They also think about how people will move around the building. Their design must take account of all these needs, in a way that makes the building easy and pleasant to use. Architects also decide what the building will look like, and how it fits into its surroundings.

A | The Petronas Towers complex in Malaysia includes an underground car park, a shopping mall and offices.

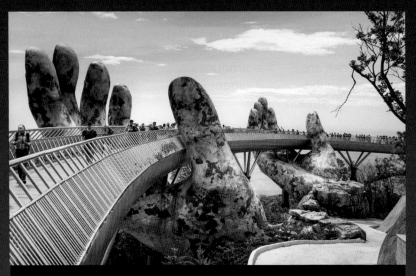

B | Some structures can also be works of art. This is the Golden Bridge in Vietnam.

Once the architects have decided on the design of the building, civil engineers use their knowledge of forces and materials to work out how to build the structure. They work closely with architects to make sure that the design is practical to build. The structure must be strong enough to withstand bad weather. In some countries, civil engineers also have to design the building to be safe in earthquakes.

Working on buildings

Architects and civil engineers need to be good at maths and computing, and at solving problems. They need university degrees and get professional training when they start work.

1
a | Write down a list of all the different types of room in your school and what they are used for.

b | What would an architect have to think about to design a school for twice as many students as your school?

2
Write down some things an architect must find out before designing a new:

a | bridge

b | shopping mall.

C | Buildings and other structures are designed using computer programs.

Most architects and civil engineers work as part of large teams. They need good communications skills, to share ideas with their team and with their clients.

Teams of architects and civil engineers work on projects in different parts of the world and with people from different countries. Scientists and engineers have certain ways of presenting information, called **conventions**. These conventions make it easier to present information in a way everyone understands. Agreeing and using conventions is an important part of communication.

3 Suggest why architects and civil engineers usually work in teams.

4 One thing that must be agreed is which measurement units to use for a project (e.g. metres, feet, pounds, kilograms). By convention, each measurements unit has an internationally agreed unit symbol.

a | Explain why it is important to decide what measurement unit to use.

b | Explain why having a convention for unit symbols is important.

D | Architects use models and plans to communicate their designs to other people.

PRACTICAL

Work in a group to design and build a bridge using only sheets of paper and sticky tape. Your bridge must stretch across a 50 cm gap between two tables and must support a 1 kg mass.

* Decide on a design for your bridge and build it.

* Test your bridge. If it supports 1 kg you have met the brief.

* Evaluate your design: if it failed, try to change your design to make it stronger. If it supported 1 kg, try to design a bridge using less material.

* Write a short report to describe your design and how you modified it.

E | Model bridges are from many materials. This bridge was built for an international 'Model Bridge with Ice Cream Sticks' competition. It supported 909 kg before breaking!

HOW DO WE KNOW THAT SPORTS EQUIPMENT IS SAFE TO USE?

In many sports, people rely on ropes or other equipment to keep them safe. All this equipment must meet certain standards. These standards make sure that the equipment is strong enough for its purpose and is safe to use.

In climbing, the ropes are tested for strength and for stretchiness. The more stretchy the rope, the smaller the impact force on the climber when the rope stops them falling.

There are no set standards for how much friction the outside of a rope must provide. Most manufacturers test their equipment for friction as well as for stretch, to make sure that people buying the rope will be happy to use it and continue to buy from them.

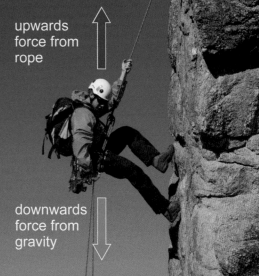

upwards force from rope

downwards force from gravity

A | The outside of the rope has to provide enough friction for the climber to be able to hold onto it, and for the knots to stay done up. But it must be smooth enough to slide through things when necessary.

B | This climber's rope is strong enough to stop him hitting the ground. The rope is also stretchy so that it reduces the impact force on the climber when it stops his fall.

1
a| How will a very stretchy rope help a falling climber?
b| Suggest a disadvantage of having a very stretchy climbing rope.

2
a| Skiers wax their skis to reduce the friction beneath them. Explain in as much detail as you can why skiers want to reduce the friction.
b| Describe three examples of where high friction is useful in sports.

3
Why are there international safety standards for things like climbing ropes but not for ski wax?

4
a| Skis are available in different sizes. Explain why a person might want to buy a bigger pair of skis. Use ideas about pressure in your answer.
b| Describe a situation where high pressure is useful in sports.

5
a| Describe the forces acting on the climber in photo A.
b| Look at photo B. Describe what happens to the climber as the rope takes his weight as he falls, and how the forces on him change.

HAVE YOUR SAY

Manufacturers have to spend money to test their products against safety standards, and this makes the items more expensive. Do you think there should be standards for adventure sport equipment?

La ANIMAL SOUNDS

Sounds are all around us. We use sound to communicate, to warn others of danger and for enjoyment. Animals also use sounds to communicate, to warn others of danger, to try to stop others entering their territory, to win a mate and to hunt. Some animals even use sound to help them to find their way around or to find **prey** when they cannot see. Other animal sounds do not seem to have a purpose.

B | Bats that hunt at night use sound to find their way around and to locate their prey.

C | Hummingbirds 'hum' because their wings flap very fast.

A | This leopard is roaring to warn other predators to keep away.

Sounds are made by something **vibrating** (moving backwards and forwards).

1 Write down two ways that humans use sounds:
 a| for communication
 b| for warning.

2 How is the sound made by the hummingbird different from the sounds made by the bat and the leopard? Give as many differences as you can.

3 Write down two different ways that you can make sounds with your body.

4 A guitar can be used to make different notes.
 a| How do you make a guitar produce sounds?
 b| How can you make high and low notes on a guitar?
 c| How can you make loud or quiet notes on a guitar?

5 Would you expect an elephant or a mouse to be able to make the lowest notes? Explain your answer.

7La MAKING SOUNDS

HOW ARE DIFFERENT SOUNDS MADE?

Some sounds are loud and some are soft. This is the **intensity** of the sound. Sounds with a high intensity are often said to have a high **volume**.

Sounds can also be high or low. This is the **pitch** of the sound. The pitch and volume of the sound depend on the way an object vibrates to make the sound.

Generally, smaller objects vibrate faster and make notes with higher pitches. The number of vibrations each second is called the **frequency**. The units for frequency are **hertz (Hz)**. A bell that vibrates 400 times per second has a frequency of 400 Hz.

The volume of a note depends on the size of the vibrations. The size of a vibration is its **amplitude**. The bigger the amplitude, the louder the note.

A | This sparrow makes high-pitched notes.

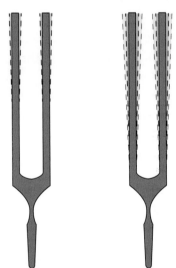

B | The tuning fork on the right was tapped harder than the one on the left. It is making a louder sound.

1   List four animals that make loud sounds.

2   What are vibrations?

3   A tuning fork vibrates 500 times per second.
   a| What is its frequency?
   b| How will it sound different from a tuning fork that vibrates 300 times per second?

C | These tubular bells vibrate when they are hit. The short bells vibrate faster than the longer ones, so they make higher notes.

FACT

Whales make many different noises. Some whale calls are louder than jet engines and can be heard over 800 km away. The photo shows a hydrophone hanging beneath a boat. It is being used to record the song of a humpback whale.

hydrophone

D

'teeth' used to make chirps

E | a male cricket

You make sounds using your voice. You have two flaps (called **vocal folds**) across your **windpipe** and these can vibrate when air moves across them. Most animals make noises in a similar way to this but there are also other ways in which animals can make sounds.

Male grasshoppers chirp by rubbing one leg against a wing. Their hind legs have teeth on them and when these are scraped against a wing it makes a sound (a bit like scraping a stick quickly along a fence).

Animals can also make sounds by hitting things. Male gorillas thump their chests or thump the ground to threaten other males.

4 A giant hummingbird flaps its wings about 12 times per second and bee hummingbirds can flap at over 80 times per second. Explain how the noise made by the wings of each species will sound different.

5 Two male gorillas are beating their chests.

a| One makes a lower sound than the other. Suggest what this could tell you about the two gorillas. Explain your answer.

b| Explain how one of them can make a louder sound than the other.

6 Henna says: 'Large animals always make lower sounds than small animals.' Explain how you could find out if she is right.

F | a male gorilla thumping his chest

I can ...

- explain what causes sounds and how to make louder sounds
- explain the link between frequency and pitch.

MOVING
7Lb SOUNDS

HOW DOES SOUND TRAVEL?

The astronauts in photo A have to talk to each other using a radio system because sound cannot travel through the empty space between them. Sound can only travel through a **medium** (a **solid**, **liquid** or **gas**). It cannot travel through a **vacuum** (a completely empty space).

All substances are made from **particles**. A vibrating loudspeaker makes the air particles close to it move backwards and forwards. These moving particles make neighbouring particles move, and so the vibrations spread out through the air. The moving vibrations form a **sound wave**. The air particles are squashed together in some places – these places have higher **pressure**. The particles are spread out in other places – these places have lower pressure. These waves are called **pressure waves** because there is a repeating pattern of high and low pressure areas.

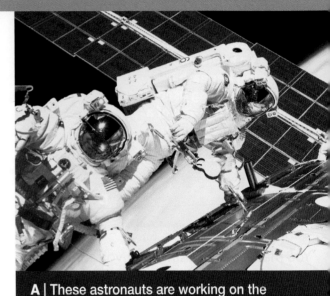

A | These astronauts are working on the International Space Station.

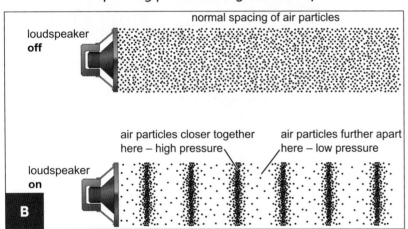

B

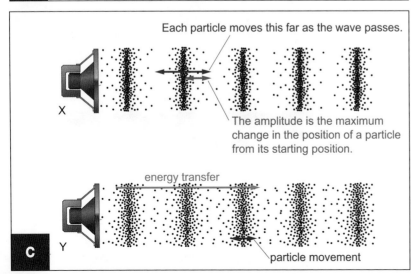

C

1 How are the particles arranged in solids, liquids and gases?

2 The astronauts in photo A can talk to each other without a radio system if they touch their helmets together. Explain why this works.

The frequency of a sound wave is the number of waves passing per second.

The amplitude of the wave is the distance moved by the air particles as the sound wave passes. The greater the amplitude, the louder the sound.

Pressure waves, such as sound waves, **transfer energy** from one place to another. They do not transfer particles. The louder the sound, the more energy it is transferring.

3 Look at the sound waves in diagram C. Which shows the louder sound? Explain your answer.

Speed of sound

Sound travels at different speeds in different materials. The vibrations are passed on more easily when the particles in a material are closer together, so sounds travel faster in solids than in liquids. Sound also travels faster in liquids than in gases.

D	Material	Speed of sound (m/s)
	air (20 °C)	343
	water (10 °C)	1450
	wood	3600
	glass	3950
	steel	6100

4 Why does sound travel faster in steel than it does in air? Use ideas about particles in your answer.

5 Look at table D. Paul says: 'The table shows that sound travels faster in metals than in other solids.'

a| Explain why this is not a good conclusion to make from the data in the table.

b| How could you find out if sound does travel faster in metals than in other solids?

E | Sound waves spread out in three directions.

Sound waves spread out from a **source**. As you get further from the source, the energy carried by the sound wave has spread out further. There is less energy for your ear to detect when you are further from the source.

FACT

You can work out how far away a thunderstorm is by counting the number of seconds between the lightning flash and hearing the thunder. Divide the number of seconds by three and that is the distance in kilometres. This works because light travels at 300 000 km/s and so reaches you very quickly but sound travels at about a third of a kilometre every second and so takes three seconds to travel each kilometre.

6 You can make your voice carry further by cupping your hands around your mouth or by shouting through a paper cone. Explain why this works.

7 The slinky in diagram F is a model representing a sound wave.

a| How does the model represent sound waves?

b| In what ways is this not a good model for sound waves?

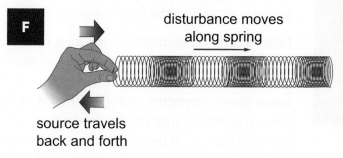

F

disturbance moves along spring

source travels back and forth

I can ...

- describe how sound moves through materials
- explain why sounds get fainter further from their source.

LINE GRAPHS AND
7Lb SCATTER GRAPHS

HOW CAN GRAPHS HELP US TO MAKE CONCLUSIONS?

A sound wave is vibrations being passed on by solids, liquids or gases. As the sound wave passes, particles in the medium move backwards and forwards. The particles that make up materials are very small, so it helps to use a model to help us to think about what is happening.

The slinky spring is a model for a sound wave. Line graph B shows how the marked point on the spring in diagram A moves as the wave passes. Line graphs are used to show how one **variable** changes as another variable changes (usually time).

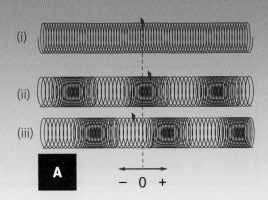

(i)

(ii)

(iii)

A

− 0 +

1	Look at graph B.
	a| What does zero distance represent?
	b| What is the amplitude of the wave in the spring?
2	The same spring is used to model a quieter sound. Describe how the graph would be different.

Positive distances show the coil has moved in the same direction as the wave is travelling.

The points are joined with straight lines or a smooth curve is drawn through them.

Negative distances show the coil has moved in the opposite direction to the wave.

Time is on the horizontal axis with the units in brackets.

B

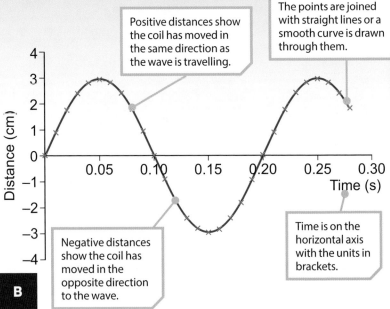

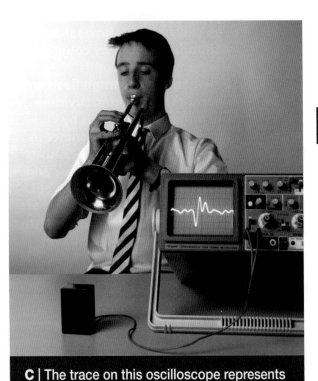

C | The trace on this oscilloscope represents the sound waves that the trumpet is making.

An **oscilloscope** can be connected to a **microphone** to show sound waves. The oscilloscope **trace** is like a line graph.

On a sound wave trace, the amplitude is the maximum distance from 0. The frequency is the number of complete waves (one up and down) that pass a point each second. In trace B, one wave takes 0.2 seconds. In each second 5 waves pass and so the frequency is 5 Hz.

Graphs can also be used to look for a **relationship** (link) between two **quantitative** variables. Graph D is a **scatter graph** that shows how the speed of sound in air changes when the temperature changes. The **line of best fit** is the best straight line that can be drawn through the points. Lines (or curves) of best fit should only be drawn when the graph shows a clear pattern.

How speed of sound depends on temperature

We usually draw a line of best fit through the points.

D

We often describe in words what the line on a graph tells us. In graph D, as you follow the horizontal axis from left to right, the temperature increases. As the temperature increases, the line on the graph goes up and this tells us that the speed of sound in air is also increasing. The description of a straight line on a graph is often written in the form: As [variable on horizontal axis] increases, [variable on vertical axis] [increases/decreases].

Graph D shows a relationship between the two variables. Relationships like this are known as a positive **correlation**. When a line of best fit on a scatter graph gets lower as you move along the horizontal axis, this is called a negative correlation.

3 Describe what graph D tells us about the speed of sound in air.

4 Draw labelled sketches to show positive and negative correlations.

5 Solid materials have different properties. The **density** is the mass of a certain volume of material. For example, iron has a higher density than wood because a piece of iron has more mass than the same sized piece of wood. Some materials are also stiffer than others.

Table E shows the density and stiffness of some different metals. For stiffness, the higher the number, the stiffer the material. Carrie says that sound travels faster in denser materials. Dave says that sound travels faster if the material is stiffer. You can find out whose hypothesis is correct by plotting scatter graphs.

Plot a scatter graph with stiffness on the horizontal axis and speed on the vertical axis. Then plot another graph with density on the horizontal axis and speed on the vertical axis.

a| What conclusion can you make from your two graphs?

b| Whose hypothesis was correct? Explain your answer.

c| How did drawing the scatter graphs help you to decide whose hypothesis was correct?

E | The properties of some metals. (You do not need to remember the units for stiffness!)

Metal	Stiffness (GPa)	Density (g/cm³)	Speed of sound (m/s)
aluminium	76	2.7	5100
copper	140	8.9	3570
iron	170	7.9	4910
magnesium	45	1.7	4602
mercury	25	13.5	1407
nickel	180	8.9	4970
silver	100	10.5	2600
titanium	110	4.5	4140
zinc	70	7.1	3700

I can ...

- present information as scatter graphs
- describe what line graphs and scatter graphs show
- identify relationships using scatter graphs.

7Lc DETECTING SOUNDS

HOW CAN WE DETECT SOUNDS?

Most animals use ears to detect sound waves. The part of your ears that you can see helps to channel the sound waves into the ear. 'Hearing' happens inside your head.

A | Owls are nocturnal. They can hunt at night because they have very sensitive hearing. They can hear much quieter sounds than humans can.

| 1 | Write down these parts of the ear in order, starting with the one that vibrates first when a sound wave arrives: bones, cochlea, eardrum. |
| 2 | a\| What are impulses?
b\| Which part of the ear sends impulses to the brain? |

Loud sounds can damage our ears, including sounds from headphones playing music. People who work in noisy surroundings often need to wear **ear protection**. Loud noises can also be annoying. We can use certain materials to **absorb** some of the energy transferred by sound waves. In our homes, soft materials like carpets and curtains help to absorb sounds.

2. The **eardrum** is a thin membrane. Sound waves make it vibrate.

3. Vibrations are passed on to tiny bones which **amplify** the vibrations (make them bigger).

4. Vibrations are passed on to the liquid inside the **cochlea**.

1. Sound wave approaches the ear and enters the **ear canal**.

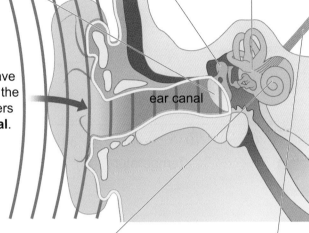

ear canal

5. Tiny hairs inside the cochlea detect these vibrations and create electrical signals called **impulses**.

6. Impulses travel along the **auditory nerve** to reach the brain. You hear the sound when the impulses reach your brain.

B | the human ear

FACT

The tufts on the head of a long-eared owl are not ears at all. Some scientists think they may help to camouflage the owl so it can hide from predators. The ear openings in owls are much further down.

ear openings in skull

Microphones

Microphones work in a similar way to ears. Sound waves make a **diaphragm** (a thin sheet of material) vibrate. Electrical circuits in the microphone detect the vibrations and convert them into changes in electrical current. Ears and microphones both change the way in which energy is being transferred.

Sound intensity meters use a microphone to measure the loudness of a sound in **decibels (dB)**. The quietest sound that humans can hear is 0 dB, normal conversation is about 60 dB and sounds are painful at above about 130 dB.

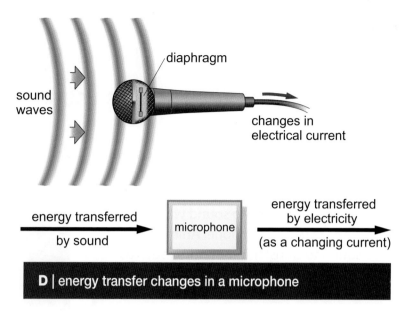

D | energy transfer changes in a microphone

Hearing ranges

Most humans can hear sounds with frequencies from 20 Hz to 20 000 Hz. This is known as the **auditory range**. Sounds with lower frequencies than we can hear are called **infrasound** and sounds at higher frequencies than we can hear are called **ultrasound**. Other animals have different auditory ranges.

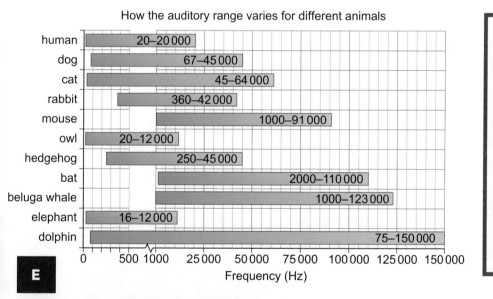

E

3 Draw a flow chart similar to the one in diagram D to show the energy transfer changes in the ear.

4 In some countries, employers must provide hearing protection if the noise level is above 85 dB. Why is this necessary?

5 How could you find out which materials are the best sound insulators? Write a plan for an investigation.

6 Look at graph E. Which animal(s) can:

a| hear infrasounds   b| hear ultrasounds?

7 Describe two differences between the hearing of owls and humans.

8 a| Cats have similar structures in their ears to humans. Describe how a cat hears.

b| Sheepdog whistles are used by some shepherds to give their dogs instructions, when herding sheep. The dogs can hear all the sounds made by the whistles but humans cannot here some of them. Suggest a frequency that a sheep dog whistle might produce that humans cannot hear.

I can ...

- describe the parts of the ear and their functions
- describe how microphones convert sound into electrical signals
- recall that different animals have different hearing ranges.

61

7Ld USING SOUND

HOW DO HUMANS AND ANIMALS USE SOUND?

We make use of sound in many different ways, including for **communication**. Sometimes the sound waves are converted to electrical signals and then back to sound waves, such as when we use a telephone. Animals also use sound to transfer information, such as warning calls.

> **1** Write down three ways in which you have used sound to communicate today.
>
> **2** Write down three different types of communication made by animal sounds.

A | The air sacs on this frog help it to make its mating calls louder.

Transferring energy

Sound waves transfer energy from one place to another. The energy transferred by sound waves is **transmitted** through some materials, or it can be absorbed or **reflected**.

The energy transferred by high frequency sound waves can be used to treat injuries. It can also be used to clean objects with complicated shapes such as jewellery or surgical instruments. The object being cleaned is put into a liquid. Ultrasound waves sent through the liquid make lots of tiny bubbles in the liquid, which help to loosen the dirt when they break.

> **3** Energy transferred by ultrasound is used to clean a watch. What does the energy do?

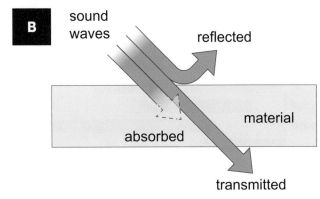

B sound waves — reflected — material — absorbed — transmitted

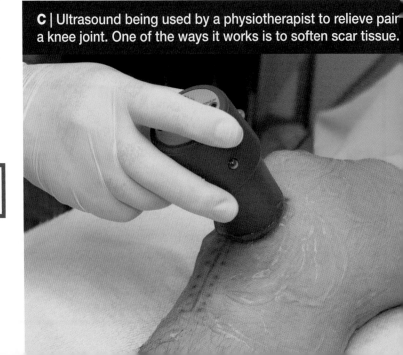

C | Ultrasound being used by a physiotherapist to relieve pain a knee joint. One of the ways it works is to soften scar tissue.

Using echoes

A reflected sound is called an **echo**. Animals such as dolphins and bats use **echolocation** to find their way around and to find their prey. These animals produce bursts of ultrasound and listen for the sound waves reflected by objects or prey. They can detect how far away the object is from the time it takes for the echo to return and they can also sense the direction of the object.

Bats use echolocation to help them to find food at night, when there is not enough light to see. Dolphins and some other sea creatures use echolocation because sound travels through water much better than light. Humans also use a form of echolocation called **sonar** to find fish in the sea and to investigate the depth of the sea.

— sound waves from bat
— returning sound waves

D | Some species of bat use echolocation to detect prey such as insects.

FACT

Some blind humans have learned to use echolocation to help them to find their way about and avoid bumping into things. They make clicks with their mouths and listen for the echoes.

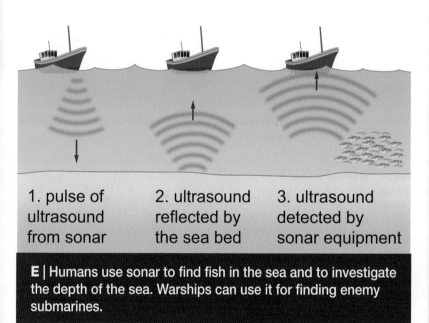

1. pulse of ultrasound from sonar

2. ultrasound reflected by the sea bed

3. ultrasound detected by sonar equipment

E | Humans use sonar to find fish in the sea and to investigate the depth of the sea. Warships can use it for finding enemy submarines.

F | Lucas Murray is blind and uses clicks to help him to play basketball as well as to find his way around.

4. Each bat can produce different frequencies of ultrasound. Explain why this is useful if there are many bats hunting together.

5. The ship in diagram E detects two echoes from a sonar pulse, one 0.05 seconds after the other. Explain what has caused these two echoes and what information the sonar equipment can work out from them.

6. Tiger moths do not use echolocation but they can detect and produce ultrasounds.

   a | Suggest how this helps them to survive.

   b | How could you check whether or not tiger moths do detect and produce ultrasounds?

I can ...

- describe some uses of ultrasound
- explain how sonar and echolocation work.

WORKING WITH SOUND

7Ld

WHAT DO ACOUSTIC ENGINEERS DO?

Acoustics is the study of sound and how it is affected by buildings and other structures. Acoustic engineers can help to develop loudspeakers and design rooms or concert halls so that audiences can hear sounds clearly. They also work to reduce unwanted sounds.

In photo A, an anechoic chamber is being used to test a loudspeaker. The walls, ceiling and floor are covered in pointed shapes that stop sounds being reflected directly back into the room. The shapes are made from soft materials to absorb the energy in sound waves. This allows engineers to gather data about many loudspeakers in the same conditions.

A | testing loudspeakers in an anechoic chamber

B | The Dubai Fountain uses water jets, lights and sound to make a spectacular show.

The lights and fountain in photo B are changing in time to music. Acoustic engineers help to place loudspeakers and control the sound so that everyone watching can hear the music clearly. At some outdoor events they may also set up temporary sound barriers, so that people living or working nearby are not disturbed by the noise.

Roads, railways and factories can all be very noisy. Acoustic engineers design noise barriers to protect nearby people from the noise. Barriers made from hard materials like metal or concrete reflect noise back into the road. Other materials, like banks of earth or wooden fences, help to absorb the noise.

1. a | Write down three different sources of noise in your school.
    b | How could these unwanted noises be reduced?

2. a | Write down three other places where there is often a lot of unwanted noise.
    b | Suggest one way of reducing the noise in these places.

3. An acoustic engineer proposes a metal or a wooden fence to act as a noise barrier next to a road. Write down one advantage and one disadvantage of each material for this purpose.

C | The barriers beside this road reduce the noise heard by people living nearby.

Acoustic engineering

Acoustic engineers need a university degree in acoustics, physics or other engineering subjects. They may go on to study further, to help them to specialise (concentrate on one area of acoustic engineering).

One specialist area is designing concert halls or theatres. Audiences hear sounds from musicians or people speaking on the stage directly, but they also hear sounds reflected from the walls and ceiling. Acoustic engineers help to design spaces such as this to give the best sound quality for the audience. They may also be asked to modify older buildings to improve their acoustics.

D | The curved walls and ceiling of the concert hall help to stop echoes of the music from the stage.

> **4** Suggest why the following employ acoustic engineers:
>
> a | a company that makes recordings of music
>
> b | architects designing a railway station.

PRACTICAL

Use a sound meter app to investigate the noise levels in your school.

- Predict which parts of the school you think will have the most noise, and which times of day they will be noisiest.

- Work in a team to record noise levels at different parts of the school at different times of day.

- Present your results in a bar chart, like the one in chart E.

- Suggest what changes the school could make to reduce the noise levels.

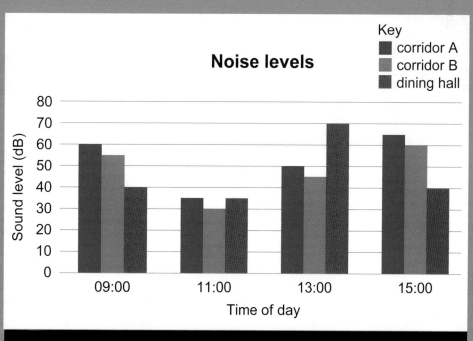

E | Presenting data in bar charts makes it easier to compare it.

COMPARING WAVES
7Le

HOW ARE SOUND WAVES LIKE WAVES IN WATER?

The ripples in the pond in photo A are small waves on the surface of the water. They are spreading out across the surface of the water from the duck at the centre. They are transferring energy from this diving duck.

Water particles move up and down as the waves pass but the water as a whole does not move. The other ducks on the pond will not be moved outwards by the waves.

A sound wave is a **longitudinal wave** because the particles vibrate in the same direction as the wave is travelling.

Waves on the surface of water are **transverse waves**. The particles in water are moving at right angles to the direction the wave is travelling. The amplitude of a transverse wave is the maximum distance the particles move up or down from their original position.

A

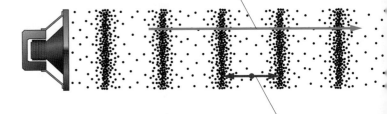

B | Sound is a longitudinal wave.

FACT

Waves on the sea are made by the wind blowing over the oceans or by earthquakes in the sea bed. The largest wave ever recorded was over 500 metres high and occurred in Alaska in 1958.

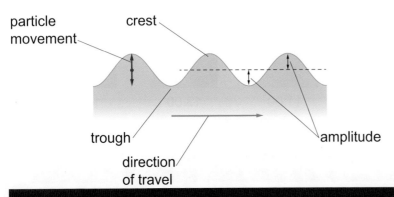

C | Waves on water are transverse waves.

1 What is the difference between a transverse wave and a longitudinal wave?

2 Which way will ducks on a pond move as waves pass them?

3 You drop a stone into a pond.

a| What happens to some of the energy that was stored in the falling stone?

b| How could you make waves on the pond with a larger amplitude?

The amplitude of waves on water gets smaller as the waves get further from their source because the energy transferred by the waves gets more spread out.

Waves on water can be reflected. This happens if the waves reach a solid barrier, such as the edge of a canal or a harbour wall.

Waves going in different directions can pass through each other. As the waves pass, their effects can add together or cancel out. This is called **superposition**, because one wave is 'on top of' another.

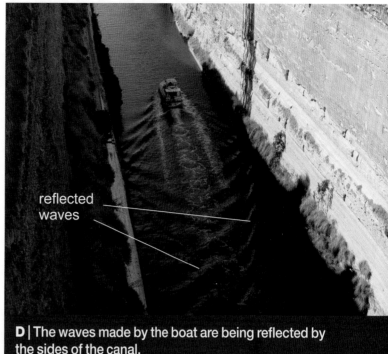

reflected waves

D | The waves made by the boat are being reflected by the sides of the canal.

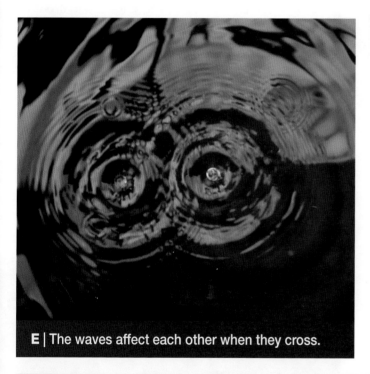

E | The waves affect each other when they cross.

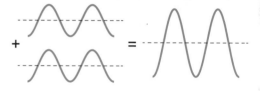

When two crests or two troughs meet they add together to make a bigger wave.

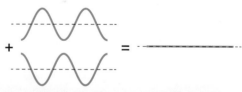

When a crest meets a trough they cancel each other out.

F | Superposition of waves can make them add together or cancel out.

4 Look at photo A. Which duck will move up and down the least as the waves pass it? Explain your answer.

5 You can think of waves on the surface of water as a model for sound waves. Are water waves or waves in a slinky spring (as shown in diagram F on page 57) the best model to help you to think about sound waves? Explain your answer.

6 People in small boats need to be careful if they are sailing near cliffs, because the waves can be bigger than in the open sea, and may be coming from more than one direction. Explain why this is.

7 Look at photo E above, and diagram E on page 57. Do sound waves or water waves get smaller fastest as they spread out from their source? Explain your answer.

I can ...

- compare longitudinal and transverse waves
- recall that all waves can be reflected
- explain what superposition means.

ANIMALS AND NOISE

HOW DO HUMAN NOISES AFFECT ANIMALS?

Sounds are all around us and we get used to most of them. If sounds are too loud, we can install soundproofing in our houses or cars, or make laws to limit the amount of noise that factories or airports are allowed to make.

Animals cannot control the noise around them. We can help our pets by keeping them indoors during noisy occasions, but it is a bit more difficult to protect wild or zoo animals.

In some cities, songbirds sing much earlier in the morning, to try to attract mates before traffic noise gets too loud. Some birds sing at different frequencies, or more loudly, in areas where there is a lot of noise. But not all animals that use sounds can adapt in this way.

A | Sometimes whales or dolphins become stranded on beaches or rocky shores. This may happen because of human-made noises underwater, such as explosions or sonar 'pings'.

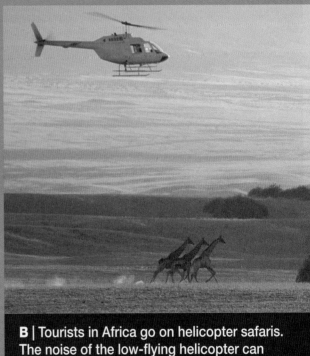

B | Tourists in Africa go on helicopter safaris. The noise of the low-flying helicopter can frighten the animals.

1 Explain how noise made by humans can affect the number of baby birds born in a year.

2 Some species of bat find it difficult to hunt in noisy areas.

   a| How can noise affect bats' hunting?

   b| How will this affect the bats' survival?

3 Naval ships use sonar to look for enemy submarines.

   a| Explain how the sonar sounds produced by the naval ships reach dolphins and divers swimming underwater.

   b| Why can the dolphins but not the divers hear the sounds?

   c| Explain how sonar noises might affect dolphins or whales.

HAVE YOUR SAY

Some people think that a noisy environment does not matter, as sounds do not usually harm animals directly. Do you agree?

EXPLORING

8Ia EXTREMES

Exploring extreme environments can help scientists to find out how the Earth and the Universe work. And humans have always wanted to explore new places just to see what is there.

About 70 per cent of the Earth's surface is covered in water. Scientists investigating the ocean floors need to use special technology to allow them to breathe and to cope with the much greater forces on objects underwater.

We can explore the solid surface of the Earth more easily, but technology helps here too. The South Pole was first visited in 1911 using teams of dogs to pull sledges. Today scientists get there using aeroplanes or vehicles fitted with caterpillar tracks. They can live there all year round, even during the Antarctic winter when the Sun never rises.

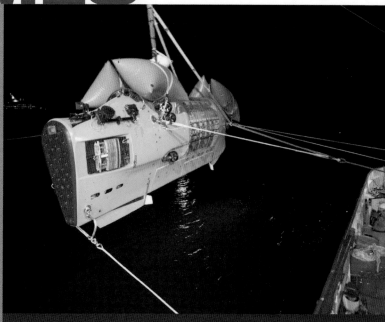

A | James Cameron's *Deepsea Challenger* has gone over 11 km down in the ocean where the forces on it are over 1000 times bigger than on the surface.

B | This is Halley station in Antarctica. The snow here never melts. To prevent the station from becoming buried, the buildings can be raised higher each year.

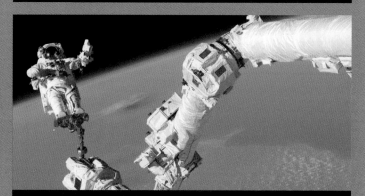

C | Astronauts need spacesuits to survive the vacuum of space.

Astronauts exploring the Moon brought back rocks that helped us to learn how the Solar System formed. Experiments in space can help to develop new materials and medical treatments.

1 Matter can exist as a solid, liquid or gas. Which state of matter is:
a| snow
b| air
c| the water shown in photo A?

2 Solids, liquids and gases have different properties. How are they different in terms of:
a| shape
b| volume?

3 Suggest some of the problems that people need to overcome in:
a| photo A
b| photo B
c| photo C.

THE PARTICLE MODEL
8Ia

HOW DO WE EXPLAIN THE PROPERTIES OF SOLIDS, LIQUIDS AND GASES?

Photo A shows a scientific expedition living on the frozen Arctic Ocean to study energy transfers. Ships are normally designed to be used on liquid water, but the ship in photo A has been specially designed to remain undamaged by the forces from solid water.

Materials can exist in three **states of matter**: solid, liquid or gas. The properties of a material are different in each of the three states.

- **Solids** keep their shape and volume; they cannot flow and are difficult to **compress** (squash into a smaller volume).

- **Liquids** keep their volume but not their shape; they can flow, take the shape of their containers and are difficult to compress.

- **Gases** can change their shape and volume; they spread out in all directions and are easy to compress.

A | the icebreaker *Xue Long* ('ice dragon') frozen into the Arctic ice

> 1   Name three different:
>   a| solid materials   b| liquids   c| gases.
>
> 2   Write down one similarity and one difference between the properties of:
>   a| solids and liquids
>   b| liquids and gases.
>
> 3   How does the arrangement and spacing of particles explain:
>   a| why it is difficult to compress solids and liquids
>   b| why gases are easily compressed?
>
> 4   How do the forces between particles explain:
>   a| why solids keep their shape
>   b| why gases expand to fill their containers?

The properties of the different states can be explained using the **particle theory** or **particle model**. This states that all matter is made up of moving particles held together by forces of attraction. The particles can be atoms or molecules. Table B shows how the forces and movement are different in the three states.

State	Forces	Spacing	Movement
solid	strong	close	vibrate in fixed positions
liquid	fairly strong	close	move around within the liquid
gas	weak	far apart	move about fast in all directions

B

Scientists think the particle model is correct because it explains many observations.

- **Diffusion**: gases or liquids mix without anything moving them because the particles are moving around all the time.

- **Brownian motion**: tiny bits of dust in air or water can be seen jiggling around around as they are hit by the moving air or water particles.

- **Expanding** and **contracting**: materials expand when heated and contract (get smaller) when cooled. This is because the particles in hotter materials move faster and so take up more space.

- **Density** changes: density is the **mass** of a certain **volume** of a material. When a material contracts, its density increases, because the same mass of particles takes up a smaller volume. A material's density decreases when it expands.

Buildings, bridges and other structures change size all the time. They have to be built with gaps in, so that, if the materials in them expand, the structure does not bend or break.

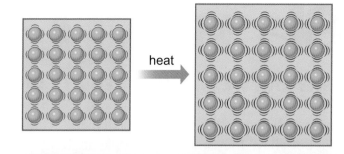

heat

C | When a solid is heated the particles vibrate further about their fixed positions. The particles themselves do *not* change size.

5 A substance cools down when energy is transferred away from it. Explain how this affects:
- a| the movement of the particles
- b| the size of the object.

FACT

Train tracks can buckle and twist in very hot weather.

D

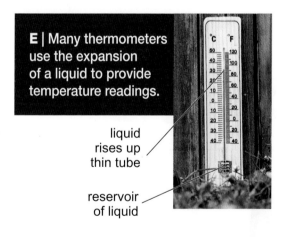

E | Many thermometers use the expansion of a liquid to provide temperature readings.

liquid rises up thin tube

reservoir of liquid

6 Look at photo E.
- a| Explain how a thermometer works.
- b| Suggest how you could make your own thermometer.

7 A bridge is built without expansion gaps. Explain what could happen to the bridge if the temperature became:
- a| much hotter than the day it was built
- b| much colder than the day it was built.

F | an expansion joint in a bridge

I can ...

- describe the properties of different states of matter
- explain the properties in terms of the particle model
- explain why materials expand and contract when the temperature changes.

CALCULATIONS
8Ia WITH DENSITY

HOW CAN WE FIND THE DENSITY OF AN OBJECT?

Photo A shows a piece of wood and a piece of iron that both have the same mass. People often say that metals are heavier than wood, but this is not correct. They usually mean that a piece of metal will have a greater mass than *the same sized* piece of wood. The mass of a piece of material with a volume of 1 cm³ is the density of the material.

A | The two cubes have the same masses but different volumes, so their densities are different.

B | When the water is heated its mass does not change but its volume increases. This means that its density decreases.

If the volume of an object changes without its mass changing (usually because it has been heated or cooled) its density will change.

Density is a quantity that cannot be measured directly. It has to be calculated using measurements of mass and volume.

Measuring volumes

Diagram C shows two ways of finding the volume of an object.

Volumes can be measured in metres cubed (m³) or centimetres cubed (cm³). These can sometimes be called cubic metres or cubic centimetres. Some measuring cylinders have the scale marked in millilitres (ml). One millilitre is the same volume as one centimetre cubed.

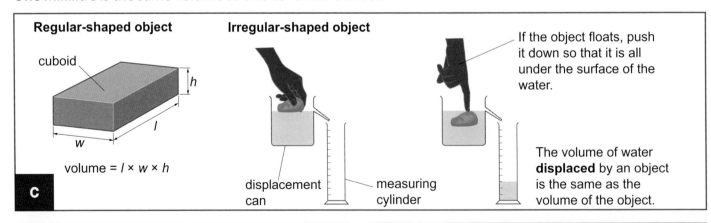

Regular-shaped object

cuboid

volume = $l \times w \times h$

Irregular-shaped object

If the object floats, push it down so that it is all under the surface of the water.

displacement can

measuring cylinder

The volume of water **displaced** by an object is the same as the volume of the object.

C

---

1 A piece of metal is a cuboid with width 2 cm, length 5 cm and height 1.5 cm. Calculate its volume.

2 Describe how to measure the volume of a piece of modelling clay.

Calculating density

The formula for calculating density is:

$$density = \frac{mass}{volume}$$

> Scientists often use ρ (the Greek letter rho, pronounced 'rowe') to represent density. We will use the letter 'd' instead.

This can be written in symbols as $d = \dfrac{m}{v}$

The units for density can be kilograms per metre cubed (kg/m^3) or grams per centimetre cubed (g/cm^3), depending on the units used for measuring the mass and volume. A worked example is shown on the right.

Calculating mass or volume

Sometimes a question may give you the mass and density of an object and ask you to calculate its volume. The triangle in diagram D shows you how to rearrange the formula.

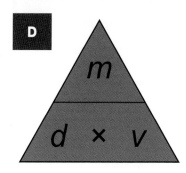

D

Cover the quantity you want to calculate, and what you can see is the formula you need.

So, the formula for calculating volume is:

$$volume = \frac{mass}{density}$$

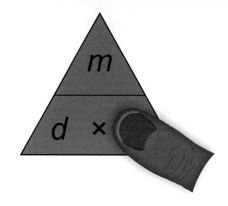

---

3 Calculate the density of the piece of iron shown in photo A.

Worked example

The volume of the wooden cube in photo A is:

$$6 \text{ cm} \times 6 \text{ cm} \times 6 \text{ cm} = 216 \text{ cm}^3$$

$$density = \frac{mass}{volume}$$

$$= \frac{64}{216}$$

$$= 0.296 \text{ g/cm}^3$$

$$= 0.3 \text{ g/cm}^3 \text{ (when rounded to 1 decimal place, 1 dp)}$$

You can also use the triangle to show how to calculate mass if you know the density and volume:

$$mass = density \times volume$$

4 The density of aluminium is 2.7 g/cm^3. You have a piece of aluminium with a volume of 50 cm^3.

a| Write down the formula you need to use to calculate its mass.

b| Work out its mass.

c| What is the volume of 810 g of aluminium?

5 A swimming pool contains 2500 m^3 of water with a density of 1000 kg/m^3 at 10° C. The water in the pool is heated to 20 °C and expands by 5.25 m^3.

a| Calculate the mass of the water in the swimming pool at 10 °C.

b| Use the particle model to explain why the water expands.

c| Will the density of the water increase or decrease when it is heated? Explain your answer.

d| Calculate the new density of the water after it has been heated.

I can ...

- state what is meant by density, and recall its units
- describe how to measure the volume of irregular objects
- use the formula relating mass, volume and density.

8|b CHANGING STATE

HOW DO MATERIALS CHANGE FROM ONE STATE TO ANOTHER?

Melting and **freezing** are **changes of state**. Some materials (including ice in some conditions) can change directly from a solid to a gas. This is called **sublimation**.

Changes such as combustion and neutralisation are **chemical changes**, because the atoms within substances become combined in different ways to form new substances. Changes of state are **physical changes**, because the chemicals in the substances do not change.

If you heat a solid to its **melting point** it forms a liquid. Particles can **evaporate** from the surface of a liquid to form a gas at any temperature. The **boiling point** of a substance is the temperature when evaporation happens *within* the liquid. The bubbles in **boiling** water are bubbles of **water vapour**.

If you cool a gas, it **condenses** into a liquid. If you cool a liquid, it starts to turn into a solid when the temperature reaches its **freezing point**. The freezing point and melting point of a substance are always the same temperature.

Graph B shows temperature against time for heating a **pure** substance. A mixture changes state over a range of temperatures because it contains substances with different melting and boiling points.

Energy is needed to overcome the forces holding particles together when solids change into liquids. When a liquid turns back into a solid, this energy is no longer needed and is transferred to the surroundings. The temperature of the substance remains the same while the liquid is changing to a solid.

A | an iceberg melting

> **1** In degrees Celsius (°C), at what temperature does:
> a| ice melt   b| water freeze?
>
> **2** Explain why diffusion is a physical change.

> **3** Look at graph B.
> a| What is the melting point of the substance shown in the graph?
> b| What is its boiling point?
> c| Why does the temperature of the substance stop rising at point X?
> d| Sketch a similar graph to show what happens when a substance cools down. Add a title and labels to explain the shape of your graph.

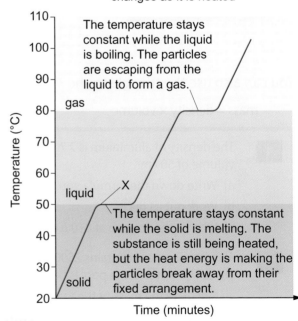

How the temperature of a pure substance changes as it is heated

The temperature stays constant while the liquid is boiling. The particles are escaping from the liquid to form a gas.

The temperature stays constant while the solid is melting. The substance is still being heated, but the heat energy is making the particles break away from their fixed arrangement.

B

A solid expands when it is heated and it expands even further when it forms a liquid. Graph C shows how the volume of a substance changes with temperature.

> **4** Think about graph C.
> a| Explain why the volume of a substance increases as it gets warmer.
> b| Describe how the volume of 1 kg of molten iron changes as it cools down and forms a solid.

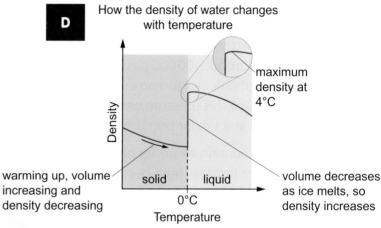

How the volume of a fixed mass of a substance changes with temperature

solid | liquid

C

melting/freezing point

Temperature

Water shows **anomalous** behaviour near its freezing point. This means that it does not behave in quite the same way as other materials. As water cools down it contracts until it reaches 4 °C and then it starts to expand again slightly. When ice forms, the ice takes up more space than the water did. Ice is less dense than water. This is why ice forms on the tops of ponds, which helps fish and other organisms to survive.

D

How the density of water changes with temperature

maximum density at 4°C

warming up, volume increasing and density decreasing

solid | liquid

0°C

volume decreases as ice melts, so density increases

Temperature

E | Water freezing inside this jar has expanded and split it apart.

FACT

This boulder was split by water getting into its cracks and expanding as it froze.

F

> **5** a| Explain the shape of the line on graph D.
> b| Describe two ways in which the changes shown in graph D are different from the changes that would occur in the case of a substance such as iron.

I can ...

- recall that a substance does not change temperature while it is changing state
- describe what happens to particles during changes of state
- describe the ways in which water and ice are different from other liquids and solids.

8Ic PRESSURE IN FLUIDS

HOW DO FLUIDS EXERT PRESSURE?

The particles in **fluids** (liquids and gases) are moving around in all directions. As they move they bump into each other and any surfaces they come into contact with. The force of the particles hitting things causes **pressure**. Pressure in liquids and gases comes from all directions.

Atmospheric pressure (the pressure of the air) at the surface of the Earth is about 100 000 pascals. One pascal (Pa) is a force of one newton on every square metre. We do not notice this pressure because fluids inside our bodies are at a similar pressure.

Car and bicycle tyres contain air under high pressure. The pressure inside is high because extra air has been pumped into the tyre so there are more particles to hit the inside walls of the tyre.

Pressure in fluids increases as the temperature increases, because the particles move faster and hit the walls of the container harder. If you compress the same amount of gas into a smaller volume the pressure also increases, because the particles hit the walls more often.

A | People diving for fun usually stay within 30 m of the surface. People who work further below the sea need special suits, like this one, to stop the high pressure from the water harming them.

1   What causes pressure in fluids?

2   Look at photo B. Explain why the two hemispheres cannot be pulled apart when some of the air has been sucked out of the space between them.

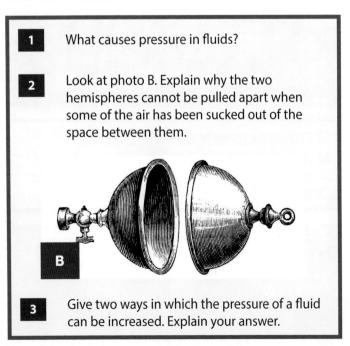

B

3   Give two ways in which the pressure of a fluid can be increased. Explain your answer.

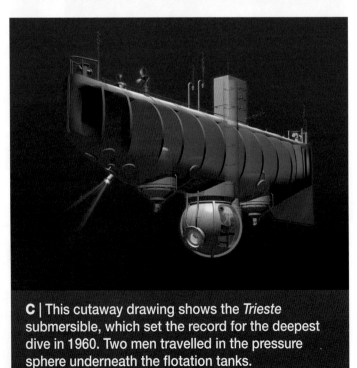

C | This cutaway drawing shows the *Trieste* submersible, which set the record for the deepest dive in 1960. Two men travelled in the pressure sphere underneath the flotation tanks.

Pressure in a fluid depends on the weight of fluid above. As you go down into the ocean there is more water above you and the pressure increases. The surface of the Earth is at the bottom of the atmosphere. If we go up a mountain there is less air above us and so the pressure gets less. There are fewer particles in each metre cubed of air.

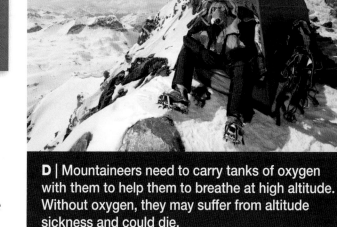

D | Mountaineers need to carry tanks of oxygen with them to help them to breathe at high altitude. Without oxygen, they may suffer from altitude sickness and could die.

This photo was taken at a height of 2413 m.

This is the same bag of crisps at sea level.

E | These photos demonstrate the effect of air pressure on a sealed bag of crisps.

4 a| Use ideas about particles to explain why there is less pressure on you from the air if you go up a high mountain.

  b| Explain why the mountaineer in photo D needs to wear an oxygen mask.

5 Look at the photos in E. Explain why the bag looks different in the two photos, using ideas about particles and pressure.

6 The steel walls of the pressure sphere on the *Trieste* (photo C) were over 12 cm thick. This is much thicker than the steel that ships are made from. Explain why the walls needed to be so thick.

7 A diver will experience twice atmospheric pressure by descending just 10 m below the surface of the sea, but you need to climb over 5000 m above sea level before air pressure is halved. Explain this statement in as much detail as you can.

I can ...

- describe how fluid pressure changes with depth or height
- describe how gas pressure can be increased
- explain some effects of pressure in different situations using the particle model.

FLOATING AND SINKING

WHY DO SOME THINGS FLOAT AND SOME THINGS SINK?

The first boats used by humans were probably just tree trunks dug out to make canoes. Later, pieces of wood were shaped and fixed together to make ships. The first ship made out of metal was not built until 1860.

When you are standing on the ground, gravity is pulling you down. An upwards force from the ground stops you sinking into the Earth. When you float in water, you feel that you weigh less. This is because there is a force from the water called **upthrust**. This pushes up against your **weight**. You still have weight, but you do not feel it. An object will float when the upthrust balances its weight.

A | Viking explorers were the first Europeans to visit North America, using wooden longships like this replica.

> **1**
> a| What two forces affect you when you float?
>
> b| How do these two forces compare in size?
>
> **2** A boy's weight is 500 N. What upthrust does he need to float?
>
> **3** A hot air balloon is floating in the air. The air gives upthrust.
>
> a| What are the two forces acting on the balloon?
>
> b| What can you say about the sizes of the two forces?

There is always upthrust on an object in a fluid, even if the upthrust is not large enough to make the object float. Photo B shows one way of measuring the upthrust.

> **4** Look at photo B. Describe how you can measure the upthrust on an object.
>
> **5** How could you find out if the size of the upthrust depends on the material the object is made from?

You can work out if something will float in a fluid if you know its density and the density of the fluid. The density of water is 1 g/cm³. If something has a density less than 1 g/cm³ it will float in water. For objects that float, the greater their density the more of the object is under the water.

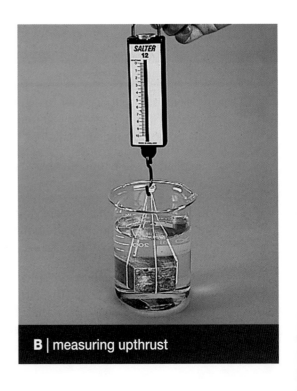

B | measuring upthrust

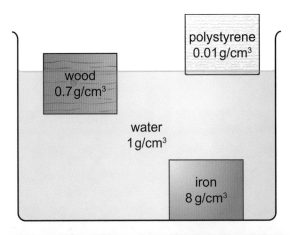

C | Objects less dense than water float in water. The lower an object's density, the higher out of the water it floats.

The density of air at sea level is approximately 0.001 g/cm³. Hot air balloons fly because the overall density of the whole balloon (including the basket and passengers and the hot air inside it) is less than the air around it. The air inside is heated to make it expand and become less dense.

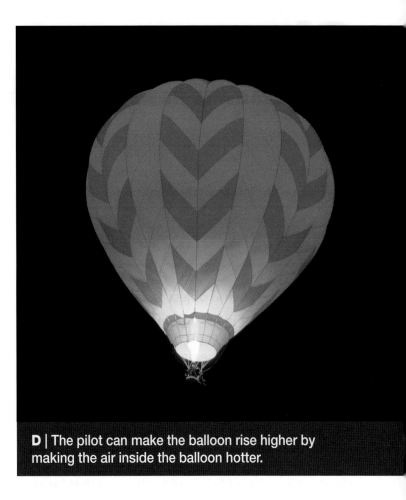

D | The pilot can make the balloon rise higher by making the air inside the balloon hotter.

FACT

Icebergs float with about 90 per cent of their volume under the surface of the water. This means that a ship sailing close to ice may hit part of the iceberg that the crew cannot see. Ice is unusual because with most materials a solid sinks in its liquid.

E | The RMS *Titanic* sank in 1912 after it hit an iceberg.

6 Look at diagram C.

  a| Explain whether a cube of iron will float in mercury (the density of mercury is 13.6 g/cm³).

  b| Explain why polystyrene will float in water but not in air.

7 Steel is denser than water, so how can a steel ship float? (*Hint*: think about what is inside the ship.)

8 Look at photo D. Explain why making the air inside the balloon hotter makes the balloon rise. Use ideas about particles in your answer.

I can ...

- state what is meant by upthrust
- explain why some objects float
- recall the factors that affect the amount of upthrust
- use ideas about density in my explanations.

8Ie DRAG

WHAT IS DRAG AND HOW CAN IT BE REDUCED?

Any object moving through water or air will have a resistance force on it that will slow it down. **Water resistance** and **air resistance** are types of **drag**.

> **1**   What is drag?

The drag on a moving object is partly caused by **friction** between the moving object and the fluid. This friction can also cause the moving object to heat up. This part of the drag is reduced by giving the object a smooth surface.

Some of the drag is caused because the object has to push some of the fluid out of the way. The faster the object is moving, the more fluid has to be pushed out of the way each second. This part of the drag is reduced by keeping the area that faces the moving air or water as small as possible, and by giving the object a **streamlined** shape. This makes it easier for the fluid to move around it.

A | The parachutes on these crates have a large area, so they produce a lot of drag.

B | This submarine has a top speed of approximately 65 km/h and a crew of 140.

C | The submersible *Alvin* is used for scientific exploration of the sea bed. Its top speed is just over 3 km/h and it has a crew of two.

2 Write down three ways of reducing drag.

3 Look at photo A. Why do the parachutes need to have a large area?

4 Look at photos B and C. Compare the features of the two vehicles that will affect their drag.

The amount of drag on a moving object depends on its speed as well as its shape. The faster the object is moving, the greater the drag.

A vehicle travelling at a steady speed has **balanced forces** on it. A forwards force from the engine is needed to balance the drag forces. If the drag is less, the vehicle will not need such a big force from the engine to travel at that speed, and it will not use up as much fuel.

The top speed of a vehicle depends on the force its engine can produce and on the drag. As the vehicle goes faster and faster the drag increases until eventually it is as big as the maximum force from the engine.

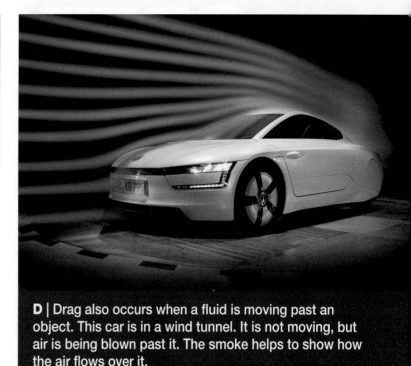

D | Drag also occurs when a fluid is moving past an object. This car is in a wind tunnel. It is not moving, but air is being blown past it. The smoke helps to show how the air flows over it.

E | a competitor in the Asian Track Championships in 2018

5 Athletes often need to make their drag as small as possible.

a| Describe two ways in which the cyclist in photo E has reduced his drag.

b| Explain how reducing his drag helps him to go faster.

6 a| Why do objects heat up if they are moving fast?

b| Use ideas about particles to explain why the drag is less if an object is moving slowly.

7 Write a 20-second radio advert explaining to drivers why they should drive more slowly.

8 a| Suggest two ways in which a car designer could increase the top speed of a new car.

b| Explain why each way would work, using ideas about balanced forces.

9 Suggest why the water speed record is only 511 km/h when the land speed record is 1227 km/h.

FACT

Golf balls have small dimples on their surface to reduce drag.

I can ...

- describe ways in which drag forces can be increased or reduced
- describe the causes of drag forces
- describe how drag changes with speed.

WHAT SKILLS ARE NEEDED TO OPERATE AEROPLANES?

There are nearly 10 000 aeroplanes in the air at any one time, carrying over a million passengers. Airline pilots are responsible for the safety of billions of passengers each year.

A | Pilots must understand and use many different instruments and displays in the cockpit.

B | Pilots need to be able to think quickly. This aeroplane's engines stopped working soon after take-off. The pilot landed in a nearby river and everyone survived.

> 1   Suggest why pilots need to study:
> a | meteorology
> b | navigation.
>
> 2   The aeroplane in photo A is an Boeing 737. Suggest why the two pilots would have to do more training before they fly an Airbus A320.

Pilots must be good at maths and physics and must pass strict medical tests. As well as learning to fly, the training at flight schools includes meteorology (weather), navigation, air law and how aeroplanes work. Their pilot's licence must be recognised by all the countries they fly to.

Air traffic control

Air traffic controllers tell pilots where they can fly, to make sure there are no collisions. They need to study many of the same things as pilots in their training.

> 3   Suggest why air traffic controllers need to study meteorology.

Communications between air traffic control and pilots are made in English, so pilots and controllers must speak English well. There are also internationally agreed conventions they use to make sure people understand.

C | Air traffic controllers use radar and computer technology to help them to keep aeroplanes at safe distances from each other.

Kansok Tower, Asia Cargo 182 with you on the localiser two niner right.

Asia Cargo 182, roger, cleared to land two niner right.

Cleared to land two niner right, Asia Cargo 182.

Maps for pilots and air traffic controllers have internationally agreed symbols on them to show things like navigation aids, routes, and obstacles such as tall masts or buildings. They need to be able to understand charts like these.

D | talk between a pilot and air traffic control

4 Why do maps for pilots show things like radio masts?

5 Explain why the wheels are moved inside the aeroplane after take-off.

6 Airliners fly at a height of about 12 km. Explain why they must have pressurised cabins and breathing masks that provide the passengers with oxygen if the cabin becomes depressurised.

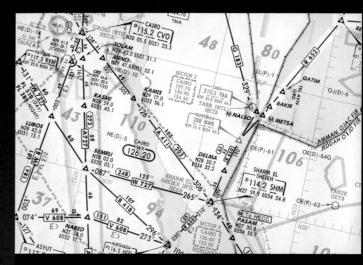

E | Maps used by pilots use special symbols.

ACTIVITY

Pilots and controllers need to understand how aeroplanes fly, so they can work out things like the length of runway a particular aeroplane will need to take off. This information is often presented as charts or graphs.

The upwards force on an aeroplane's wing is called lift. The lift produced by a wing is proportional to the density of the air. The lift also depends on speed – the faster an aeroplane is flying, the greater the lift.

Graph F shows how air density changes with height. Air density also depends on temperature. Hot air is less dense than cold air.

1 Compare the density of the air at 12 km with the density at sea level.

2 Explain how the lift from a wing changes when an aeroplane:

a | slows down

b | climbs to a greater height.

3 Explain why an aeroplane has a higher take-off speed on a hot day.

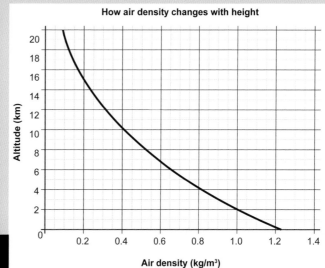

F

HUMANS AT THE EXTREMES

HOW CAN WE SURVIVE IN EXTREME CONDITIONS?

In 2012, Felix Baumgartner broke the world record for skydiving. He jumped from a balloon at about 39 km above the Earth and reached supersonic speeds as he fell. This is also the record for the highest balloon flight. He needed to wear a special pressure suit to keep him alive.

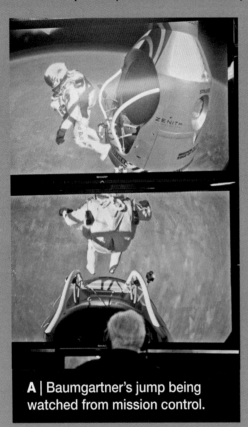

A | Baumgartner's jump being watched from mission control.

1 As Baumgartner's balloon went up through the atmosphere, it got bigger. Explain why this happened, using ideas about particles and pressure.

Divers exploring the oceans used to suffer from decompression sickness. Experiments on animals and humans allowed scientists to work out safe ways of reducing the pressure as they came back to the surface so that divers would not be harmed.

People who work on boats in the Arctic or Antarctic often wear immersion suits. These help them to survive for longer if they end up in the water. This gives them more chance of being rescued. Some of the information used to develop these suits was obtained from experiments on human prisoners.

B | An immersion suit helps a person to survive in cold water.

2
a| Name one substance in each state of matter in photo B.
b| Describe the arrangement and movement of particles in each state.
c| How does the particle model explain the properties of the three states?

3 Sketch a graph to show how the temperature changes with time when a piece of ice is left to melt in a warm room. Label your graph to explain what is happening to the particles.

4 In photo B, ice is floating on liquid water. Explain why this is unusual. Use ideas about particles and density in your answer.

HAVE YOUR SAY

Should experiments ever be carried out on animals? Should they be carried out on humans?

We see things when light reflects off them and enters our eyes. But sometimes our eyes can mislead us. Lights, mirrors and colours can control what we see.

Light travels in straight lines from a **source**. In photo C the source of light is a spotlight. The hands are **opaque**, so light cannot travel through them and they forms a **shadow**.

A | We can see the beams of the spotlights because some of the light is reflecting off dust in the air.

B | This image looks three dimensional when you look at it through glasses with red and blue lenses.

C | This hand shadow only works when a spotlight shines on the hands from a particular direction.

1   Write down four different sources of light.

2
a| What does 'transparent' mean?
b| Write down the names of three materials that are transparent.
c| Write down the names of three materials that are opaque.

3   Look at photo A. Write a paragraph to explain how people watching can see the buildings and the water.

4   Look at photo C.
a| Explain why we can see a shadow on the wall.
b| Why does the shadow have no colour?
c| Draw a diagram to show how we can see the hands.

8Ja LIGHT ON THE MOVE

HOW DOES LIGHT TRAVEL?

Light is a way of transferring energy from one place to another. Light travels much faster than sound. Light can also travel through a **vacuum** (a completely empty space), which sound cannot. Table B compares light waves and sound waves.

B	Light	Sound
Type of wave	**transverse**	**longitudinal**
Speed	300 000 000 m/s in air	330 m/s in air
Travels through:	vacuum, gases, some liquids, some solids	**matter** (solids, liquids and gases)

1 Look at photo A. Explain why you see the flashes before you hear the bangs.

We can show how light travels by drawing **rays**. The rays have arrows to show in which direction the light is travelling.

A | These flashes are made by exploding fireworks. Energy is transferred from the explosions by light and sound.

C | The rays show how the audience can see the person on the stage.

2 Draw a sketch with light rays on to show how you can see:
a| a programme on TV   b| the pages of a book.

Light can pass straight through **transparent** materials. We say light is **transmitted** through these materials. When light reaches an opaque material, some of it is **reflected** and some is **absorbed** (taken into the material). When an object absorbs energy it warms up.

A **translucent** material, such as frosted glass, allows light through it but the rays leave the glass in many different directions. They are **scattered**. You cannot see clearly through translucent materials.

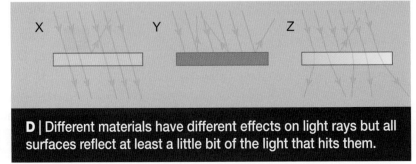

D | Different materials have different effects on light rays but all surfaces reflect at least a little bit of the light that hits them.

Pinhole cameras

A camera obscura is a room with a small hole in one wall. People inside the room can see an **image** of the outside world on the wall opposite the hole. A **pinhole camera** is a small version of a camera obscura.

A pinhole camera forms an image on the screen because light from the object travels in straight lines.

4 | You are given three pieces of card with holes in them, a piece of cotton thread and a candle. Explain how you could use this apparatus to show that light travels in straight lines.

5 | Someone is singing in another room with the door closed. Explain why you can hear them but not see them.

6 | Look at diagram F. Explain why the image formed in a pinhole camera is upside down.

The Camera Obfcura.

E | Artists often used a camera obscura to help them with their paintings.

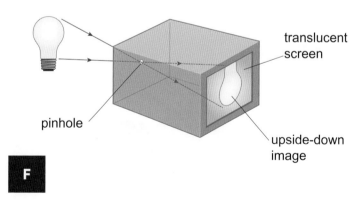

translucent screen

pinhole

upside-down image

F

FACT

The way a pinhole camera works was first described by the Arabic scientist Ibn al-Haytham (965–1040). He was also the first scientist to show by experiment that we see when light enters our eyes. Earlier thinkers had said that our eyes emit (give out) light that allows us to see.

I can ...

- compare light and sound waves
- describe what happens to light when it hits different surfaces
- describe how to demonstrate that light travels in straight lines.

DRAWINGS AND
8Jb CONVENTIONS

HOW DO WE USE RAY DIAGRAMS TO INVESTIGATE LIGHT?

Light from the Sun or from a light bulb spreads out in all directions. When we investigate how mirrors or other objects affect light, we need to use a narrow beam of light. Lasers are too expensive and not safe enough to use in school, so we use **ray boxes** instead.

A **plane mirror** is a flat mirror. You can investigate what happens when a ray of light hits a mirror using a ray box. The method described is called **ray tracing**.

A | Lasers produce very narrow beams of light. We can see where the beam of light goes because some of the light is reflected by dust in the air.

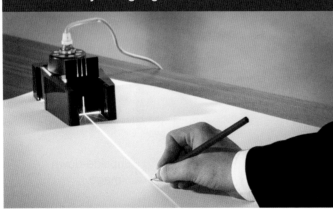

B | placing a ray box on a piece of paper to mark where the rays of light go

---

1 Why do we need to use ray boxes and paper when we investigate light?

2 Suggest why we can only see the rays from a ray box where they shine on the paper.

Method

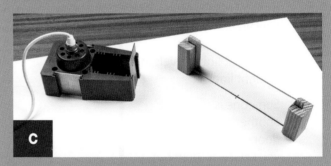

C

A | Stand a plane mirror on a piece of paper and point a ray box at the mirror. Draw a line on the paper along the back of the mirror. This will help you to make sure the mirror goes back to the same place if you move it accidentally.

B | Make a mark on the paper in the middle of the front of the mirror.

C | Switch on the ray box and aim the ray of light at the mark in the middle of the mirror. Mark where the rays of light are going by putting small crosses along the centre of the ray of light.

D | Carefully join the crosses using a ruler. You may need to move the mirror to do this, so make sure you put it back in the same place afterwards.

E | Repeat steps D and E with the ray box in three different positions. Point the ray of light to the same mark at the middle of the mirror each time.

F | Draw a line at right angles to the mirror where the mark is. This line is called the **normal.** Use a protractor to measure the angles between the light rays and the normal.

Scientists use standard **conventions** when drawing **ray diagrams**. This means that any scientist can understand the diagram.

Rays of light are shown by straight lines. The arrow shows the direction in which the light is travelling.

The normal is a line at right angles to the mirror. This is usually drawn as a dotted line. The angles of the light rays are measured from the normal.

The light travelling towards the mirror is called the **incident ray**.

The light travelling away from the mirror is called the **reflected ray**.

The angle between the incident ray and the normal is the **angle of incidence**.

This is called the **angle of reflection**.

D

The back of the mirror is often shown like this.

3 Table E shows some results from the investigation described in the Method above. Write a conclusion for the investigation.

E	Angle of incidence	Angle of reflection
	21°	20°
	30°	30°
	44°	45°
	55°	55°
	64°	65°
	72°	72°

4 Why is it important to use agreed symbols and conventions in science?

5 A curved piece of glass called a lens is fitted to the ray box to make the ray of light narrower and brighter. Explain how this can help to give more accurate results in this investigation.

I can ...

- explain why agreed conventions are used in ray diagrams
- use the correct names for rays reaching and leaving a mirror and the angles between them and the normal
- use ray tracing to investigate mirrors.

8Jb REFLECTION

WHAT HAPPENS TO LIGHT WHEN IT HITS A REFLECTIVE SURFACE?

Most mirrors are made of glass with a very thin layer of metal at the back. It is the metal that reflects the light. Mirrors reflect light evenly because the metal is very smooth. The angle of reflection (*r*) is equal to the angle of incidence (*i*). This kind of reflection is called **specular reflection**.

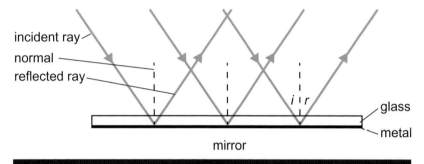

Law of reflection
angle of incidence = angle of reflection

incident ray
normal
reflected ray

i | *r*

glass
metal
mirror

B | specular reflection

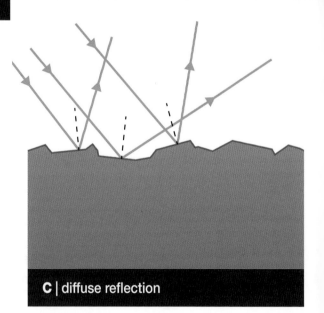

A | This man is standing in a lift with mirrors on the walls.

> **1** Which material is best at reflecting light: metal or glass? Explain how you worked out your answer.
>
> **2** Light hits a plane mirror with an angle of incidence of 20°. What will the angle of reflection be?

All materials reflect some of the light that reaches them. Even transparent materials like glass reflect some light. The light reflected by most opaque materials is scattered, so that it travels in all directions. This is called **diffuse reflection**. It happens because the surface of most materials is rough, so the light reflects at a lot of different angles.

C | diffuse reflection

> **3** Explain why you cannot see an image reflected by a piece of paper.
>
> **4** Explain why you can see your reflection better in a piece of metal if you polish the surface.

Images in mirrors

Diagram D shows how we see an image in a plane mirror. Rays of light spread out in all directions from a source of light. However, when we draw ray diagrams we only draw a few rays, to keep the diagram simple.

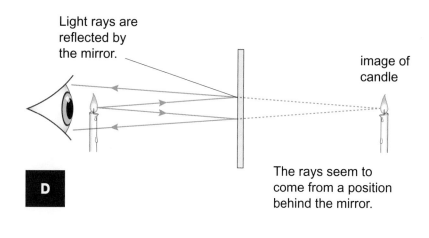

Light rays are reflected by the mirror.

image of candle

The rays seem to come from a position behind the mirror.

D

The image in a plane mirror:

- is the same size as the object
- is the same distance behind the mirror as the object is in front of it
- has left and right swapped over.

> **5** You stand 2 m in front of a plane mirror. Explain how far you are from where the image appears to be.
>
> **6** Suggest why the lines on the right-hand side of diagram D are shown as dotted lines.

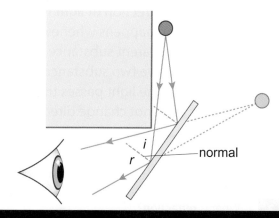

normal

E | You can use a mirror to look at something round a corner.

FACT

The Salar de Uyuni, in South America, is a salt flat (a dried out salt lake) with an area of over 10 000 km². Every year it becomes covered in a thin layer of water and forms the world's largest mirror.

F

> **7** The water in photo F is reflecting light.
>
> a| Is this specular or diffuse reflection? Explain your answer.
>
> b| Draw a ray diagram to show how light coming from the sky forms an image of the vehicle in the water.
>
> c| Explain why you will not see an image in the water on a windy day.

I can ...

- describe how mirrors and rough surfaces reflect light
- describe how an image is formed in a mirror using a ray diagram.

8Jc REFRACTION

HOW DO LENSES WORK?

Lenses are used in cameras to make sure the image is clear. They are also used in microscopes to make small things look bigger, and in telescopes to make distant objects look closer. Many people wear spectacles with lenses to help them to see more clearly, and lenses are used in theatres to focus beams of light from spotlights.

Lenses bend light as light passes through them. This change of direction of light is called **refraction**. Refraction happens whenever light travels from one transparent substance to another. It only takes place where two substances meet (at their **interface**). If the light passes through the interface at 90° it does not change direction.

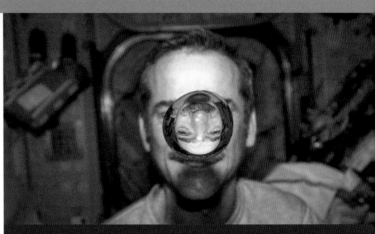

A | On the International Space Station, drops of water form spheres. This water is acting as a lens.

> **1** Why are lenses needed in:
> a| cameras   b| telescopes   c| microscopes?
>
> **2** What is refraction?

Refraction happens because light travels at different speeds in different materials. It travels more slowly in substances such as water or glass than it does in air. When light travels from air to a material such as glass or water it changes direction towards the normal. When it travels out into the air it changes direction away from the normal.

B | You can investigate the path of light through glass blocks using a ray box. You can mark the points where it enters and leaves and join these points with a straight line.

C

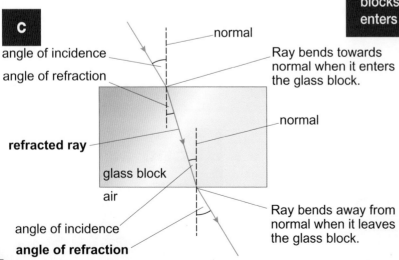

normal

angle of incidence

angle of refraction

Ray bends towards normal when it enters the glass block.

normal

refracted ray

glass block

air

Ray bends away from normal when it leaves the glass block.

angle of incidence

angle of refraction

> **3** Draw a ray diagram to explain the following terms:
> a| the normal   b| the angle of incidence
> c| the angle of refraction.
>
> **4** Describe how to compare the angles of incidence and refraction for a ray of light entering a glass block. (*Hint*: look back at pages 88–89.)

When you look into a pond or water in a swimming pool, objects on the bottom often appear to be closer to you than they really are. Diagram D shows why this happens.

> **5** Look at diagram D. Explain why an object in water appears to be closer than it really is.

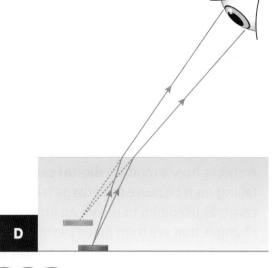

D

The **focal length** is the distance between the centre of the lens and the focal point.

The point where the rays meet is called the **focal point**.

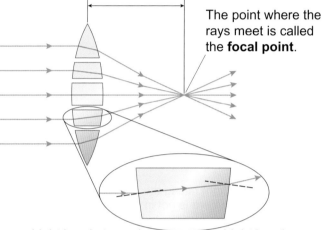

Light bends towards the normal as it goes into the lens.

Light bends away from the normal as it leaves the lens.

E | a model to explain how a converging lens works

Lenses

Lenses are curved pieces of glass or other transparent material. The lens in diagram E is a **converging lens**, because it makes the rays of light come together. It is easier to think about how a lens works if you think of it as being made up of lots of separate bits of glass.

> **6** Describe the shape of a converging lens.
>
> **7** Converging lenses can be fat or thin.
>
> **F**
>
> a| What would happen to rays of light if they shone through a lens fatter than the one in diagram E? Draw a diagram similar to diagram E to work out the answer.
>
> b| Would this fatter lens have a longer or shorter focal length than the lens in diagram E?
>
> **8** Light spreads out in all directions from a bulb. Suggest how a converging lens can be used in a theatre spotlight to make a parallel beam of light. Include a diagram with your answer.

FACT

On a hot day you can often see what looks like water on a dry road. This is a mirage and it happens because the hotter air near the ground bends rays of light coming from the sky.

G | There is no water in this desert.

I can ...

- recall some uses of lenses
- describe how light changes direction at the interface of two different substances
- use a model to explain how lenses work.

8Jd CAMERAS AND EYES

HOW DO CAMERAS AND EYES WORK?

Cameras and eyes work in similar ways, but there are some important differences. Diagram A shows how a modern **digital camera** works. The **sensor** in the camera detects light falling on it because the energy transferred by the light causes electrical changes. Older cameras used film to record an image. Light hitting photographic film causes chemical changes that are then made permanent by developing the film with other substances.

The lens focuses the light. The position of the lens can be adjusted so that the camera can focus on close or distant objects.

The sensor changes energy transferred by light into electrical signals. These are stored on a **memory card**.

The image is also produced on a screen so the photographer can check the picture they are taking.

The **shutter** stops light hitting the sensor when the camera is not in use. The shutter opens when a photo is being taken.

A

The **aperture** is a hole that can be adjusted to allow different amounts of light into the camera.

Eyes work in a similar way to cameras. Diagram B shows some of the parts of the eye. Light reaching the eye is refracted as it passes through the cornea, and this focuses the light. The lens also helps to focus light. The image that forms on the **retina** is upside down, just as it is in a camera. Your brain allows you to see the image the right way up.

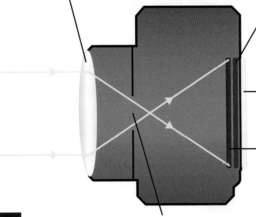

Muscles can change the shape of the lens so that the eye can focus on objects at different distances.

Special cells in the retina change the energy transferred by light into electrical impulses called nerve impulses.

blood vessels

The **iris** is the coloured part of the eye. It has a hole in the middle called the **pupil**. The iris can change the size of the pupil to control the amount of light entering the eye. This helps to prevent damage to the eye if the light is very bright.

pupil

The lens also helps to focus the light.

The transparent covering of the eye is called the **cornea**. It focuses the light.

B Nerve impulses are sent to the brain along the **optic nerve**.

1 Which part of a camera:
  a| focuses light   b| detects light?

2 Look at diagram F on page 87, and compare a pinhole camera with a digital camera. Write down:
  a| two similarities   b| three differences.

There are two different types of specialised cell in the retina. The outer parts of the retina contain many **rod cells**, which can detect quite low light levels, but do not detect different colours. The centre of the retina has mainly **cone cells**. There are three types of cone cells, which detect red, green and blue light. These three colours are the **primary colours** of light. All the other colours we see are mixtures of these three colours. Photo C shows the **secondary colours** we see when two different primary colours are combined. All three primary colours mix to form white light (a tertiary colour).

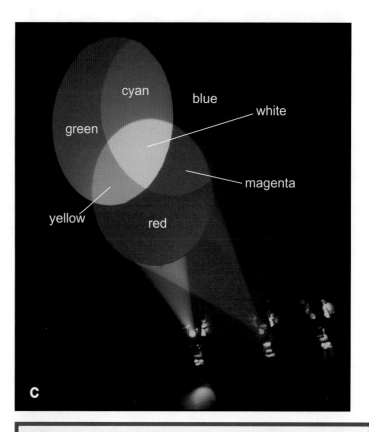

C

FACT

Photo D shows a tennis ball changing shape as it hits a racket. The photo was taken in a tiny fraction of a second. Our brains cannot process images this quickly and so we can never directly see an image like this, even though about a third of the brain is involved in interpreting information from the eyes.

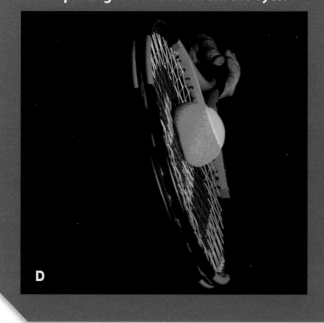

D

I can ...

- recall the parts of cameras and eyes and state their functions
- describe some ways in which the energy transferred by light leads to chemical or electrical effects.

HOW DO OPHTHALMOLOGISTS WORK?

Ophthalmologists and optometrists help us to look after our eyes. They must have good communications skills to talk to their surgical teams and their patients (to find out what problems people have and to explain treatments).

Ophthalmologists are doctors with special training. They study at university to get a degree in medicine, and then take further training to get a professional qualification.

Ophthalmologists examine patients and apply their knowledge to diagnose problems and diseases. They can treat eyes using medicines or surgery.

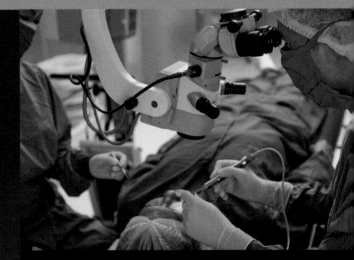

A | Ophthalmologists use technology to operate on eyes.

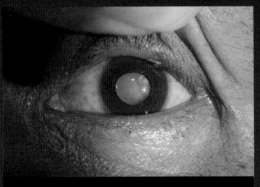

B | An eye with a cataract. The lens has turned cloudy.

As we get older our eyes can suffer from cataracts (photo B). Ophthalmologists cure cataracts by replacing the lens with an artificial one.

Macular degeneration (when the centre of the retina is damaged) can also affect eyesight. Electronics engineers are working to develop microchips that can be implanted into the retina to help patients with macular degeneration.

> **1** Explain how the following conditions prevent a person seeing clearly:
> a | cataracts
> b | macular degeneration.
>
> **2** Look at photo A. Describe one piece of technology that an ophthalmologist would use during a cataract operation.

Short and long sight

Some people can see close objects clearly, but not distant ones. This is called short sight and happens because the eyeball is too long (as shown in diagram C).

> **3** A long-sighted person can see distant objects clearly but not close ones. Draw a labelled diagram to show how long sight happens.

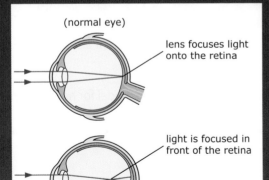

(normal eye)

lens focuses light onto the retina

light is focused in front of the retina

(eyeball too long)
(short sight)

C | normal vision and short sight

Optometrists test eyes for conditions such as short or long sight and prescribe glasses or contact lenses. They may also detect problems such as cataracts and send the patient to an ophthalmologist for further diagnosis and treatment.

Optometrists study at university then do further training at work. It is quicker to qualify as an optometrist than an ophthalmologist.

D | Optometrists use charts similar to this to measure how clearly someone can see. These charts are a standard size all over world, so that optometrists can compare different people's eyesight.

4 Explain why optometrists need to have good communication skills.

5 Write down one treatment that an ophthalmologist can provide that an optometrist cannot.

ACTIVITY

Choose one of the eye problems described on this page and make a poster for an optometrist to display. Your poster should describe:

- the problem
- its cause
- how it can be treated.

PRACTICAL

You will need an optometrists' chart.

1 Stand 6 metres from the chart and cover one eye. Note the lowest row you can read clearly. Repeat with the other eye.

If you can read the row marked 6 m, you are said to have 6/6 vision. This is normal vision. If you can only read down to the row marked 15 m, you have 6/15 vision. This means you can read at 6 m what a person with normal eyesight can read at 15 m.

2 Work with a partner. Stand close to the chart and look at the bottom row of letters. Move your head closer to the chart until you cannot read that row any more. Ask your partner to measure the distance from your nose to the chart. You can use this measurement to compare how well different members of the class can see close objects.

3 A person can only read the top three rows on the chart from 6 m away. Explain whether they are short sighted or long sighted.

8Je COLOUR

HOW DO WE GET COLOURED LIGHT?

We think of daylight as **white light**. But white light is made up of different **frequencies** of light. We see the different frequencies as different colours. Rainbows form when white light from the Sun is split up by drops of rain in the air.

You can split up white light with a **prism**. When white light passes through a prism the different frequencies are refracted (change direction) by different amounts, so the colours spread out. The colours of the rainbow are called a **spectrum**. Red is refracted the least and violet the most. This separating of the colours is called **dispersion**. The colours in the spectrum are red, orange, yellow, green, blue, indigo and violet.

A | A rainbow is produced when water droplets in the air refract sunlig

FACT

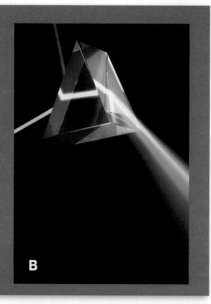

Many people used to think that prisms added the colours to light. Isaac Newton (1642–1727) showed that the colours could be made back into white light with a lens and a second prism, so the first prism had only split them up.

B

1. List the colours in the spectrum.

2. How is a rainbow formed?

3. Newton used a prism to make a spectrum on a piece of card with a long, narrow slit cut in to it. He placed the card so that only the green light in the spectrum went through the slit.

   a| Explain what Newton saw when this green light went through another prism.

   b| Explain what other scientists of his time might have expected to see.

C | Lenses also split up the colours in white light. Photographs taken with cheap cameras often show coloured fringes around objects. Good-quality cameras use combinations of lenses to avoid this effect.

Objects around us appear to be different colours because they absorb and reflect different parts of the spectrum. A white object looks white because it reflects all the colours. When you look at a post box in white light (normal daylight) it looks red because it reflects the red frequencies and absorbs the others. Black objects absorb all the colours in white light.

D

> **4** Which colours in white light does a blue object:
> a| reflect   b| absorb?

Making coloured light

Coloured light can be made from white light using **filters**. As white light passes through a filter, some of the colours are absorbed. A red filter only allows red light to be transmitted through the filter and all the other colours are absorbed.

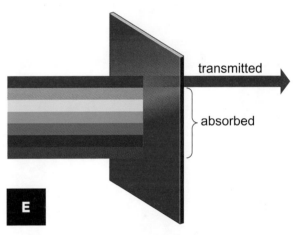

E

F | The left-hand part of the diagram shows what the man looks like in white light. In the right-hand part of the diagram only red light is reaching the man. The red and white parts of his costume reflect red light, and the other parts absorb it.

If a coloured light shines onto an object then the object's colour may appear to change. This is because there are fewer colours to be reflected in the light falling on it.

> **5** Explain how a filter makes blue light.
>
> **6** Which colours of light are being reflected by the different parts of the man's clothing in the left-hand part of diagram F?
>
> **7** Look at the right-hand part of diagram F.
> a| Explain why the sleeves and trousers look red.
> b| Explain why the body and hat look black.

I can ...

- describe how to make a spectrum
- explain why coloured objects appear coloured.

INVISIBILITY CLOAKS

WHAT WOULD BE THE BENEFITS AND DRAWBACKS OF BEING INVISIBLE?

A | Cuttlefish can change the colour of their bodies to match the surface they are swimming over. Can you see the cuttlefish in the lower photograph?

Many animals have colouring that helps them to look similar to their backgrounds. This helps them to hide from predators or can help predators to move slowly towards their prey without being seen. Some animals can even change colour, depending on their background.

Humans also camouflage themselves and their vehicles. You may have seen films where characters can make themselves invisible – scientists have been working on invisibility cloaks for many years! Most of these devices work by bending light reflected by objects in the background around the object being hidden. So far the only working devices can hide things from one direction only and for only one frequency of light.

B | A set of carefully angled glass blocks can make objects invisible. Scientists are working on new materials that can mimic this effect and be used as a fabric to cover objects, and make them invisible.

1 a| Explain how you can see the model cat in photo B.

b| Sunlight is white light. Explain why the collar on the cat appears red.

2 Describe the differences between the way light is reflected by a mirror and by the model cat in photo B.

3 a| What is the name of the process that bends light?

b| When does this normally happen?

4 Photos A and B were taken using cameras.

a| List the parts of a camera.

b| Describe what each part does.

5 a| List the parts of your eye.

b| Describe what each part does.

HAVE YOUR SAY

How would you use an invisibility cloak? Should anyone be allowed to have one?

LIVING IN EXTREMES

Humans live in many different environments all over the world. Some places where humans live are very hot and some are very cold.

Coober Pedy is a town in the middle of Australia where the temperature can reach 45 °C in areas with no direct sunlight. Almost all the buildings are underground, dug out of the rock.

The temperature of the human body is 37 °C. If the insides of our bodies get more than a few degrees warmer or cooler than this, we can die. Our bodies have ways of keeping us at the right temperature, such as sweating and shivering. However, we cannot live in very hot or very cold places without helping our bodies to stay at the right temperature. One way is to use buildings to shelter from heat or cold.

A | Living underground in Coober Pedy helps people to keep cool.

The walls of buildings can reduce the transfer of energy by heating, to stop the temperature inside changing too much. We can also use energy transferred by electricity to warm the insides of houses or to cool them, using air conditioning.

B | Inuit people build igloos for temporary shelter on hunting expeditions. Air trapped inside blocks of snow reduces the energy transferred by heating to the surroundings.

C | Energy transferred by electricity is used to keep this swimming pool warm.

1 Write down four different ways in which energy can be:

a| transferred

b| stored.

2 Photo C shows water in solid and liquid form, and the air also contains water vapour. Use the particle model to:

a| explain the different properties of solids, liquids and gases

b| describe how the movement of particles changes when energy is transferred into or out of a substance

c| describe what happens when a substance changes state.

3 Explain the difference between evaporation and boiling.

TEMPERATURE
8Ka CHANGES

WHAT IS THE DIFFERENCE BETWEEN INTERNAL ENERGY AND TEMPERATURE?

The particles that everything is made from are always moving. The energy stored in the movement of particles is called **internal energy**. It is sometimes called **thermal energy** or 'heat' energy. Energy is measured in **joules (J)**.

Temperature describes how hot or cold an object is. It is usually measured in **degrees Celsius (°C)**.

Temperature and internal energy are not the same. We can measure temperature with a thermometer, but we cannot measure the amount of internal energy something contains in the same way.

The amount of internal energy stored in something depends on:

- its temperature
- the material it is made from
- its mass.

A | Each spark given off by the sparkler is at a very high temperature, but the sparks do not store enough internal (thermal) energy to burn your hand.

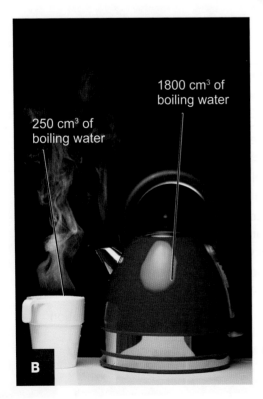

1800 cm³ of boiling water

250 cm³ of boiling water

B

1 a| What is the difference between internal energy and temperature?

 b| What units are used to measure them?

2 Why do you not get burnt by the sparks from a sparkler?

3 Look at photo B.

 a| Which contains the greatest mass of water: the kettle or the mug?

 b| Is the water in the kettle or mug storing the greatest amount of energy? Explain your answer.

 c| Why do you think it takes longer to boil a kettle full of water than to boil only enough to fill the mug?

FACT

The coldest place on Earth is in Antarctica. A temperature measurement made by satellite recorded a temperature of −98 °C in 2013.

Energy stored in a substance can be transferred by heating. Energy flows from a hotter object to a cooler one. The bigger the difference in temperature, the faster the energy is transferred. The cool object becomes hotter and the hot object becomes cooler until they are both at the same temperature.

4 Look at photo C. The temperature of the air in the room is −5 °C. The temperature of the drinks is 70 °C.

a| Will energy flow from the drinks to the room or from the room to the drinks? Explain your answer.

b| One of the drinks is left for 10 hours. Explain what its final temperature will be.

C | A room in an ice hotel; ice hotels are built every winter in some countries where the temperature stays below 0 °C for several months.

Cooling by evaporation

Evaporation is a way of transferring energy. A liquid evaporates fastest at its boiling point, but it can evaporate at any temperature. The fastest moving particles in a liquid are the ones that escape to form a gas. The particles that are left are storing less energy as movement and so the temperature of the remaining liquid is lower.

5 Your body produces sweat when you are hot.

a| What temperature is the sweat when it is first produced? Explain your answer.

b| Explain how sweating helps to cool you down.

6 Look at photo D. Explain how the fountains help to keep the gardens cool.

7 Jatin says, 'We do not know what the coldest temperature on the Earth is.' Give as many reasons as you can why he is right.

D | This palace in Spain was built 700 years ago. The fountains help to keep the gardens cool.

I can ...

- explain how internal energy and temperature are different
- identify the direction in which energy will be transferred
- explain what happens to particles when a liquid evaporates.

TRANSFERRING
8Kb ENERGY

HOW IS ENERGY TRANSFERRED BY HEATING?

Energy can be transferred by heating in several ways: evaporation, **radiation**, **conduction** and **convection**.

Radiation

When you stand near something hot, such as a fire, your skin feels warmer. Energy is transferred from hot objects by radiation (sometimes called **infrared radiation**).

All things give out or **emit** infrared radiation. The hotter the object, the more infrared radiation it emits. When radiation hits something, it can be **absorbed** (taken into the object) or **reflected**.

Infrared radiation transfers energy by waves, in a similar way to light. It does not need a **medium** to travel through, and it can also go through transparent substances like air or glass. Infrared radiation can also be focused. Energy travels to the Earth from the Sun by infrared radiation and this energy will burn paper if you focus it using a magnifying glass.

Thermal imagers are instruments that measure infrared radiation and convert the data into maps of temperatures. Thermal imaging can be used for filming things at night.

A | This man is being warmed by infrared radiation.

> **1** Describe three ways in which infrared radiation and light are similar.
>
> **2** Explain which will emit the most radiation: a mug of hot water or a mug of cold water.

Conduction

Energy can be transferred through many solid materials by conduction. When a solid is heated, the particles vibrate more. These vibrations are passed through the solid. Energy is transferred easily through metals in this way. Metals are good **thermal conductors**. Materials such as wood and plastics are good **thermal insulators** – energy is not transferred through them by conduction very well.

> **3** a| Why are saucepans usually made from metal?
>
> b| Why are saucepan handles usually made from wood or plastic?

B | Infrared radiation can be focused.

Conduction usually happens best in solids because the particles are very close together. Conduction does not take place very well in liquids. It hardly happens at all in gases because the particles are a long way apart.

The energy in the hot part of the bar is transferred along the bar, making these particles vibrate more.

These vibrating particles transfer some of their energy to the next particles in the bar.

As energy is transferred to the metal bar, its particles vibrate faster.

C

> **4** Explain how energy is conducted through a solid object. Use ideas about particles in your answer.
>
> **5** Why are solids better thermal conductors than liquids?

Convection

Energy is transferred through **fluids** (liquids and gases) by convection. When part of a fluid is heated it expands and becomes less dense than the fluid around it. It floats upwards through the remaining fluid. Cooler fluid moves in to take its place and a **convection current** forms. Convection currents can also form when part of a fluid is colder than its surroundings.

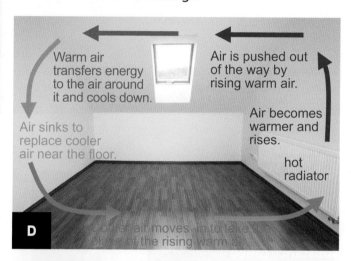

Warm air transfers energy to the air around it and cools down.

Air is pushed out of the way by rising warm air.

Air becomes warmer and rises.

Air sinks to replace cooler air near the floor.

hot radiator

Cooler air moves in to take the place of the rising warm air.

D

FACT

This temperature map was made using infrared measurements from satellites. The different temperatures in the oceans cause convection currents in the air above. We feel the movement as wind.

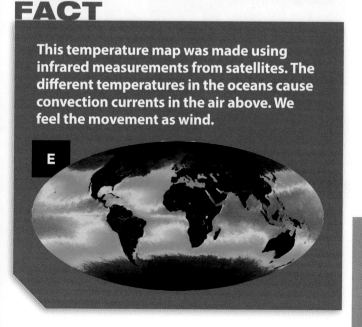

E

> **6** Look at photo D.
> a| How is energy transferred from the hot water inside the radiator to the air in the room?
> b| How is energy transferred to the side of the room opposite to the radiator?
>
> **7** a| Why will air sink if it is colder than the air around it?
> b| Sketch a diagram of an ice lolly. Add arrows to show the direction of the convection currents caused by the cold lolly.
>
> **8** Explain why energy cannot be transferred through space by conduction or convection.
>
> **9** Look at photo F. Is the food being cooked by conduction, convection or radiation? Explain your answer.

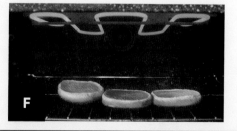

F

I can ...

- describe how energy is transferred by radiation, conduction and convection
- use the particle model to explain energy transfers in matter.

CONTROLLING
8Kc TRANSFERS

HOW CAN WE CONTROL ENERGY TRANSFERS?

In cold climates, people can keep their houses warm by burning fuel for heating. Insulation can help to keep the warmth inside the house and save money on fuel bills. Brick, wood and other building materials are good insulators.

Air is a very poor conductor because the particles are far apart. Air does allow convection to take place, so air is a good thermal insulator only when it cannot move. Carpets, feathers and wool all contain a lot of trapped air.

A | This house is being built from bales of straw. Air trapped inside the bales makes them a good insulating material. The straw will be covered with plaster.

1 a| Draw a table to show which of these materials are thermal conductors and which are thermal insulators:

wool   plastic   aluminium foil
paper   copper   feathers   wood

b| Which two contain trapped air?

2 Look at the containers in photo B. Describe how you could use apparatus like this to find out which materials make the best insulators.

B

FACT

One of the best insulating materials is a substance called Aerogel, which is over 99 per cent air. This also makes it extremely light. Because it is such a good insulator, it can be used in very thin sheets where there is not much space. These could be used to insulate buildings on the Moon or on other planets.

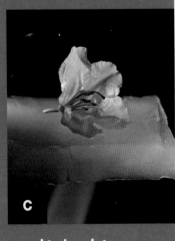

C

D | This infrared image shows where energy is being transferred from the building. Red shows the hottest parts and blue the coolest.

In hot countries, the challenge is to stop a house warming up too much. There were different ways of doing this long before air conditioning systems were invented.

Light colours and shiny surfaces reflect infrared radiation, so painting houses white helps to keep them cool in summer. They are also poor emitters of radiation. Dark colours absorb and emit infrared radiation well, so **solar panels** (used to heat water) are painted black.

E | These houses in Thailand are painted white to keep them cool but the solar panels for the water heating are black.

3 Look at photo D. Suggest the two most important things that could be done to reduce energy transfers from this building.

4 A black car and a white car are parked next to each other on a sunny day. Explain which car will:

a| become the hottest inside

b| cool down the fastest when the sun sets.

5 Elephants often spray themselves with water. Explain two ways in which this can help to keep them cool. (*Hint*: Look back at page 103.)

6 Insulated mugs that people use when camping often have lids.

a| Suggest two ways in which the lid helps to keep a hot drink warm for longer.

b| Explain how the mug can help to keep hot drinks hot and keep cold drinks cool.

7 Some people stick aluminium foil onto the walls behind radiators. Suggest how this helps to keep the house warm.

8 Diagram F shows a vacuum flask.

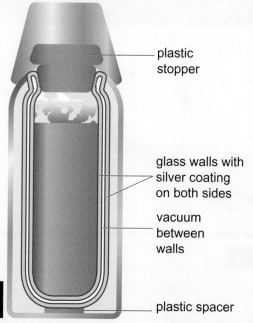

- plastic stopper
- glass walls with silver coating on both sides
- vacuum between walls
- plastic spacer

F

Explain which parts of the flask are designed to reduce energy transfers by:

a| radiation   c| convection

b| conduction   d| evaporation.

I can ...

- recall ways of reducing energy transfers.

ACCURACY AND
8Kc PRECISION

WHAT ARE ACCURACY AND PRECISION?

A scientific investigation is usually carried out to test a hypothesis and reach a conclusion. A **valid** conclusion is one that relates to the original question being investigated and is only based on the evidence. A valid conclusion needs good-quality data that is **accurate** and **precise**.

Accuracy

A measurement is accurate if it is close to the true value of the thing being measured. Measuring devices that have smaller divisions on their scales can measure more accurately than ones with larger divisions, if they are set up correctly.

B | This is a clinical thermometer, used in hospitals to take a patient's temperature. Each division represents 0.1 degree.

A | Each division on this thermometer represents 10 degrees. It is used to check the temperature inside an oven.

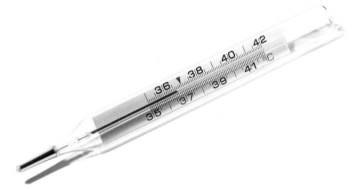

I need to measure the temperatures to the nearest 0.1 degree, because the differences in temperature will be very small.

I can measure the roof insulation to the nearest centimetre, because the layers are quite thick.

> **1**
> Look at photos A and B.
> a| Describe the differences between the two thermometers.
> b| Explain how each thermometer is suited to its use.

Accurate measurements are not always better. They may be harder to make, take more time or use complicated apparatus. You must choose a level of accuracy by thinking about the results you need in order to draw a conclusion, and how easy it will be to do the experiment. You may also have to justify a level of accuracy. This means you have to say why you use or do not use more accurate measurements.

c

Precision

Measurements are precise if several measurements of the same thing give the same results. The closer together repeated measurements are, the more precise the data is (and the smaller its range). You cannot tell how precise your measurements are if you only take one reading – this is why scientists often repeat an experiment several times.

Errors

Sometimes measuring instruments have **systematic errors**, which means that all the readings from these instruments are incorrect by a similar amount. For example, if you forget to zero a balance before finding the masses of some objects, all the readings will be incorrect by the same amount. A systematic error like this reduces the accuracy of your results but does not affect the precision.

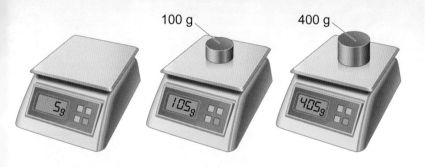

D | an example of systematic error

Results can also have **random errors**. For example, when measuring temperature, you might look at the thermometer scale from a slightly different angle each time you read it. Instruments with a digital readout avoid this problem.

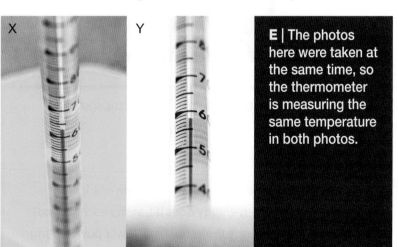

E | The photos here were taken at the same time, so the thermometer is measuring the same temperature in both photos.

2
a| Below are the results obtained when different students measured the time it took to boil the same volume of water using a Bunsen burner:

> 10.5 minutes, 10.4 minutes, 10.5 minutes, 10.5 minutes, 10.6 minutes

What can you say about the precision of these results?

b| In the same investigation, measurements from the whole class were used to work out a mean time for heating of 10.9 minutes. Explain what this tells you about the accuracy of the results in part a.

3 Look at the photos in E.
a| Write down the temperatures shown by thermometers X and Y.
b| Suggest the true temperature.
c| How can you avoid this kind of error?

4 Look at the results given in question 2.
a| What kind of error could be responsible for the differences between the five readings in part a?
b| What kind of error could explain the difference between these students' results and the class mean?

5 Sally wants to measure how much a brass rod 15 cm long expands when she heats one end using a Bunsen burner. Ben is measuring how far water will rise up a thin tube when it is heated.

Explain who will need to use the most accurate measuring instrument.

I can ...

- state the meanings of accuracy and precision
- explain how to avoid random and systematic errors.

8Kd POWER AND EFFICIENCY

HOW MUCH ENERGY DO DIFFERENT APPLIANCES USE?

In many parts of the world, energy for heating and cooking is obtained by burning fuel in an open fire. In many countries, we can use gas or electricity for heating and cooking, and we also use electricity to run many other **appliances**.

> **1** Write down three different electrical appliances that:
> a| transfer energy by heating
> b| are used for things other than heating.

Different appliances transfer different amounts of energy. For example, an electric shower needs to heat the water running through it very quickly, so it transfers a lot of energy in a short time. It can transfer up to 10 000 J of energy each second.

A | A reconstruction of an Iron Age roundhouse from about 600 BCE. The central fire was for heating and cooking and filled the hut with smoke!

The amount of energy transferred per second is the **power** of the appliance. The units for power are **watts (W)** or **kilowatts (kW)**.

> 1 watt = 1 joule transferred every second
>
> 1000 W = 1 kW

We can find out how much energy different appliances transfer by looking for their **power ratings**.

The appliance in photo B has a power rating of 3000 W and so it transfers 3000 joules of energy each second.

The higher the power rating, the more energy the appliance transfers each second. Cookers, electric fires and other heating appliances usually have higher power ratings than other appliances.

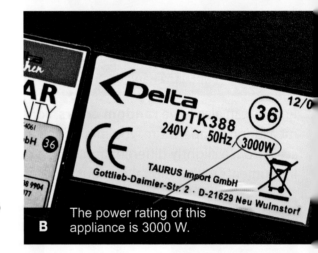

B The power rating of this appliance is 3000 W.

> **2** What is the power rating of an electric shower transferring 10 000 J/s:
> a| in watts
> b| in kilowatts?
>
> **3** An electric kettle has a power rating of 3 kW.
> a| How much energy does it transfer each second?
> b| Suggest why the kettle has a lower power rating than an electric shower.

Efficiency

Appliances do not transfer all the energy supplied to them into useful forms of energy. Some of it is wasted. The amount of useful energy transferred compared with the total amount supplied is the **efficiency** of an appliance. Wasted energy usually makes the surroundings warmer.

We can use a **Sankey diagram** to show energy transfers. The width of each arrow represents the proportion of the energy.

C | This type of light bulb is not very efficient. Only 10 per cent of the energy it receives is transferred as useful energy.

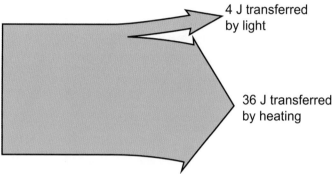

D | a Sankey diagram for the light bulb in photo C

40 J supplied each second by electricity

4 J transferred by light

36 J transferred by heating

Energy cannot be created or destroyed, so the total amount of energy supplied must be equal to the total amount transferred or stored.

We can calculate efficiency using the following formula:

$$\text{efficiency} = \frac{\text{useful energy transferred}}{\text{total energy supplied}} \times 100\%$$

Example

The energy transfers of the bulb shown in photo C are shown in diagram D. The efficiency of the bulb is:

$$\text{efficiency} = \frac{4}{40} \times 100$$
$$= 10\%$$

The efficiency of an appliance can never be more than 100 per cent, as you can never get more useful energy out than the total amount of energy you put in.

FACT

In many parts of the world, people still cook on open fires. A simple stove like this can increase the efficiency of the fire to over 50 per cent.

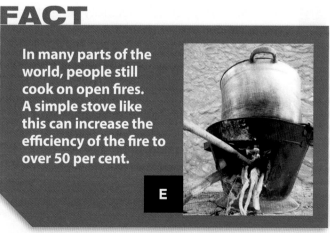

E

---

4 A modern efficient light bulb transfers 9 J of energy by light every second. It uses 20 J of energy to do this.

a| Calculate its efficiency.

b| Sketch and label a Sankey diagram to show the energy transfers.

5 All the energy used by a kettle ends up stored as thermal energy in the water, the kettle or the surroundings. Kettles are about 80 per cent efficient.

a| A kettle uses 200 kJ of energy to boil water. How much of this energy ends up stored in the water inside the kettle?

b| Sketch and label a Sankey diagram to show the energy transfers.

c| It is more efficient to boil water in a kettle than in a saucepan. Suggest why this is so.

I can ...

- describe what power and efficiency mean
- calculate efficiencies
- interpret Sankey diagrams.

HOW CAN WE HELP PEOPLE AFTER A DISASTER?

Natural disasters include earthquakes, floods and hurricanes. They can injure and kill thousands of people.

Some deaths occur during the disaster itself. However, many people are made homeless, and can become ill or die from cold, starvation or disease. There are international organisations that can help the people.

Disaster coordinators

After a disaster, such as an earthquake, disaster response coordinators need to organise emergency workers to rescue people from collapsed buildings. They also need to organise the delivery of shelter, food, water and medical aid. Coordinators gather as much information as they can about what has happened and what supplies are needed. They can list the supplies in a table or spreadsheet and put them in order of importance.

A | In April 2015 an earthquake destroyed many buildings in Kathmandu, Nepal. Nearly 9000 people were killed, and more than 600 000 buildings were destroyed. Many people had to live in tents after the disaster.

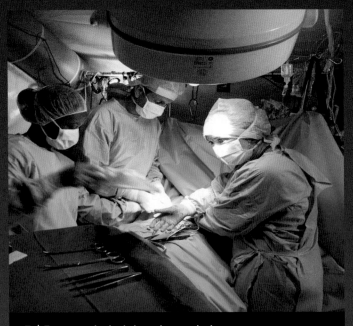

B | Doctors help injured people in emergency medical tents. A nurse will triage patients by deciding who needs the most urgent treatment.

1 Suggest what kinds of information a disaster coordinator could obtain from:

a | satellite photos

b | the government of the country where a disaster has occurred

c | people in the disaster area.

2 Look at photo A. The average minimum temperature in Kathmandu in April is around 12 °C. Explain why homeless people there needed tents.

3 a | Suggest why portable electricity generators are needed in disaster areas.

b | Portable generators run on petrol or diesel fuel. Explain why the generators need to be as efficient as possible.

4 A coordinator wants to use renewable resources to generate electricity for a temporary hospital. Write down some information she needs before she can decide which form of renewable energy to use.

Keeping vaccines cold

After a natural disaster, drinking water is often contaminated by human waste, causing illness. Vaccines are medicines that can be given to people to stop them becoming ill. However, vaccines must be kept cold or they will not work.

> **5** Look at photo C.
> a | Describe how insulation is used to make the cool box as efficient as possible.
> b | Suggest why both types of equipment might be needed in a disaster area.

C | Portable solar-powered cool boxes or solar powered refrigerators can be used to keep vaccines cold.

ACTIVITY

In December 2004 a tsunami (huge wave) killed over 200 000 people in coastal areas in Indonesia and around the Indian Ocean.

In April 2015, an earthquake in Nepal killed nearly 9000 people in cities and villages throughout the country.

Your team's task is to make plans for helping remote villages after disasters such as the ones in 2004 and 2015.

1 Find out about the places shown in photos D and E. Record information about each place that will help you in your planning.

2 Make a table to list all the different people, equipment and supplies you need to transport to the villages. Explain any differences between the tables for the two countries.

3 Decide the best way of transporting people and supplies for each country.

4 You may not have enough vehicles to transport everything. Discuss the importance of the things in your tables and give each item a score (1 for most important, 5 for least). Rank the items in each table in order of importance.

5 Everyone in your group should be prepared to justify your chosen transport method and order of importance to others in your class.

D | a ruined village in Thailand

E | destroyed villages in Nepal

8Ke PAYING FOR ENERGY

HOW DO WE PAY FOR ENERGY?

Most of the energy we use has to be paid for. Some of the energy we use is bought as fuel, such as petrol or diesel for cars or gas for cookers and boilers. When we burn a fuel, energy stored within the chemicals is transferred by heating.

For electricity and gas, we pay for the amount of energy transferred. Energy companies use a unit called a **kilowatt-hour (kWh)** to measure energy. A kilowatt-hour is the amount of energy transferred in 1 hour by an appliance with a power of 1 kW. For example, using a 2 kW electric fire for 4 hours would use 8 kWh of energy:

$$\text{energy use (kWh)} = \text{power rating (kW)} \times \text{time (hours)}$$

Your electricity use this period	
Reading last time	1763
Reading this time	2547
	784 Units
784 Units at 15.0p	**£117.60**
VAT at 5%	£5.88
Total charges	**£123.48**

B | A kilowatt-hour is usually called a 'Unit' in electricity bills.

FACT

In many countries, part of the price people pay for petrol, gas and electricity is tax. Some governments also charge a 'carbon tax', depending on the amount of carbon dioxide burning fuels produce. The carbon dioxide is contributing to climate change. This extra tax is to encourage businesses to improve their efficiency so that they use less fuel overall.

A | Energy bills for heating and cooling our homes can be reduced by designing houses well. These houses have solar cells on their roofs to generate electricity.

> **1** A 1 kW electric fire operates for 5 hours.
> a| How much energy does it use in kilowatt-hours?
> b| Suggest why energy companies do not use joules to measure energy.

We can save money on electricity and gas bills by not using as much energy. Insulating houses and using more efficient appliances can help with this.

> **2** Why will using a more efficient appliance help you to use less energy?

C | New appliances have energy labels to show how efficient they are. More efficient appliances are usually more expensive than less efficient ones.

Sometimes buying a new, more efficient appliance or improving the insulation can cost more money than it will save you. The **payback time** tells you how long it will take to save the money that an efficiency measure costs:

$$\text{payback time} = \frac{\text{cost of change}}{\text{saving per year}}$$

For example, diagram D shows some ways in which a homeowner could save money:

$$\text{payback time for cavity wall insulation} = \frac{350}{100}$$
$$= 3.5 \text{ years}$$

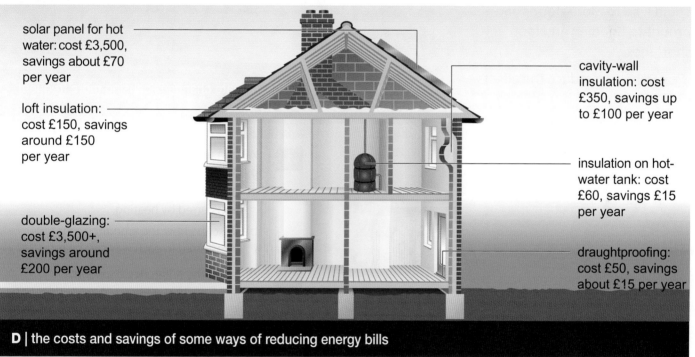

solar panel for hot water: cost £3,500, savings about £70 per year

loft insulation: cost £150, savings around £150 per year

double-glazing: cost £3,500+, savings around £200 per year

cavity-wall insulation: cost £350, savings up to £100 per year

insulation on hot-water tank: cost £60, savings £15 per year

draughtproofing: cost £50, savings about £15 per year

D | the costs and savings of some ways of reducing energy bills

3 Why should you work out the payback times before choosing a new appliance?

4 Use the data in diagram D to calculate the payback time for:
a| loft insulation
b| draughtproofing.

5 Suggest why the information in diagram D does not give exact values for the savings for each modification.

6 Mrs Holman is choosing a fridge. Fridge A costs £120 and costs £27 per year to run. Fridge B costs £150 and costs £22 per year to run. Which one should she buy? Explain your answer.

I can ...

- explain how power companies charge for energy used
- describe what a payback time tells you
- work out payback times.

HOW DOES OUR ENERGY USE AFFECT THE PLANET?

Electricity is essential for the way we live. Most of our electricity comes from power stations that burn fuel and produce carbon dioxide. Carbon dioxide is also produced when we burn gas for heating or use petrol in cars. Most scientists agree that extra carbon dioxide in the atmosphere is causing the Earth to become warmer. **Climate change** could lead to more storms and droughts, flooding and food shortages.

We can help to reduce the effects of climate change by reducing the amount of carbon dioxide we produce. We need to do this by burning less **fossil fuel**.

A | Some people think that climate change is causing more frequent storms.

1 We can use less energy for heating or cooling by insulating our homes better.

a| Describe four ways in which energy can be transferred by heating.

b| Describe how the amount of energy transferred in each way can be reduced.

2 Describe the difference between:

a| energy and temperature

b| energy and power.

3 a| Why is it better to use more efficient appliances?

b| How can you calculate the efficiency of an appliance?

B | Some low-lying countries like the Maldive Islands will become uninhabitable as sea levels rise. The Maldive government held an underwater meeting to draw attention to the problem.

HAVE YOUR SAY

Some governments encourage people to improve the insulation of their homes by helping to pay for it. Do you think it is right for a government to spend taxpayers' money in this way?

The positions of the **Sun**, the **Moon** and the **stars** have been observed and recorded for over 5000 years. The observations were used to work out a calendar so that farmers knew when to plant crops. Many observations were used for religious reasons.

People have known that the **Earth** is a sphere for thousands of years, but until about 500 years ago most people believed that the Earth was at the centre of everything. They thought that the Sun moved, causing day and night.

A | Stonehenge is believed to be over 5000 years old. The rising Sun in the middle of summer shines between the most important stones.

B | This photo of the Earth was taken by the astronauts on *Apollo 8*. They were also the first people to see the side of the Moon that faces away from the Earth.

We now use a **model** of the **Solar System** in which the Sun is at the centre, with the Earth and other **planets** moving around it on paths called **orbits**. In this model, the planets are also spinning, which explains why the Sun appears to move across the sky and we get day and night.

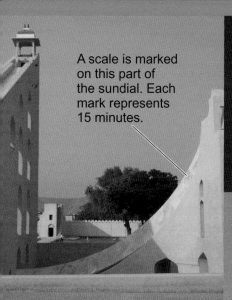

A scale is marked on this part of the sundial. Each mark represents 15 minutes.

C | Sundials have been used to tell the time for thousands of years. This one, in India, is 27 m tall and the shadow it makes moves at 1 mm per second.

1   What shape is the Earth?

2   a| Name three planets in the Solar System.

    b| What is the difference between a planet and a moon?

3   Ecuador is on the opposite side of the Earth from Malaysia. Explain why:

    a| it is approximately 24 hours between sunrises for most places on the Earth

    b| it is daytime in Ecuador when it is night time in Malaysia.

4   Explain how the sundial in photo C works.

8La GATHERING THE EVIDENCE

HOW WAS OUR MODEL OF THE SOLAR SYSTEM WORKED OUT?

Today, astronomers use spacecraft and very powerful telescopes to explore and observe the Solar System. Early astronomers could only use their eyes and so only made observations of the five planets visible from Earth without using a telescope (Mercury, Venus, Mars, Jupiter and Saturn).

An Egyptian astronomer called Ptolemy (90–168) worked out a model of the Solar System with the Earth in the centre. In this model, the Moon, Sun and planets moved in circles around the Earth. Most astronomers accepted this model for the next 1500 years because it could explain many of their observations.

> **1** Explain why Ptolemy only knew about six planets (including the Earth).
>
> **2** How would Ptolemy's model explain why we have day and night?

B | The Moon appears to be different shapes at different times. Ptolemy's model and our modern model can both explain the **phases of the Moon.**

Later astronomers from Arabia, Egypt and Europe made more accurate observations of the movements of the planets, and discovered that Ptolemy's model did not explain the observations very well. In 1543, a Polish astronomer called Nicolaus Copernicus (1473–1543) published a book that suggested that the Earth and the other planets moved in circles around the Sun.

Copernicus' model was not accepted straight away, partly because it still did not explain all the observations very well. However, observations by Galileo using one of the first telescopes provided more evidence to support Copernicus' model.

> **3** We see the Moon because it reflects light from the Sun.
> a| How much of the Moon is lit up by the Sun?
> b| Suggest why the Moon looks different as it moves around the Earth.

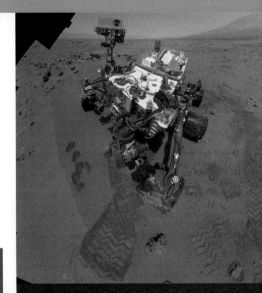

A | This is a 'selfie' of the *Curiosity* rover, which landed on Mars in 2012 to take measurements and carry out experiments.

C | Galileo Galilei (1564–1642) used one of the first telescopes to collect evidence to support Copernicus' idea. Telescopes allowed astronomers to make more accurate measurements.

The model used today was first suggested by Johannes Kepler (1571–1630). In this model, the Sun is still at the centre of our Solar System, but the planets move around the Sun in **elliptical** orbits (an ellipse is like a squashed circle). Most of the planets have **moons** orbiting them.

4 Why did Kepler have more accurate information about the movements of the planets than Ptolemy?

5 a| Write down one difference between the models suggested by Copernicus and Kepler.

b| Write down three differences between Ptolemy's model and the model of the Solar System we use today.

c| Why is the model suggested by Kepler the model we use today?

Spacecraft

Luna 2 was the first space probe to reach the moon. It crashed into the Moon in 1959. Later probes made soft landings and some even brought back some Moon rocks to the Earth. Before this, scientists could only investigate other planets by looking at them through telescopes.

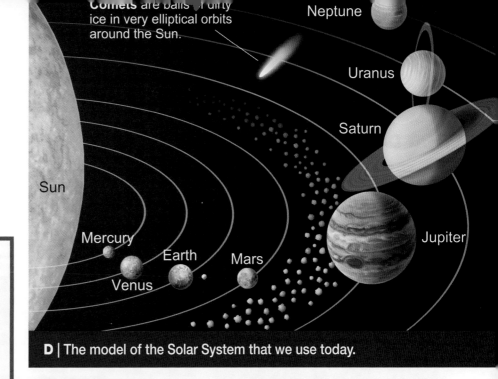

Comets are balls of dirty ice in very elliptical orbits around the Sun.

Sun

Mercury

Venus

Earth

Mars

Jupiter

Saturn

Uranus

Neptune

D | The model of the Solar System that we use today.

E | Harrison Schmitt collecting Moon rocks: the Moon is the only body in the Solar System (other than Earth) that has been visited by humans.

FACT

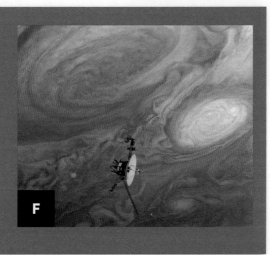

The space probe *Voyager 1* is the most distant spacecraft from Earth. It was launched in 1977 and is now over 19 billion kilometres away. It has sent images of Jupiter and Saturn back to Earth.

F

6 Describe three different ways of investigating the planets that were not available to scientists in Kepler's time.

I can ...

- describe some ways of investigating the planets
- compare different models of the Solar System.

WORKING IN SPACE

WHAT DO ASTRONAUTS DO IN SPACE?

The first astronauts were all jet aircraft pilots with a good knowledge of engineering. The early space flights, such as the Vostok and Gemini programs, concentrated on developing the technology to put humans into orbit around the Earth. The Apollo program developed the technology to send humans to the Moon.

After the first Moon landings in 1969, more Apollo missions were sent to different parts of the Moon to study its rocks. The first scientist to become an astronaut was Harrison Schmitt, a geologist who went to the Moon in 1972 (photo E on page 119).

A | Being an astronaut is not a safe occupation. Kalpana Chawla flew two Space Shuttle Missions as an engineer responsible for launching satellites. She died when the Space Shuttle Columbia broke up just before landing in 2003.

B | The International Space Station has been inhabited continuously since 2000.

Scientists in space

Today's astronauts work on the International Space Station (ISS). Astronauts all have a university degree in engineering, science or mathematics. They must also have experience working in science, or be qualified jet pilots, and pass strict physical examinations before being accepted for training.

During training, astronauts learn how the ISS works and how to perform some medical procedures. They also do survival training. They need to be able to work as a team and speak Russian and English. Astronauts are often asked to make speeches or presentations, so they also get training in public speaking.

1. Suggest why astronauts need training in:
   a | medical procedures
   b | survival.

2. Find out why ISS astronauts need to speak Russian and English.

Tasks carried out by astronauts on the ISS include:

- exercise
- carrying out scientific experiments.
- repair and maintenance of the space station

Astronauts may have to solve problems to repair parts of the space station. They apply their knowledge by thinking about the similarities and differences between Earth and the space station.

Astronauts in the ISS float around as if they have no weight. Astronauts often do experiments to investigate the effects of this weightlessness on the human body.

C | Astronauts train for the tasks they will do. These astronauts are practising a space walk in a tank of water.

3 Look at photo C. Suggest why astronauts train under water.

4 All water on the ISS is recycled.

a | Apply your knowledge of how the human body works to suggest two sources of water to be recycled.

b | Explain why the water is recycled.

5 Food and liquid can float around in the ISS, which can damage equipment. Apply your knowledge of eating and drinking on Earth to suggest ways to eat safely on the ISS.

D | Malaysian astronaut Dr Sheikh Muszaphar Shukor visited the International Space Station in 2007. He carried out scientific experiments on cancer cells.

ACTIVITY

In the future, humans may set up bases on the Moon or on Mars. The bases will need electricity for heating and lighting, to run computers and machinery that keeps the air breathable and to help grow food.

You are going to use your knowledge of energy resources to suggest how to generate electricity on the Moon.

- Think about what you already know about energy resources on Earth.
- What is different about resources on the Moon? Can all the resources we use on Earth be used on the Moon?

1 Design a Moon base and label your design with ways in which electricity will be generated.

2 Prepare a short presentation explaining the key reasons why you chose the energy resources for your Moon base.

8Lb SEASONS

WHAT CAUSES THE SEASONS?

The weather in some parts of the world is very different at different times of the year. These changes happen because the Earth's axis is tilted.

1 Describe two ways in which the place in photo A is different in the summer compared with winter.

2 Describe the difference between summer and winter in:
a| the length of daylight
b| the temperature.

A | The same place in summer (top) and winter (bottom).

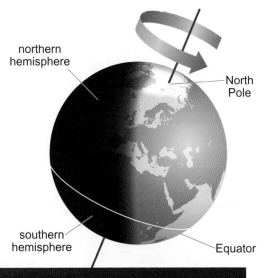

B | The Earth is divided into two halves or hemispheres by an imaginary line called the Equator. Europe, North America, part of Africa and most of Asia are in the northern hemisphere.

In summer, the Sun is high in the sky at midday and days are longer than nights. In the winter, the Sun is not very high in the sky at midday and nights are longer than days.

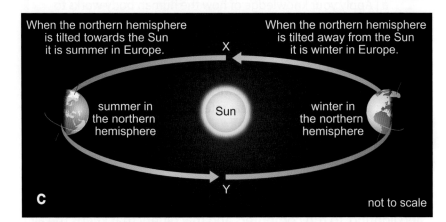

When the northern hemisphere is tilted towards the Sun it is summer in Europe.

When the northern hemisphere is tilted away from the Sun it is winter in Europe.

X

summer in the northern hemisphere

Sun

winter in the northern hemisphere

Y

C

not to scale

3 Explain what a hemisphere is.

4 Look at diagram C.
a| What season will it be in the northern hemisphere when the Earth is at position X?
b| What season will it be in the northern hemisphere when the Earth is at position Y?
c| Explain your answers.

5 Explain why days are longer than nights in summer.

> **6** Draw a diagram similar to diagram D. Add labels to explain why nights are longer than days in the winter in the UK.

The Sun feels hotter in the summer than it does in the winter. Some people think that this is because the Earth is closer to the Sun in summer, but this is not true in the northern hemisphere. The northern hemisphere is slightly closer to the Sun in winter. This means that the southern hemisphere is closer to the Sun during its summer, which is one reason why summers are often a little hotter in the southern hemisphere than they are in the northern hemisphere.

The Sun feels hotter in summer compared with winter because it is higher in the sky. This means the heat from the Sun is more concentrated. Summer days are also warmer than winter days because the Sun is shining for longer and has more time to warm up the air and the ground.

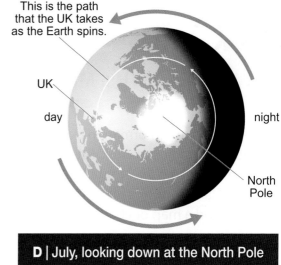

This is the path that the UK takes as the Earth spins.

UK

day

night

North Pole

D | July, looking down at the North Pole

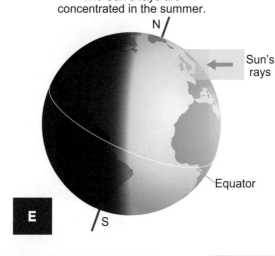

The Sun's rays are concentrated in the summer.

N

Sun's rays

Equator

S

E

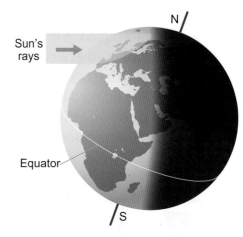

The Sun's rays are spread out in the winter.

N

Sun's rays

Equator

S

FACT

In some parts of the world there are days when the Sun never sets. A place like this is sometimes called the 'Land of the Midnight Sun'.

F | photos of the Sun taken at 10 minute intervals

⚠ **!** Never look directly at the Sun. This could permanently damage your eyesight.

> **7** New Zealand is on the opposite side of the Earth from the UK. Which season is it in New Zealand when it is summer in the UK?

> **8** a| Look at diagram D. If you were near the North Pole, how long would daylight last in summer?
>
> b| Use a diagram to help you explain what happens in winter at the North Pole.

> **9** If you live near the Equator, the Sun always feels hotter than it does in countries away from the Equator. Use a diagram to help you to explain why.

I can ...

- use the tilt of the Earth's axis to explain the changes in the seasons
- use a model to explain the pattern of light and dark at the Earth's poles.

8Lc MAGNETIC EARTH

WHAT IS THE EARTH'S MAGNETIC FIELD?

Modern ships use information from satellites and radios to work out where they are and which way to steer. Until the middle of last century, sailors had to use a compass and a map or chart to help them navigate.

Magnetic materials were discovered thousands of years ago. It was found that pieces of rock that contained a lot of iron would always point north if they were hung from a thread. A magnet that points north can be used as a **compass**. When people made bar magnets, they named the end that pointed north the **north-seeking pole**. We call the other end of the magnet the **south-seeking pole**. These names are usually shortened to north pole and south pole.

A | The Northern Lights are caused when particles streaming away from the Sun are concentrated near the North Pole by the Earth's magnetic field.

---

1   What is a compass?

2   Why is one end of a magnet called the north-seeking pole?

If you put two magnets near each other, the north pole of one magnet will **attract** the south pole of the other. Two north poles (or two south poles) will **repel** each other.

The space around a magnet where it has an effect is called its **magnetic field**. A **field** in physics is a space in which a particular force has an effect. You can find the shape of a magnetic field using iron filings or a small compass.

B | You can see the shape of the magnetic field of a bar magnet using iron filings.

C | The shape of a magnetic field is represented by **field lines**. The direction of the field is always from the north pole of the magnet towards the south pole.

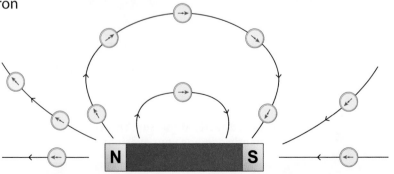

3 Describe two ways of finding the shape of a magnetic field.

4 Draw the shape of the magnetic field around a bar magnet.

5 Suggest how you could find out the shape of the magnetic field when two bar magnets are close to each other.

Diagrams C and D show the shape of the magnetic field of a bar magnet. The field is strongest where the lines are close together. The field gets weaker as you get further from the magnet. The field is all around the magnet.

The magnetic field has a direction. This direction is the way the north pole of a compass moves near another magnet. North poles repel each other, so the direction of the magnetic field is away from the north pole of the bar magnet and towards the south pole.

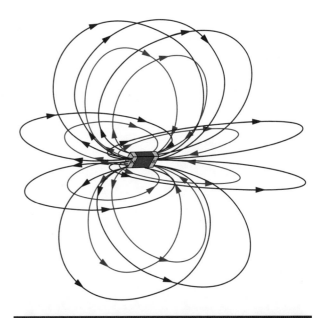

D | The magnetic field of a magnet is all around the magnet.

E | Compasses point north because the Earth has a magnetic field. Compasses point towards the north magnetic pole, which is near the North Pole. A model for helping us to understand how compasses work is to think of the Earth as having a huge bar magnet inside it.

FACT

Many animals, including salmon, turtles and some birds, can detect the Earth's magnetic field. The animals use this sense to help them navigate long distances when they migrate.

6 Diagram E is a model to help us think about the Earth's magnetic field. Explain why the bar magnet is drawn with its south pole near the Earth's North Pole.

7 The Earth's magnetic field is caused by movements in the liquid part of the Earth's core.
 a| Write down two advantages of using the model in diagram E to explain the Earth's magnetic field.
 b| Write down one disadvantage.

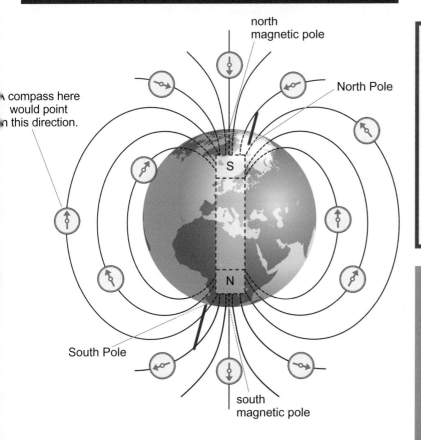

north magnetic pole

North Pole

A compass here would point in this direction.

S

N

South Pole

south magnetic pole

I can ...

- explain how to arrange magnets so they attract or repel each other
- describe the Earth's magnetic field and how it affects compasses
- describe how to find the shape of a magnetic field.

GRAVITY
8Ld IN SPACE

HOW DOES GRAVITY AFFECT THE SOLAR SYSTEM?

A | This *Soyuz* rocket is taking astronauts to the International Space Station. Its engines produce a large force to push the rocket upwards against the Earth's gravity.

When any two objects are near each other they exert a tiny force that tries to pull them together. This force is called **gravity**. The bigger the mass of the object, the stronger the force it exerts.

Even your body attracts things around you by gravity, but the force you exert is too small for you to notice. The Earth has an enormous mass, so it exerts a large force. This force pulls you towards the centre of the Earth. The force of gravity pulling on you is your **weight** and is measured in newtons (N).

When the Earth was formed from rocky particles, the gravitational attraction between the particles pulled them all together to form a sphere.

The space around the Earth where its gravity attracts things is the Earth's **gravitational field**. The **gravitational field strength** at the surface of the Earth is about 10 newtons per kilogram (N/kg) and is represented by the letter *g* in italics. This means that the Earth's gravity pulls on every kilogram with a force of 10 N. The gravitational field strength is different on other bodies in the Solar System.

weight (N) = mass (kg) × gravitational field strength (N/kg)

Example

Calculate the weight of a 5 kg mass on the Earth:

$$weight = mass \times g$$
$$= 5 \times 10$$
$$= 50 \ N$$

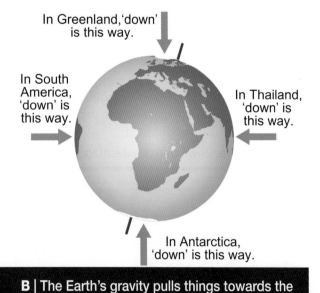

In Greenland, 'down' is this way.

In South America, 'down' is this way.

In Thailand, 'down' is this way.

In Antarctica, 'down' is this way.

B | The Earth's gravity pulls things towards the centre of the Earth.

1   Why is a motorbike heavier than a bicycle?

2   a| Calculate the weight of a 2 kg mass on the Earth.
    b| The gravitational field strength on the Moon is 1.6 N/kg. Calculate the weight of the 2 kg mass on the Moon.

3   Callisto is a moon of Jupiter. The mass of Callisto is three times less than the planet Mercury, although both are the same diameter. State whether the force of gravity on Callisto is more than, less than or the same as on Mercury. Explain your answer.

C | The spacecraft that took the *Curiosity* rover to Mars had small rockets to push against the gravity on Mars. This allowed it to descend very slowly as it lowered *Curiosity* on wires. The gravitational field strength on Mars is only 3.8 N/Kg.

FACT

If you climbed to the top of Mount Everest you would weigh about 1 N less than you do now, because you would be further from the centre of the Earth.

Gravity and orbits

The Earth is moving around the Sun at approximately 100 000 km/h. If there were no gravity from the Sun, the Earth would fly off into space. The force of gravity between the Sun and the Earth keeps the Earth in its orbit. Gravity keeps the other planets and comets in orbit around the Sun.

The force of gravity gets weaker when the two objects attracting each other get further apart.

4	a|	What stops the Earth from moving away from the Sun?
	b|	What stops the Moon from moving away from the Earth?

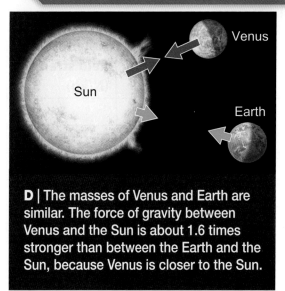

D | The masses of Venus and Earth are similar. The force of gravity between Venus and the Sun is about 1.6 times stronger than between the Earth and the Sun, because Venus is closer to the Sun.

Anything that orbits a planet is called a **satellite**. The Moon is a **natural satellite** of the Earth. **Artificial satellites** are kept in orbit around the Earth by the Earth's gravity. Their uses include photographing the Earth and transmitting TV programmes.

5	Photo E was taken in the International Space Station (ISS), which is in orbit around the Earth. Explain how you know that there *is* gravity acting on the ISS.
6	Neptune is about 4.5 billion kilometres from the Sun. Explain how this shows that the Sun's gravitational field extends at least that far.

E | Astronauts in space are sometimes described as being 'weightless' or in 'zero gravity'. This does not mean there is no gravity in space.

I can ...

- calculate weight
- recall the factors that affect the strength of gravity
- describe how gravity affects objects in space.

MAKING
8Ld COMPARISONS

HOW CAN WE COMPARE THINGS NUMERICALLY?

Model Solar Systems are popular tourist attractions. Map A shows the distances between the different bodies if a model were built across London with a scale of 1:350 000 000. This is a **ratio** and shows that 1 metre in the model represents 350 000 000 metres (or 350 000 km) in the Solar System.

B	Body	Diameter (km)	Gravitational field strength (N/kg)
	Mercury	4880	3.7
	Venus	12 092	8.9
	Earth	12 742	9.8
	Mars	6779	3.7
	Jupiter	142 838	23.2
	Saturn	120 412	9.0
	Uranus	51 095	8.7
	Neptune	49 439	11.0

We can use ratios to directly compare the planets in the Solar System. For example, we can work out the ratio of the diameters of Earth and Neptune.

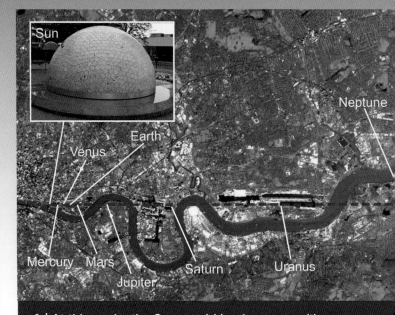

A | At this scale, the Sun would be 4 m across (the same size as the model in the city of Anchorage, shown). The model of the Earth would be 3.6 cm across and 430 m from the Sun. The model of Neptune would be 14 cm across and nearly 13 km from the Sun.

The Earth's gravitational field strength is 9.8 N/kg. This is often rounded to 10 N/kg to make calculations easier.

Example

C

Diameter of Earth (km)   Diameter of Neptune (km)

12742 : 49439

÷12742 ↳ 1 : 3.88 ↰ ÷12742

1 : 4 to nearest whole number

1 Look at the caption for photo A and the ratio calculation in C. Explain which is the easier way to compare the sizes of Earth and Neptune.

It is easier to understand the ratio if one of the numbers is a 1. Simplify the ratio by dividing both sides by the smaller number.

There are other ways of using numbers to compare things. You can compare numbers by writing one as a fraction of another and converting to a decimal.

Example

Write the diameter of Mars as a fraction of the diameter of the Earth and convert it to a decimal.

$$\frac{\text{diameter of Mars}}{\text{diameter of Earth}} = \frac{6779}{12\,742}$$

$$= 0.532$$

> **2** Compare the gravitational field strength of Mars with that of Earth using a decimal.

The diameter of Mars is just over half as big as the diameter of the Earth.

D | These models of the four inner planets are all to the same scale: 1 cm on this photo represents approximately 2900 km on the planets.

Per cent means out of 100. A **percentage** is a way of comparing things with 100. You can convert a decimal to a percentage by multiplying by 100.

Example

Compare the diameter of Mars with the diameter of Earth using a percentage.

$$\frac{6779}{12\,742} = 0.532$$

$$0.532 \times 100 = 53.2\%$$

Sometimes you may need to convert a percentage to a decimal.

Example

The gravity at the surface of the Moon is only 16 per cent of the gravity at the surface of the Earth. Write this as a decimal.

16 per cent is 16 out of 100.

This is $\frac{16}{100}$ which you can write as 0.16.

> **3** Compare the gravitational field strengths of Mars and Earth using a percentage.
>
> **4** Compare the diameter of Mercury with the diameter of Jupiter using:
> a| a fraction
> b| a percentage.
>
> **5** Compare the gravitational field strengths of Mercury and Jupiter using:
> a| a fraction
> b| a percentage.
>
> **6** The diameter of Neptune is only 35 per cent of the diameter of Jupiter. Write this as a decimal.
>
> **7** How would you describe the scale of photo D as a ratio?

I can ...

- calculate ratios and percentages
- convert fractions to decimals
- express one number as a percentage of another.

BEYOND THE SOLAR SYSTEM

8Le

WHAT IS BEYOND OUR SOLAR SYSTEM?

Before compasses, people used stars to guide them. Polaris is a star that is always above the North Pole. **Constellations** (patterns of stars) can be used to find Polaris which lets you work out which direction is north.

Stars are huge balls of gas that give out large amounts of energy (some of which can be seen as light). The Sun is a star. The stars you see at night do not seem very bright compared with the Sun because they are much further away. The stars are around us all the time. We cannot see them during the day because light from them is very faint compared with light from the Sun.

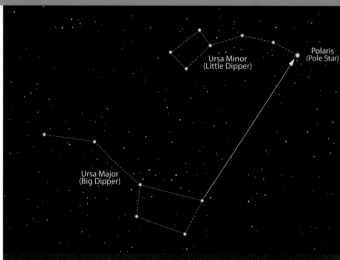

A | The constellation called Ursa Major is always visible on clear nights in the northern hemisphere. You can use it to help you to find Polaris.

1. What is a star?

2. Why does the Sun look much brighter than the other stars?

3. Why can't we see stars during the day?

4. If astronomers watch the stars all night, they have to keep moving their telescopes as the stars seem to move across the sky. Why does this happen?

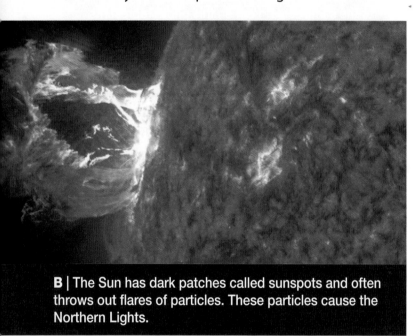

B | The Sun has dark patches called sunspots and often throws out flares of particles. These particles cause the Northern Lights.

FACT

The astronomer Abd al-Rahman al-Sufi (903–986) was the first astronomer to record an observation of the Andromeda galaxy, the nearest large galaxy to the Milky Way. He described it as a 'small cloud'.

D

C | A long-exposure photo shows how the stars appear to move during the night.

Galaxies

When people first observed the stars they also saw blurred patches of light. When telescopes were invented, people could see these patches of light more clearly. Some of them were large groups of stars, called **galaxies**.

The Sun is in a galaxy called the **Milky Way**. The bright band of stars in photo E is part of the Milky Way. It is the part of our galaxy that we can see from Earth. There are millions of other galaxies, and each of these galaxies contains millions of stars. All these galaxies make up the **Universe**.

The stars are a very long way apart. Scientists measure these distances in **light years**. One light year is the distance travelled by light in 1 year. It is approximately 10 000 000 000 000 km (ten million million kilometres).

The nearest star to the Sun is called Proxima Centauri. It is 4.22 light years away. It would take a rocket from Earth over 12 000 years to reach Proxima Centauri.

The stars in a constellation are not close together, and only look close when seen from Earth. Stars are not in fixed positions in our galaxy, so in millions of years the constellations seen from Earth will look different.

E | The bright band of stars is the Milky Way, seen from Earth.

F | We cannot see the shape of the Milky Way directly, but observations suggest that it is this shape. This photograph of Barred Spiral Galaxy NGC 1300 was taken by the Hubble Space Telescope.

---

5 Does a light year measure distance or time?

6 The first list of blurred objects in the sky was produced by Charles Messier (1730–1817) in 1771.

a| Suggest why he only listed 100 objects.

b| Explain why astronomers today can observe millions of galaxies.

7 Explain what the Milky Way is and why we cannot see its shape directly.

I can ...

- describe stars, galaxies and constellations
- describe the Milky Way
- explain what a light year is.

SHOULD WE BE SPENDING MONEY ON STUDYING SPACE?

The *Galileo* space probe orbited Jupiter from 1995 to 2003 and sent back a lot of data about Jupiter and its moons. The whole mission cost about $1.5 billion. The European Space Agency spends about three times that amount each year on exploring space. The money comes from European taxpayers. That is enough to build more than 10 hospitals every year.

A | An artist's impression of NASA's *Galileo* in orbit around Jupiter.

B | An artist's impression of Europa, one of Jupiter's moons: Europa is thought to have a liquid ocean beneath an icy crust. This means it is possible there may be some life there.

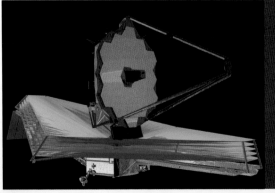

C | The James Webb Telescope will study the formation of stars and galaxies. It will cost over $9 billion.

1. What are the differences between:
   a| a star and a planet
   b| a planet and a moon?

2. Which parts of our Solar System have humans visited?

3. a| Describe some observations of the planets that can be made from the surface of the Earth.
   b| Describe two ways in which new technology has improved our knowledge of the Solar System.

4. a| Write down two factors that affect the strength of gravity between two objects.
   b| How does the Sun's gravity affect the planets in the Solar System?

HAVE YOUR SAY

Do you think that money should be spent on finding out more about the planets and the stars?

9la MOVING THINGS

Photo A shows a lighthouse being moved in the United States. Modern equipment and machinery are needed to move large buildings like this. Smaller houses are sometimes moved using lorries.

Machines such as those used to move the Cape Hatteras lighthouse have only existed for a few centuries. Before then, moving and lifting things had to be done using only human or animal power, or by using energy from the wind or moving water.

B | Stonehenge, in southern England, was built over 4000 years ago. The largest stone has a mass of 50 tonnes.

A | The Cape Hatteras lighthouse in North Carolina, USA, has a mass of almost 5000 tonnes. It was moved 460 metres inland because of coastal erosion.

C | We do not know how ancient peoples built their large structures. This photo shows students testing a possible way in which the 50 tonne stones in Stonehenge might have been moved.

1 Look at photo A. Name the forces acting on the building as it is being moved, and describe what they are doing.

2 Look at photo C. The students are using rollers beneath the stone they are pulling to reduce friction.

a| How does friction affect the movement of an object?

b| Describe two ways of reducing the friction between two surfaces without using rollers or wheels.

3 The students moving the stones are using energy.

a| Where do humans get their energy from?

b| Where does this energy originally come from?

c| Draw a diagram to show the energy transfers between the original source of energy and the students.

9Ia FORCES AND MOVEMENT

HOW DO FORCES AFFECT OBJECTS AND THE WAY THEY MOVE?

When an object is pulled along the ground, the force of **friction** between the object and the ground makes it difficult to move. Friction can be reduced using rollers or wheels. In snowy countries, sleds have been used for thousands of years to move heavy loads.

> **1** Look at photo A. Suggest why sleds are only used when there is snow on the ground.

If the forwards force on a moving sled is the same size as the force of friction, the forces on the sled are **balanced**. The sled will continue to move at a constant speed.

A | This sled is being used to transport logs.

If the horses pull harder the forces on the sled will be **unbalanced**. The difference between the forward and backwards forces is the **resultant** force. In this case, the resultant force will be acting in a forwards direction and the sled will **accelerate** (get faster). As well as changing the speed, unbalanced forces can also change the direction in which something is moving and its shape.

In photo B, the shape of the metal horseshoe is being changed using a force from the hammer. Some changes of shape are not as obvious as this. For example, in photo A the leather in the horse's harness will stretch as it pulls the sled. Even things like metal wires stretch a little when they are pulled.

B | The shape of this horseshoe is being changed so that it fits the horse's hoof.

Some of the stones used in Stonehenge come from Preseli, in South Wales, over 250 km away. Many archaeologists think these stones were transported using boats on rivers and the sea. Early boats were paddled using oars, but later boats had sails to use the wind to move them.

A boat moving through the water has several forces acting on it.

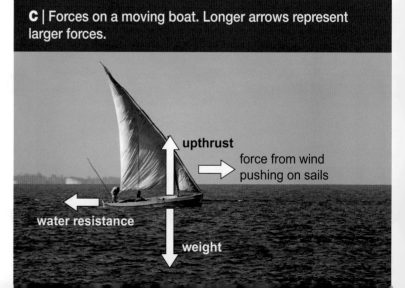

C | Forces on a moving boat. Longer arrows represent larger forces.

upthrust

force from wind pushing on sails

water resistance

weight

Water resistance and **air resistance** are forms of **drag**. Drag forces act to slow down objects moving through **fluids**. The size of the drag force increases as the speed of the object increases, because more of the fluid has to be pushed out of the way each second.

2 Look at photo C. Write down the force that:

a| is caused by gravity

b| is helping to make the boat go forwards

c| will increase if the speed of the boat increases.

3 The weight of the boat in photo C is 2000 N. How big is the upthrust? Explain your answer.

4 Explain what will happen to the speed of the boat if the wind gets stronger.

5 Explain why a sailing boat will slow down if the wind speed reduces.

Top speed

The top speed of a ship or other vehicle depends on the maximum force that can move it forwards and on the friction or drag acting to slow it down. As a ship gets faster, the water resistance increases. Eventually the water resistance is as large as the force from the sails and this means that the ship cannot accelerate any more. It is now at its top speed for that amount of wind.

Falling objects also reach a maximum speed. As the object starts to fall there is no air resistance because it is not moving. As it accelerates, the air resistance increases until it balances the weight of the object. The speed at which this happens is called **terminal velocity**. Velocity is the speed in a particular direction.

 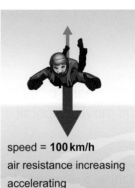 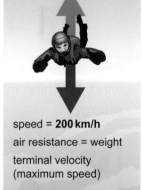

speed = **0**
no air resistance
accelerating

speed = **100 km/h**
air resistance increasing
accelerating

speed = **200 km/h**
air resistance = weight
terminal velocity
(maximum speed)

D | The terminal velocity of the skydiver is when the air resistance is equal to their weight.

FACT

The *Cutty Sark* was one of the fastest sailing ships, with a maximum speed of over 30 km/h. It brought tea from China, and the first tea to arrive in England each year sold for the highest prices.

6 A racing car has a higher top speed than a family car. Give two reasons for this.

7 Look at diagram D.

a| Explain what will happen to the air resistance of the skydiver when they open their parachute.

b| Explain why the skydiver will reach a new, lower, terminal velocity.

I can ...

- recall the names of different types of force
- explain the effects of balanced and unbalanced forces
- explain why moving objects have a top speed.

9b ENERGY FOR MOVEMENT

WHICH ENERGY RESOURCES CAN BE USED TO MOVE THINGS?

The earliest forms of transport often used animals to carry things, or to pull sleds or carts with wheels. The energy needed by humans and animals comes from their food. The energy in the food originally came from the Sun. Today we also directly use energy from the Sun (**solar energy**) to heat water and to produce **electricity**.

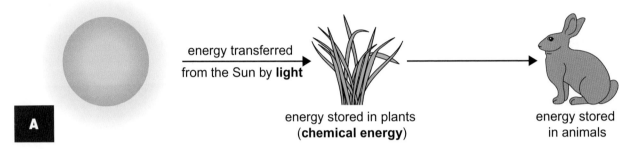

energy transferred from the Sun by **light**

A

energy stored in plants (**chemical energy**)

energy stored in animals

Ships were moved using oars, or using energy from the wind. Anything that is moving contains a store of **kinetic energy**.

1 Write down three examples of substances or objects that are stores of chemical energy.

2 Explain how the galley in photo B could be said to be using solar power.

3 Write down one factor that affects the amount of kinetic energy stored in an object.

B | Galleys were ships with oars and sails.

Just over 200 years ago, some forms of transport started to use energy stored in coal. Coal is a **fossil fuel**, formed underground over millions of years from the remains of plants. Fossil fuels are a very convenient way of storing large amounts of energy, but they are a **non-renewable resource** because they will run out one day. Today we also use energy stored in oil and natural gas for transport. Energy released by burning fuels can be transferred by **heating** to be used for cooking or keeping our homes warm.

4 Explain how energy stored in coal originally came from the Sun.

C | A similar locomotive was built by Richard Trevithick in 1801. It used the energy stored in coal. This is a modern replica.

Other energy stores

Smaller amounts of energy can be stored using weights and springs. The clock in photo D uses weights to keep it going. A weight on a chain gradually falls and transfers energy to the clock. Energy stored in raised objects is called **gravitational potential energy**. Some clocks use **elastic potential energy** (or **strain energy**) stored in a wound-up spring. Elastic materials can store energy when they are **deformed** (change shape).

Internal (or **thermal**) **energy** is the energy stored in the movement of particles. There is more of this energy in things that are hot. Energy is transferred from hot objects to cooler objects by heating.

> **5** An archer uses a bow to shoot an arrow.
>
> a| How is energy stored just before she shoots?
>
> b| What happens to this energy as she shoots?
>
> **6** a| Give two examples of objects or substances that store gravitational potential energy.
>
> b| Describe two factors that affect the amount of gravitational potential energy stored in an object.

pendulum

weights

D | a pendulum clock

Transferring energy

Many modern devices use energy transferred by electricity. Electricity cannot be stored, but has to be generated using **renewable resources** such as wind, moving water or solar energy, or from non-renewable resources such as fossil fuels or **nuclear energy**.

Energy is never created or destroyed, but only transferred. This is the **law of conservation of energy**. However energy is not always transferred usefully. The **efficiency** of an energy transfer compares the useful energy transferred to the total energy transferred. Wasted energy is usually transferred to the surroundings by heating, and often by **sound** as well. This energy is **dissipated** (spread out). The greater the efficiency, the less energy is wasted.

> **7** Write down three energy resources that are:
> a| renewable   b| non-renewable.
>
> **8** Early steam engines had efficiencies of only a few per cent.
> a| What energy store did steam engines use?
>
> b| Was most of this energy transferred as wasted or useful energy? Explain your answer.
>
> c| Suggest two ways in which energy might have been wasted.
>
> **9** A man pushes his daughter on a swing to make her start moving.
> a| Draw an energy transfer diagram (similar to diagram A) to show the energy transfers.
>
> b| Explain why the swing eventually stops moving after the man stops pushing it.

FACT

Uranium nuclear fuel can release over 80 million million joules of energy per kilogram. Petrol only releases about 46 million joules per kilogram when it burns.

I can ...

- recall ways in which energy can be stored and transferred
- recall the law of conservation of energy
- state the meaning of efficiency.

WHAT SKILLS ARE NEEDED TO SAIL SHIPS SAFELY AROUND THE WORLD?

The largest ships in the world are container ships 400 m long, which travel at over 40 km/h. Ships carry over 10 billion tonnes of cargo every year.

Roles on ships

The people who operate machinery on board, steer the ship or keep a lookout for other ships are called ratings. They need to be good at maths and science, and usually do a short training course at college before going to sea.

Deck officers are in charge of a ship. They choose the route, make decisions about safety (such as changing routes to avoid bad weather) and make sure that cargo is loaded correctly. Deck officers usually study marine engineering or nautical studies at college or university. They carry on learning and do more training at sea in order to get internationally recognised qualifications. They must be good at communication and teamwork, and need to speak English.

Engineer officers on ships maintain and run the engines and all the other machinery. They need a degree in marine or mechanical engineering. Deck and engineering officers need internationally recognised certificates to allow them to work at sea.

A | The Panama Canal crosses Central America, connecting the Atlantic and Pacific Oceans.

B | Deck officers use radar and other technology for navigation and to avoid collisions.

1. Suggest why deck officers need to:
   a | speak English
   b | be good at maths and physics
   c | have good eyesight.

2. Explain why deck officers need to study meteorology (weather) and sea currents as part of their training.

3. Suggest why deck officer qualifications need to be internationally recognised.

Efficient ships

Transporting cargo by ship is much more efficient than using lorries or aeroplanes, but ships do cause pollution. Most large ships burn oil to power their engines. Burning oil adds carbon dioxide to the atmosphere, and produces other pollutants, such as sulfur dioxide. Oil spills at sea pollute water and beaches, and kill wildlife.

4 Explain why a lot of cargo is sent around the world by aeroplane, even though ships are more efficient.

C | Smoke from burning fuel oil

E | This kite produces a forward force, so less engine power is needed.

Some marine engineers help to build and develop ships and their engines, including ways to reduce the carbon emissions from ships. The ships in photos D and E combine existing ideas about wind power to move ships in innovative ways. Marine engineers analyse and evaluate potential solutions. They do this by recording and comparing the advantages and disadvantages of each solution.

D | The four spinning rotors on this ship cause a forward force when the wind blows from one side.

5 Explain why the ships in D and E still need normal engines.

6 Some naval ships and submarines use nuclear reactors as their power sources, and do not produce carbon emissions. Suggest why:

a | nuclear power is useful for a submarine

b | cargo ships do not use nuclear power.

ACTIVITY

Three different systems that could reduce carbon emissions from cargo ships are: spinning rotors, kites and solar cells used to power electric motors.

1 Evaluate each idea. Your evaluation could consider these points:

- how much it will cost to install the equipment on a ship
- how much the propulsion will be affected by the weather.

Summarise your evaluations in a table, showing the advantages and disadvantages.

2 A shipping company uses small cargo ships that make short trips to deliver goods to many ports on the Baltic Sea. Decide which system would be best for one of these ships, giving your reasons.

9|c SPEED

HOW DO WE CALCULATE SPEED?

Speed is a way of saying how far you can travel in a certain time. This time can be a second (s), a minute (m), an hour (h), or even longer.

To work out a speed, you have to measure a distance and a time. The units you use for speed depend on the measurements you take. For example, if a car travels 200 kilometres in 4 hours, its speed would be in **kilometres per hour** (km/h). Other units for speed that are often used are **metres per second** (m/s) and **miles per hour** (mph).

$$\text{speed} = \frac{\text{distance}}{\text{time}}$$

Many moving objects do not travel at a constant speed. For example, cars can travel faster on motorways than in towns, and may have to stop at junctions. The **mean (average) speed** for a journey is the total distance travelled, divided by the total time taken.

A | The Shanghai maglev train can travel at 430 km/h.

Convert a speed in m/s to km/h by dividing by 1000
(1000 m = 1 km) then multiplying by 3600 (3600 s = 1 hour).

Convert a speed in km/h to m/s by multiplying by 1000 then dividing by 3600.

Example

$$50 \text{ km/h} = 50 \times \frac{1000}{3600} = 13.9 \text{ m/s}$$

1 You are growing a little taller each year. What units could you use to measure how fast you are growing?

2 A horse and rider cover 54 km in 9 hours.

a| Calculate the mean speed.

b| Explain why the fastest speed during the journey was higher than your answer to part a.

3 The fastest human can run at 44 km/h. Convert this speed to m/s.

Distance–time graphs

You can show how fast someone travelled during a journey using a **distance–time graph**. This is sometimes called a displacement–time graph. **Displacement** is the distance *in a straight line* between an object and its starting point. Graph B (opposite) shows a journey by coach and horses.

A steep line on a distance–time graph shows that something is moving quickly. A shallow line shows it is moving slowly. If the line is horizontal the object is not moving at all.

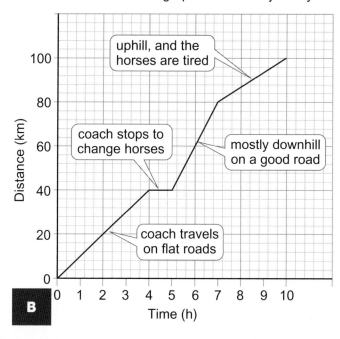

Distance–time graph for a coach journey

uphill, and the horses are tired

coach stops to change horses

mostly downhill on a good road

coach travels on flat roads

B

Distance (km) / *Time (h)*

4 Look at graph B.

a| How far did the coach travel?

b| How long did it stop when they changed the horses?

c| During which part of the journey was the coach moving fastest?

5 Calculate the speed of the coach for the first 4 hours of the journey.

6 Sketch a distance–time graph to show your journey to school.

Relative speeds

When you talk about how fast you can walk or run, you are measuring your speed over the ground. However you can also walk along a train while it is moving. If you walk at 2 m/s towards the front of the train and the train is travelling at 50 m/s, your speed **relative** *to the ground outside* is 52 m/s. If you walk towards the back of the train, your speed relative to the ground is 48 m/s.

If two trains are travelling towards each other, and both are moving at 100 km/h, they are moving at 200 km/h *relative to each other*.

Sailors and pilots have to think about relative motion all the time, because water and air are usually moving.

FACT

If you are sitting down reading this you are not moving relative to the ground. But you are moving at a speed of about 108 000 km/h relative to the Sun!

C | This man is only moving slowly relative to the train, but he could be moving at up to 50 m/s relative to the ground.

D | The speed of a boat depends on its speed through the water and on how fast the water itself is moving.

boat moving at 5 m/s through the water

← river flowing at 2 m/s

7 Look at photo D.

a| How fast is the boat moving relative to the riverbank?

b| If the river was flowing in the opposite direction to that shown, how fast would the boat be moving relative to the riverbank?

I can ...

- describe the meanings of speed and mean (average) speed
- use the formula relating speed, distance and time
- represent simple journeys on a distance–time graph.

9|c EQUATIONS AND GRAPHS

HOW DO WE DRAW AND INTERPRET DISTANCE–TIME GRAPHS?

Calculating distances and times

The text in the box describes Samina's cycle ride. We can use this description to construct a distance–time graph to show her ride.

A

> Samina cycled at 16 km/h for half an hour, then at 8 km/h for the next half hour. She covered the last 6 km at 24 km/h.

We need to know the distance and time for each part of the journey. We can rearrange the formula for speed:

distance = speed × time $\text{time} = \dfrac{\text{distance}}{\text{speed}}$

1 Calculate how far Samina travels in the second half hour of her ride.

2 Calculate how long Samina took to complete the last part of her ride.

3 Use your answers to questions 1 and 2 to draw a distance–time graph to show Samina's ride. Your vertical axis should go up to 20 km and your horizontal axis should go up to 1.5 hours. Remember to give your graph a title.

Example

How far does Samina travel during the first half hour?

distance = speed × time
= 16 km/h × 0.5 hours
= 8 km

Calculating a gradient

You can use a distance–time graph to compare the speeds at different points in a journey.

You can also use information from a distance–time graph to calculate speeds. The **gradient** of a line is a way of describing how steep it is in numbers. The larger the value of the gradient, the steeper the line.

For distance–time graphs, the gradient of a line represents the speed. On graph B, the gradient will be how far the object travels in 1 second.

$\text{gradient} = \dfrac{\text{vertical change}}{\text{horizontal change}}$

this represents the distance

this represents the time

so the equation is calculating the distance travelled per second

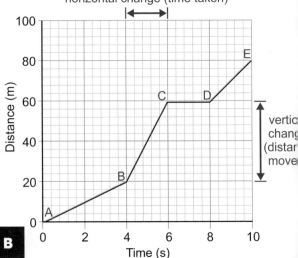
Distance–time graph for a toy car

C | These radio-controlled cars can cover 100 metres in around 5 seconds.

4	Calculate the gradient of the following lines on graph B:
	a|A–B b|D–E.

Speed–time graphs

You can show how fast someone travelled using a speed–time graph. Graph D shows Samina's ride. The horizontal lines show where she is travelling at a constant speed. The sloping lines show where she is changing speed (accelerating).

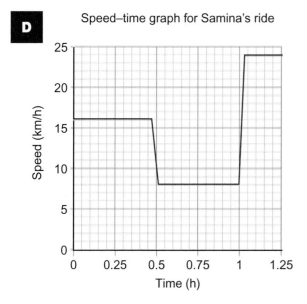

D   Speed–time graph for Samina's ride

Example

Graph B shows how a radio-controlled car moves.

Calculate the speed of the car between points B and C by working out the gradient of the line.

Vertical difference (distance) = 60 m – 20 m

= 40 m

> Start with the end of the section of the line you are interested in and read its value from the vertical scale, then subtract the value for the beginning of that section of line.

Horizontal difference (time) = 6 s – 4 s

= 2 s

> Find the value on the horizontal axis for the end of the section you are looking at, and subtract the value for the beginning of that section of the line.

gradient = $\dfrac{40 \text{ m}}{2 \text{ s}}$

= 20 m/s

> Remember that the units for speed depend on the units used to measure the distance and the time.

5	Look at graph D. At what time is Samina:
	a| speeding up
	b| slowing down?

6	Use the information on this page and your answers to question 4 to draw a speed–time graph for the toy car. Your vertical axis should go up to 20 m/s. The horizontal axis will be the same as graph B.

I can ...

- use the formula relating speed, distance and time
- draw and interpret distance–time graphs
- calculate the gradient of a line on a graph
- draw and interpret speed–time graphs.

9ld TURNING FORCES

HOW CAN YOU INCREASE THE SIZE OF A FORCE?

You can move heavy objects using a **lever**. A lever is a long bar that turns around a **pivot** or **fulcrum**. When you push down on one side you are applying an **effort** and the object on the other end moves up. This object is called the **load**. The longer the lever, the easier it is to move the load.

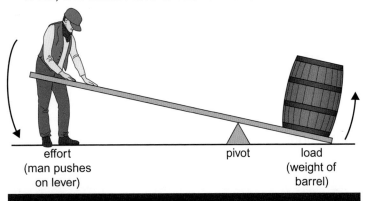

effort
(man pushes
on lever)

pivot

load
(weight of
barrel)

A | The effort force moves further than the load.

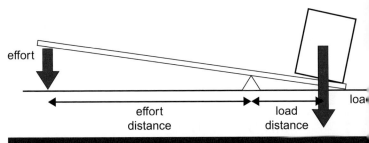

effort

effort
distance

load
distance

load

B | The effort is smaller than the force needed to lift the weight of the load directly.

There are many simple levers in the home. Most levers work by changing a smaller force into a larger one. The lever acts as a **force multiplier** if the effort distance is greater than the load distance. When the load is lifted, the effort force is smaller than the force at the other end of the lever pushing up on the load. The force has been multiplied. However, the effort force has to move through a greater distance than the load.

Some levers can act as **distance multipliers** instead. In this case a large effort force moves a small distance, and the load you are moving moves a greater distance.

pivot

load

effort

C | A bottle opener is a lever. It is a force multiplier.

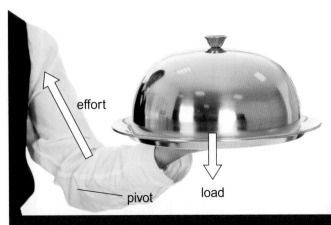

effort

pivot

load

D | Your arm is a lever. It is a distance multiplier.

Turning forces

The spanner in diagram E is being used to turn the nut. The turning effect of a force is called a **moment**. The size of the moment depends on the size of the force and the distance between the force and the pivot. Moments are measured in units called **newton metres (N m)**.

moment of the = force × perpendicular distance
force (N m)   (N)   from the pivot (m)

E The distance is always measured at right angles (perpendicular) to the force.

> **4** The spanner is 0.2 m long and the force is 20 N. Calculate the moment of the force.

We can use ideas about moments to explain how levers work. Look at diagram F. If the moment due to the effort is equal to the moment caused by the load, the lever will not move. If the effort moment is greater than the load moment, the load will move in the direction shown.

> **5** Look at photos C and D. Explain why:
> a| the bottle opener is a force multiplier
> b| an arm is a distance multiplier.

effort	load
moment = 220 N × 2 m	moment = 400 N × 1 m
= 440 N m	= 400 N m

F | The box will move up because the moment from the effort is bigger than the moment from the load.

In equilibrium

The crane in diagram G is acting as a lever. The crane is balanced, because the clockwise moment is balancing the anticlockwise moment. We say it is **in equilibrium**. If the man in diagram G pulls a little harder, the forces will not be balanced and the barrel will rise.

> **6** Look at diagram G. Which force is the load and which is the effort?
>
> **7** Look at diagram G. The rope holding the barrel is moved so that it is only 0.5 m from the pivot.
>
> a| Will the anticlockwise moment be larger or smaller than before? Explain your answer.
>
> b| Calculate the new anticlockwise moment. Show your working.

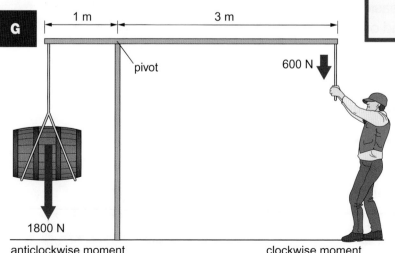

G

anticlockwise moment
= 1800 N × 1 m
= 1800 N m

clockwise moment
= 600 N × 3 m
= 1800 N m

I can ...
- describe how a simple lever can multiply forces or distances
- identify the load, effort and pivot on a diagram of a lever
- describe the factors that affect the size of a moment
- explain why something will balance if the moments are equal and opposite.

9Ie MORE MACHINES

WHAT OTHER SIMPLE MACHINES MAKE IT EASIER TO MOVE THINGS?

A **machine** is anything that can help us to work with forces. Most machines help by allowing us to use a smaller force to move an object. Levers are simple machines. Another type of simple machine is a **ramp**. It needs less force to push an object up a slope than it does to lift it directly. The shallower the slope, the less force is needed.

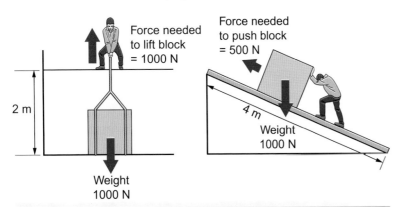

Force needed to lift block = 1000 N

Force needed to push block = 500 N

2 m

4 m

Weight 1000 N

Weight 1000 N

B | A ramp reduces the force needed to lift an object, but the object has to be moved further.

A | No-one knows how the Ancient Egyptians built the pyramids. Some archaeologists think that ramps were used to help move the huge blocks of stone up to the top.

1 Write down two more examples of where ramps are used.

FACT

It is estimated that over 2 million blocks of stone were used to build the Great Pyramid at Giza, in Egypt. Most of the stones had a mass of 2500 kg or more.

Pulleys can also be used to help us to move things. In diagram D, pulley X makes lifting the load easier because we can pull down on the rope instead of lifting the object directly, but it does not change the force needed. Pulley Y halves the force needed to pull the object, but the rope has to be pulled twice as far as for pulley X. Pulley Z reduces the force needed even further.

C | Pulleys and levers make it easier to control the sail and to steer.

2 Suggest two other uses of pulleys.

3 Look at the pulley in photo C. The woman would need less force to control the sail if the rope went round more pulleys. Suggest why this is not done.

tiller (a

pulleys

Rio2014

rud

Work

In physics, **work** means the amount of energy transferred when a force moves something. Work is measured in joules (J). The formula for calculating work done is:

work done = force × distance moved in the
(J)   (N)   direction of the force (m)

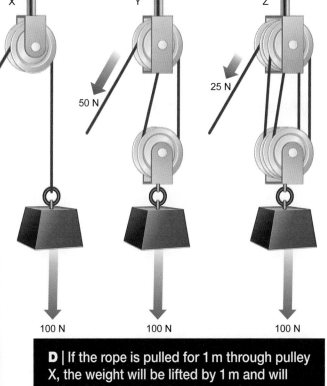

| D | If the rope is pulled for 1 m through pulley X, the weight will be lifted by 1 m and will gain 100 J of gravitational potential energy.

Example

Look at pulley Y in diagram D. The force on the rope is 50 N, and the rope is pulled through a distance of 2 m.

How much work is done?

work = 50 N × 2 m

= 100 J

In pulley Y, the force from the rope lifts the weight upwards, and the *weight* moves up by 1 m. The energy transferred (work done) by pulling on the rope is all transferred to the weight. The weight has 100 J more gravitational potential energy than before it was lifted.

In a similar way, energy is transferred (work is done) when a force is used to stretch a spring. This energy is stored as elastic potential energy in the stretched spring.

Conservation of energy

In diagram D, pulley Z allows the weight to be lifted using a force of 25 N, but the rope has to be pulled for 4 m to lift the weight by 1 m. The same is true of all machines – if a smaller force is needed to move something, the force has to move through a greater distance.

You would expect that the same work is done to lift the weight even when the pulley allows you to use a smaller force. However, friction causes a little *more* work to be done when smaller forces are used.

4 Look at diagram B. Calculate the work done to:

a| lift the block directly upwards

b| push the block up the ramp.

c| Comment on your answers to parts a and b.

5 Look at diagram B. Explain why it will need more energy to lift the block using the ramp than it will to pull it directly upwards.

6 A heavy box is pulled along the floor. The work done is 200 J. Explain the final form of this energy store.

I can ...

■ describe how simple machines can magnify forces

■ describe the factors that affect the total work done.

SUPPLYING THE ENERGY

WHAT TRANSPORT IDEAS DID NOT LAST?

Steam engines had to carry a supply of coal with them. In the 1840s several engineers built railways where the engines were beside the track instead of part of the train. This meant the trains did not have to carry fuel. These 'atmospheric' railways had a long tube laid along the track with a slot. Air pumped into the tube from pumping stations along the track pushed on a piston attached to the train. Unfortunately the atmospheric railways had problems with air leaking out of the pipe, and they turned out to be more expensive to run than steam locomotives. They only ran for a few years.

A | A train on the 'atmospheric railway' in Devon in the United Kingdom.

Although diesel-powered trains still have to carry their energy store with them, many modern trains use energy transferred to them by electricity. The train does not emit any polluting gases.

1. Suggest some advantages and disadvantages of an atmospheric railway compared to a steam-powered railway.

2. Suggest some advantages and disadvantages of modern electric trains compared to diesel-powered trains.

3. Mr Wong travels 70 km from Kuala Lumpur to Seremban. The journey takes 1.5 hours by train. The train stops for 10 minutes in the middle of the journey. Draw a labelled distance–time graph to show this journey.

4. Engines are machines. Simple machines include levers, pulleys and ramps.

   a| Write a sentence or two for each of these simple machines to explain how they can help us to move things.

   b| Explain why a machine that magnifies a force needs as much energy as doing the same task without the machine.

B | Electric trains can only run on tracks where overhead wires or an extra 'live' rail have been installed.

HAVE YOUR SAY

It is expensive to install overhead electricity wires along railway lines, so only busy main lines are electrified. Should governments invest money in electrifying *all* railway lines in the UK?

9Ja MISSION TO MARS

The Moon is the most distant body that has been explored by humans. Sending humans to Mars or beyond is more complicated than sending them to the Moon. The distance is much greater, and astronauts would have to live in space for many months or even years.

It takes a large force to move spacecraft from the surface of the Earth into space. All the equipment, food and fuel for the whole mission has to be lifted. Rockets burn fuel such as hydrogen or kerosene, but in the future there may be other ways of launching astronauts and equipment into space, such as using giant magnetic 'guns'.

A | The Curiosity rover has been exploring Mars since 2012. It receives instructions from engineers and scientists on Earth, but it also has computers that help to control its wheels and instruments.

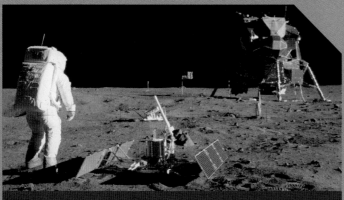

B | Buzz Aldrin doing an experiment on the Moon in 1969.

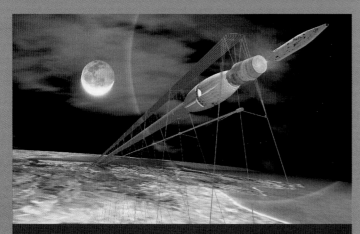

C | This artist's impression shows a possible magnetic launcher for spacecraft. This uses electrical and magnetic effects to produce large forces.

1
a| What is the force that pulls objects towards the Earth?

b| Name two factors that affect the size of this force, and describe how they affect it.

2
a| What are the two ends of a magnet called?

b| What is a magnetic field?

c| Explain why compass needles point north.

3 Electronic devices (such as computers on the Curiosity rover) use electric currents.

a| Describe the apparatus you need to make an electric current flow.

b| Describe how to measure an electric current.

c| What does voltage mean?

d| Describe how to measure a voltage.

9Ja FORCE FIELDS

WHAT KINDS OF FORCE FIELD ARE THERE?

In science fiction films, a force field is often shown as a kind of invisible wall. The meaning of **force field** in physics is a space where a **non-contact force** has an effect.

Magnetic fields

The space around a magnet where it can attract magnetic materials is called a **magnetic field**. A bar magnet has two ends, called the north pole and the south pole. Two north poles or two south poles will repel each other. A north pole and a south pole will attract each other.

> **1** Draw two bar magnets in an arrangement where they will:
>
> a| attract each other
>
> b| repel each other.

You can find the shape of a magnetic field using iron filings or small compasses. The arrows show the direction a north pole would move. The field is strongest where the lines are closest together.

> **2** State where the magnetic field of a bar magnet is:
>
> a| strongest
>
> b| weakest.

The Earth's magnetic field helps to protect it from charged particles emitted by the Sun. However, the shape of this field is altered by the Sun.

> **3** Explain why the full name of the north end of a magnet is the 'north-seeking pole'.

A | This imaginary 'force field' is protecting the woman.

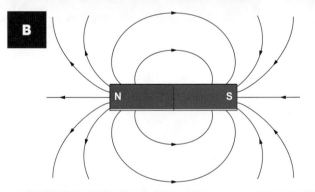

B

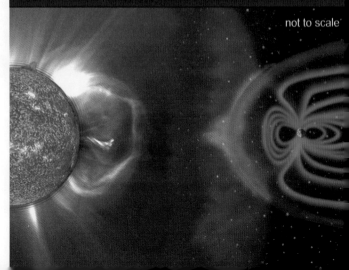

C | The shape of the Earth's magnetic field is deformed by the charged particles coming from the Sun. Astronauts travelling to Mars or beyond will need to be protected against these particles.

not to scale

Gravitational fields

Any object that has **mass** has a **gravitational field** around it. When two objects are in each other's gravitational field, they attract each other.

The **gravitational field strength** (*g*) of the Earth is approximately 10 N/kg. This means that the force of attraction between the Earth and a 1 kg mass is 10 N. We call this force the **weight** of the object:

weight (N) = mass (kg) x *g* (N/kg)

 All objects attract each other.

 If one or both of the objects has more mass, the force is bigger.

 If the objects are further apart, the force is smaller.

D | The force of gravity between two masses depends on the strength of their gravitational fields, and on how far apart they are. The gravitational field strength of the Earth decreases as you move further from the centre of the Earth.

---

4 The Curiosity rover is exploring Mars. It has a mass of 900 kg.

a| Calculate its weight on Earth.

b| The gravitational field strength of Mars is 3.7 N/kg. What is the rover's weight on Mars?

---

5 Rhea is a moon of Saturn and Oberon is a moon of Uranus. They have similar diameters, but the mass of Oberon is approximately 1.3 times the mass of Rhea.

a| Explain which moon will have the greater force of gravity on its surface.

b| Suggest why two moons of similar diameter were chosen for this question.

Storing energy

It takes energy to move an object away from the Earth, because of the forces of attraction between the two objects. The energy needed to move the object is stored in its mass as **gravitational potential energy** (**GPE**). The greater the mass, or the higher it is moved, the more gravitational potential energy it stores.

FACT

The idea of a space elevator was first suggested in 1895. We do not yet have the technology to build one.

E | A 'space elevator' could be an alternative way of putting objects into orbit around the Earth. The 'climbers' going up the cable would gain GPE as they moved upwards.

6 Describe two different ways of increasing the amount of gravitational potential energy stored in a bucket.

I can ...

- state what is meant by a force field
- describe the shape of a magnetic field
- recall the factors that affect the strength of gravity
- calculate the weight of a mass.

9Jb STATIC ELECTRICITY

WHAT CAUSES STATIC ELECTRICITY?

People sometimes get small shocks when touching metal railings, doorknobs or car doors. Shocks like this are caused by **static electricity**. A charge of static electricity can build up when two different materials rub together. Sparks caused by static electricity can cause fires or damage electronic equipment.

Separating charges

Atoms consist of a central **nucleus** with small particles called **electrons** moving around it. The nucleus contains positively charged **protons** and uncharged **neutrons**. It has an overall **positive charge** and

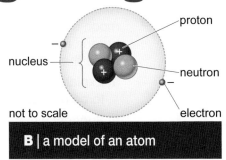

B | a model of an atom

each electron has a **negative charge**. The total positive and negative charges in an atom are usually the same, so they balance each other and the atom has no overall charge

| 1 | Where are electrons found in an atom? |
| 2 | Why do most atoms have no overall charge? |

A | Artist's impression of a dust storm on Mars. These can last for months, and can generate a lot of static electricity that could interfere with electronic systems in spacecraft.

When you rub two insulating materials together some electrons may be transferred from one object to the other. The positive charges cannot be transferred because the protons are fixed in the nuclei of the atoms. The object that ends up with more electrons has an overall negative charge. The object that has lost electrons has an overall positive charge.

C | The effect of rubbing two different insulating materials with a cloth. The charges stay where they are when they have been transferred.

When you rub an acetate rod with a piece of cloth, some of the electrons in the acetate move onto the cloth.

The acetate now has more positive than negative charges, so it has an overall positive charge and the cloth has an equal negative charge.

When you rub a polythene rod, some of the electrons in the cloth move onto the polythene.

3 Why are only the negative charges transferred when you rub an insulating material?

4 Look at diagram C.

a| Explain why the polythene rod has an overall negative charge after it has been rubbed.

b| Explain why the cloth will have the same amount of positive charge as the rod has negative charge.

Positive and negative charges can become separated when a conducting material (such as metal) is rubbed. However, the charge spreads out over the whole of the metal object, so we do not usually notice the charge.

FACT

Lightning happens when clouds build up a very large charge of static electricity. The potential difference (voltage) between the cloud and the ground can be as high as 100 million volts.

Attract and repel

Something with a charge of static electricity can attract uncharged objects. The force is not very strong, so you only notice this effect with small things such as pieces of tissue paper or hair (see photo D).

Two charged objects can attract or repel each other. If the charges are the same (two positively charged objects, or two negatively charged ones) they will repel each other. If the two objects have opposite charges they will attract each other.

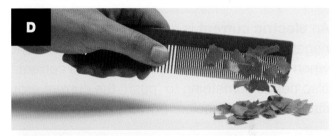

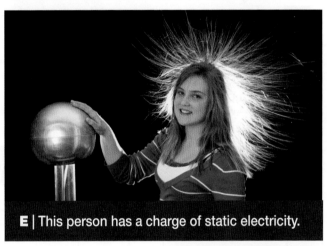

E | This person has a charge of static electricity.

5 Look at diagram C. Explain what will happen when two charged rods are suspended close to each other if:

a| they are both acetate rods

b| one is acetate and one is polythene.

6 Look at photo E. The silver dome is part of a machine that makes static electricity, which has passed into the girl. Explain why the girl's hair is sticking out.

Electric fields

The space around a charged object where it has an effect is an **electric field**. The field is strongest close to the object. Diagram F shows one way of representing the electric field around the end of a rod with a negative charge.

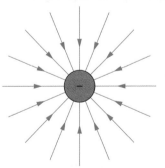

F | Electric field around a negative charge. The arrows show the direction in which a positive charge would move.

7 Look at diagram F. Draw a similar diagram to show the electric field around a positive charge. Explain your answer.

I can ...

- explain why an insulating material can be given a charge by rubbing
- describe how electrically charged objects affect each other
- describe an electric field.

9Jc CURRENT ELECTRICITY

HOW CAN CURRENT ELECTRICITY BE CONTROLLED?

All spacecraft need computers. These control the engines and all the instruments. For spacecraft that carry astronauts, the computers also keep the air inside breathable and at the correct temperature. Electric circuits turn motors and fans on and off at the correct times.

An **electric current** is a flow of electrons, which are negatively charged particles. An electric current only flows when there is a complete circuit for the current. A circuit also needs something to 'push' the current around the circuit, such as a cell or power pack.

A | Astronauts in a Soyuz spacecraft. This is used to take astronauts to and from the International Space Station.

1 The wires in a circuit are often made of copper. Explain why this material is used.

2 We represent electric circuits using standard symbols. Draw the symbols for:
a| a cell   b| a bulb.

FACT

Astronauts in space cannot survive without electricity. In some countries, if the mains electricity supply failed, some physically weak people could start dying after only a few days from contaminated water or shortage of food.

B | Circuits can be **series circuits** or **parallel circuits**.

Series circuits	Parallel circuits
The current is the same everywhere in the circuit.	The current through the cell splits up when it comes to a junction.
All the bulbs go off when the switch is opened.	Each bulb can be controlled individually.
If you add more bulbs in series, the current in the circuit is reduced and the bulbs are dimmer.	If you add more bulbs in parallel, the bulbs all stay at the original brightness. The current through each bulb stays the same.

3 A series circuit has two bulbs in it. One bulb is removed and the gap in the circuit is joined up. Explain what will happen:
a| to the current in the circuit
b| to the brightness of the remaining bulb.

4 A parallel circuit like the one in table B has one of the switches closed. Explain how the current in different parts of the circuit will change if the other two switches are also closed.

5 Copy the parallel circuit in table B and add one switch to it that will turn all the bulbs on and off at once.

Measuring electricity

We use an **ammeter** connected in series to measure the current flowing through a circuit. The units for current are **amperes** (A).

The **voltage** across a cell is a measure of the energy provided by the cell. We measure voltage using a **voltmeter** connected in parallel to a component; we say that a voltmeter is connected *across* a component. The units for voltage are **volts** (V).

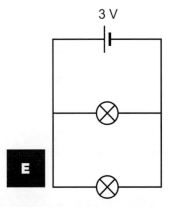

D | A 'multimeter' can be used to measure different quantities. Here it is being used as a voltmeter. The probes are being used to measure the voltage across a component on the circuit board.

The voltage across a component is a measure of the energy transferred by that component. In circuit C the bulb is transferring more energy than the motor, because the voltage across it is higher. The voltages across all the components add up to the voltage across the cell.

In a parallel circuit, the voltage across each branch of the circuit is the same as the voltage provided by the cell. In circuit E both bulbs have a voltage of 3 V across them.

---

6 Look at circuit C. The voltage of the cell is increased to 12 V.

a| What will happen to the current in the circuit?

b| Explain how the voltages across the bulb and motor will change.

I can ...

- explain how switches can be used to control different parts of a circuit
- recall how current behaves in series and parallel circuits
- describe how voltage behaves in series and parallel circuits.

WHAT SKILLS ARE NEEDED TO WORK WITH ELECTRICITY?

We all depend on electricity in many ways. We use it in our homes and schools, and the products we buy in the shops are made and transported with the help of electricity.

> **1** Write down three different things electricity is needed for:
>
> a | in a car
>
> b | in a supermarket.
>
> **2** Look at photo A. Suggest why the plastic covering on the wires has different colours.

A | Electronic engineers help to design the wiring for aeroplanes. This electrician is assembling the wiring for an aeroplane.

B | These electrical engineers are working in a hydroelectric power station. They act on data about electricity use in a region, and increase or decrease the supply from their power station.

Electricians

Electricians install and maintain the wiring in houses. Some electricians specialise in the wiring in cars and aeroplanes.

In most countries an electrician must have a qualification. This shows that they understand the many safety requirements. They usually study at college and train with an experienced electrician.

Electrical engineering

Electrical engineers work with the way electricity is generated and transmitted in a country, and within buildings. Electronics engineers design and maintain smaller electrical circuits, such as the ones that control cars, aeroplanes or computers.

Engineers need to be good at maths and physics. They need a degree in electrical or electronic engineering and will usually do further training when they start work.

C | A multimeter can be used to measure resistance. If there is a high resistance between two ends of a connecting wire, there is probably a break in the wire.

D | electricians mending power lines

3 Explain why it is important that electricians understand safety regulations.

4 State two risks from unsafe electrical wiring.

People who work with electricity need to be good at problem solving. They may need to:

- find the best way to wire a house using the shortest length of cable
- find out why a circuit does not work, and fix it.

Electricians need to take a systematic approach (following a fixed method) to make sure they have checked all the possible causes of a fault. They use checklists to keep track, and this allows someone else to check their work.

5 Write down a list of the things an electrician needs to think about when planning the wiring for a house.

6 When a car is towing a trailer, the brake lights on the trailer should come on at the same time as the brake lights on the car.

a | The brake lights on a car's trailer are not working. Write a list of all the possible causes of the fault.

b | The brake lights on the car are working. What does this tell the electrician about the location of the fault?

c | Suggest how the electrician could check one of the possible causes.

☐ **Observe and ask:** was there a bang, are there signs of burning, can you see anything loose?

☐ **Problem area:** can you work out where the fault is most likely to be?

☐ **Identify possible causes:** make a checklist of all the possible causes?

☐ **Priorities:** chek the most likely cause first, this will save time?

☐ **Test and repair.**

Torch checklist of what to fix
☐ flat battery
☐ broken bulb
☐ broken switch
☐ bad connections between components
☐ broken wires

E | checklists for electrical fault finding

PRACTICAL

Your teacher will give you an electrical circuit that does not work. Your task is to find the faulty component and replace it.

1 Write down all the possible reasons why the circuit is not working. Put them in order, starting with the problem that you think is the most likely, and make a checklist.

2 List the equipment you will need to test the circuit.

3 Test the circuit, and identify the fault or faults. Make a list of your findings.

4 Check your conclusion by replacing the faulty components.

9Jd RESISTANCE

HOW CAN WE CALCULATE THE RESISTANCE OF A COMPONENT?

Spacecraft are controlled by computers and other electronic systems. The currents in the components inside a computer are very small, only tiny fractions of an amp. But the current inside a heater can be over 10 amps.

The size of the current flowing in a circuit depends on the voltage of the cell or power pack, and on how easy it is for current to flow through the components in the circuit.

> **1** What are the units for measuring:
> a| current   b| voltage?

A | Hot food in the International Space Station is prepared using an electrical food warmer.

The **resistance** of a component is a way of saying how easy or difficult it is for current to flow through it. The current in a circuit can be controlled by changing the resistance of the components. Resistance can be added to a circuit using components called **resistors**.

Factors affecting resistance

The resistance of a wire depends on how long it is, how thick it is and on the metal it is made from.

- Longer wires have a higher resistance than shorter wires.

- Thin wires have a higher resistance than thick wires.

All metals conduct electricity, but some metals conduct it better than others. Copper, silver, gold and aluminium are the best conductors.

Insulating materials have very high resistances.

B | This electric fence will give a small shock to people or animals touching the wire.

> **2** Name three different materials that have a high resistance.
>
> **3** Look at photo B.
> a| Explain why the plastic handle is needed to allow people to move the wire.
> b| What can you say about the resistance of plastic materials?

Calculating resistance

The units for measuring resistance are **ohms**, and the symbol is the Greek letter omega (**Ω**).

Voltage, resistance and current are related by this formula:

voltage (V) = current (A) × resistance (Ω)

The voltage of a cell is what helps to 'push' charges around a circuit. This formula shows that the voltage you need to supply to a circuit increases if you need a large current or if the circuit has a high resistance.

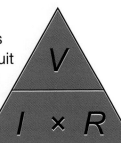

Example

What voltage do you need to make a 2 A current flow around a circuit with a resistance of 5 Ω?

voltage = current × resistance

$V = I \times R$

$= 2\,A \times 5\,\Omega$

$= 10\,V$

D | The formula can be rearranged using this triangle. *V* represents voltage, *I* represents current and *R* represents resistance.

4 Calculate the voltage needed to make a 5 A current flow through a circuit with a resistance of 20 Ω.

The formula can be rearranged to work out the resistance of a component from a current and a voltage.

Example

What is the resistance of a bulb when the voltage across it is 10 V and the current is 0.5 A?

resistance = $\dfrac{\text{voltage}}{\text{current}}$ $\left(R = \dfrac{V}{I}\right)$

$= \dfrac{10\,V}{0.5\,A}$

$= 20\,\Omega$

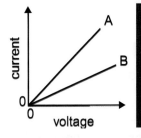

E

5 What is the resistance of a component that has a current of 3 A through it when the voltage is 18 V?

6 Describe how you could show that the resistance of a wire depends on its length.

7 Look at Graph F. Which resistor has the higher resistance? Explain your answer.

FACT

Some materials become superconductors when they are very cold, effectively having zero resistance at these temperatures. The photo shows an MRI scan of a head. MRI scanners need superconducting materials to work, which have to be cooled to nearly −270 °C.

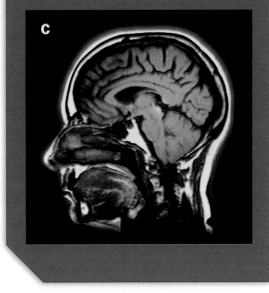

C

The resistance of a component is the ratio of the voltage (potential difference) across it to the current flowing through it. A graph of current against voltage is a straight line.

F | Current–voltage graph for two resistors. The graph shows that current is directly proportional to voltage.

I can ...

- describe some factors that affect resistance
- use the formula relating voltage, current and resistance.

ROUNDING NUMBERS

HOW AND WHY DO WE ROUND NUMBERS IN SCIENCE?

We round numbers to make estimates or to make calculations simpler. For example, on page 151 the gravitational field strength of the Earth was given as 10 N/kg. A more accurate value for the average gravitational field strength is 9.80665 N/kg.

We use a value of 10 N/kg in *Exploring Science* because this is accurate enough to explain ideas about mass and weight. This is the value rounded to the nearest whole number.

A | In 2014 the Philae spacecraft landed on a comet. Gravity on the comet is only about 0.0007 N/kg.

Decimal places

The gravitational field strength can be rounded to different numbers of **decimal places**.

When you have rounded a number, it is useful to show how many decimal places it is rounded to. Otherwise someone reading it does not know if 9.8 is the exact value, or if it was rounded from a higher or lower number, such as 9.84 or 9.75.

> **1** The mass of an apple is 0.25834 kg. Write its mass:
>
> a| to one decimal place   b| to three decimal places.
>
> **2** Look at photo A. Suggest why engineers did not round the value of gravity on the comet to 1 d.p.

1 d.p. — 9.8|0665   9.8
↖ less than 5, round down

2 d.p. — 9.80|665   9.81
↖ 5 or more, round up

3 d.p. — 9.806|65   9.807
↖ 5 or more, round up

B

Rounding in calculations

The box below shows an answer to an exam question.

> **Exam question:** A current of 0.7 A flows through a component when the voltage is 1.5 V. What is its resistance?
>
> **Answer:** resistance = voltage/current
> = 1.5 V/0.7 A
> = 2.142857143 Ω

The numbers used to calculate this answer are both given to one decimal place. This means that the actual voltage could really have been anything between 1.45 V and 1.54 V.

> **3** Suggest two different values for current that could be rounded to give 0.7 A to one decimal place.

The number of digits after the decimal point in the exam answer makes it appear that the value for the resistance is far more accurate than it really is. The answer to a calculation should always be rounded to an appropriate number of decimal places. This is usually the same number of decimal places as the numbers given in the question.

> **4** The answer to the exam calculation should be rounded to one decimal place. What should the answer be?
>
> **5** In a different version of the exam paper the voltage and current were given as 1.50 V and 0.70 A. Explain what the answer should be in this case.

Significant figures

Rounding numbers to a certain number of decimal places does not work very well when the numbers are very large or very small.

For example, the current through an electronic component could be 0.000 483 A. If you round this to two or even three decimal places, you get a value of zero. For large or small numbers, what matters is the number of **significant figures**. The first significant figure is the digit with the highest place value. The second significant figure has the next highest place value, and so on.

C

Small numbers	Large numbers
0.000 483	5 183 760 000
↑	↑
1st significant figure = 4 ten thousandths	1st significant figure = 5 billion

Round to 2 significant figures (2 s.f.):

0.000 48│3	5 │83 760 000
↗	↑
less than 5 so round down	5 or more, so round up
0.000 48	5 200 000 000
	↖ add zeros so the 5 is still in the billions position

D | a Falcon 9 rocket taking off

> **6** A Falcon 9 rocket had a launch mass of 505 846 kg.
>
> a| What is the mass to 1 s.f.?
>
> b| What is the mass to 2 s.f.?
>
> c| Suggest who would use the accurate value in the question, and who might use one of the rounded values you worked out in your answers.
>
> **7** The speed of light in deep space is 299 792 458 m/s. This value is often quoted as 300 000 000 m/s.
>
> a| Round this number to 1 s.f., 2 s.f, 3 s.f. and 4 s.f.
>
> b| Explain why you cannot say to how many significant figures the value of 300 000 000 m/s is given.

I can ...

- round numbers to a given number of decimal places
- round numbers to a given number of significant figures.

9Je ELECTRO-MAGNETS

HOW CAN ELECTRICITY PRODUCE MAGNETISM?

Apollo astronauts used lunar rovers to help them to explore the Moon. The rovers were powered by electric motors that used energy stored in batteries. Electric motors use **electromagnets** to make them spin.

Electromagnets

A wire with an electric current flowing through it has a magnetic field around it. The strength of the field increases if the current increases. The direction of the field changes if the direction of the current changes.

When the wire is wrapped into a coil, the magnetic field is a similar shape to the magnetic field of a bar magnet. The directions of the north and south poles of an electromagnet depend on which way the current is flowing through the wires.

You can increase the strength of an electromagnet by:

- increasing the number of coils of wire
- increasing the current in the wire
- using a magnetic material as a 'core' inside the coil of wire.

A | Only six people have driven a vehicle on the Moon.

1	a| What happens to an electromagnet if you switch the current off?
	b| How is this different to a bar magnet?
2	Describe three ways of reducing the strength of an electromagnet.
3	Describe how you could show that the strength of an electromagnet depends on the current in the coil.

Electromagnets have many uses. **Relays** (as shown in diagram C) can improve safety by using a small current to switch on a circuit that carries a much bigger current. This means that people do not have to touch any part of the circuit carrying the large current.

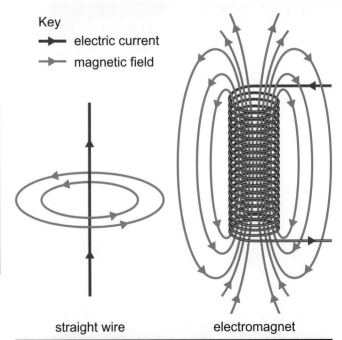

Key
→ electric current
→ magnetic field

straight wire   electromagnet

B | The magnetic field around a wire and an electromagnet. There is only a magnetic field while the current is flowing.

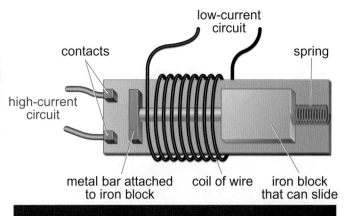

C | an electromagnetic relay

> **4** Look at diagram C. Explain what happens when a current flows in the low-current circuit.

Electric motors

A current flowing through a wire creates a magnetic field around it. If the wire carrying the current is placed in the magnetic field of a magnet, the two magnetic fields affect each other and the wire experiences a force. This is known as the **motor effect**. The direction of the force depends on the directions of the current and the magnetic field. This only happens when the wire cuts across the magnetic field.

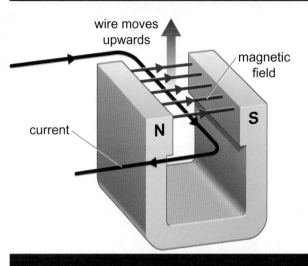

D | the motor effect

> **5** Suggest two ways in which the force shown in diagram D could be made bigger.

An **electric motor** consists of a coil of wire in a magnetic field. The magnetic field can be produced by permanent magnets (as shown in diagram E), or by electromagnets. When a current flows through the coil of wire, the combination of the magnetic field from the magnets and from the coil makes the coil spin.

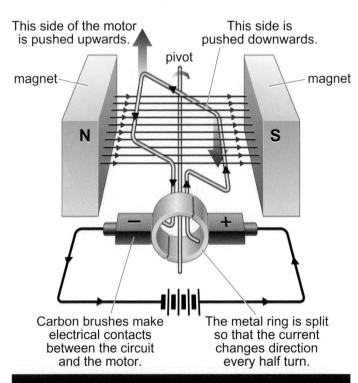

E | This is a simplified diagram of an electric motor, as a real motor would have a lot more turns of wire on the coil.

> **6** Explain what effect you think the following factors will have on the motor in diagram E:
>
> a| increasing the current in the coil
>
> b| making the magnetic field weaker
>
> c| changing the direction in which the current flows.

FACT

Some motors are small enough to fit inside human cells. However, these nanomotors use electrostatic effects, not electromagnets.

I can ...

- describe an electromagnet and its magnetic field
- describe how the strength of an electromagnet can be changed
- describe some applications of electromagnets.

WHAT ARE THE RISKS OF SPACE FLIGHT?

Since humans first started travelling into space, 18 astronauts have died in space, and 11 more have died during training accidents on the ground. In addition there have been accidents during test flights of rockets.

But accidents are not the only risks. Astronauts do not feel weight in space, and this leads to their muscles wasting away and their bones becoming thinner.

In 2012, a Dutch company called Mars One announced plans to send four astronauts on a one-way trip to Mars. More astronauts would join them later. Their journey would be made into a reality TV show. Thousands of people applied to go to Mars, even though they would not be coming back.

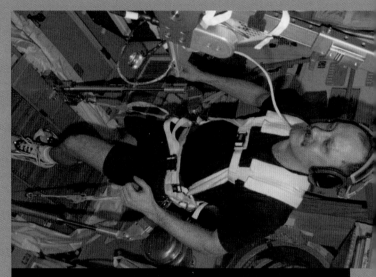

A | Astronauts on the space station have to exercise for around 2 hours every day to try to keep their bones and muscles healthy.

1. Gravitational field strength on Mars is 3.7 N/kg. Suggest what will happen to astronauts' bones and muscles if they live on Mars for a year. Explain your answer.

2. a| Describe the three types of force field you have studied in this unit.

   b| Write down two similarities and one difference between them.

3. The air and temperature inside the Mars One base will be controlled by electric heaters and fans.

   a| Describe what resistors are used for in electric circuits.

   b| Describe how to find the resistance of a component.

4. Fans are moved by electric motors.

   a| Describe the components of an electric motor.

   b| Describe two ways to make an electric motor spin faster.

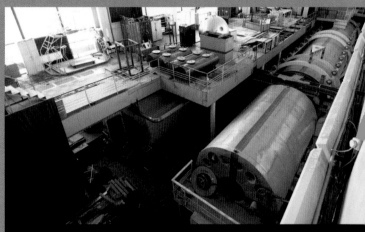

B | These tubes are living modules from a 520 day experiment to see how people might cope with living on Mars.

Should humans be allowed to take the risk of travelling to Mars to explore the planet? Should 'space tourists' be allowed to go to Mars?

WHAT DO PHYSICISTS DO?

A physicist is a scientist who researches questions connected with the properties of matter and energy. Questions vary from what is inside atoms to working out what happened when the Universe began.

Like all scientists, physicists make observations that lead to asking questions. Then they make a hypothesis and use it to make a prediction. The ways they gather data to test their predictions can be very different.

A | The Large Hadron Collider is a 27 kilometre long 'accelerator'. Tiny particles are accelerated to nearly the speed of light and smash into each other. What happens next can tell particle physicists about what atoms are made from.

B | Astronomers cannot carry out experiments with stars. They make hypotheses using observations, but they can only test these by making more observations.

1 a | Draw a flow chart to show the scientific method used by most scientists.

   b | Which of these steps may be done differently by astronomers compared to particle physicists?

2 Write down two scientific questions that:

   a | can be investigated by experiments in a laboratory

   b | can only be investigated by making more observations.

3 a | Write down two differences between the weather in the summer and in the winter in the UK.

   b | Explain why one of these differences occurs.

C | Meteorologists study the weather. They can carry out some experiments, such as on the properties of air, but many hypotheses can only be tested by making more observations.

9Ka DIFFERENCES

HOW DO DIFFERENCES MAKE THINGS HAPPEN?

Potential difference

Lightning can strike between a cloud and the Earth or between two clouds. Clouds become charged with static electricity because hailstones and ice crystals rub against each other as they move inside the cloud. If the difference in the charges (the **potential difference**) between two places is large enough, the air between them can conduct electricity and we see a lightning strike.

1 Potential differences are also needed to make electrical circuits work.

a| What supplies the potential difference in a circuit?

b| What does the potential difference across a component show?

A

Temperature differences

Temperature differences cause energy transfers by heating, such as when a hot drink cools down because it is warmer than the surrounding air.

Temperature changes can cause substances to change state. An ice cube taken out of a freezer is at a temperature below its melting point. As energy is transferred to it from its surroundings its temperature will rise until it reaches 0 °C. Its temperature will remain at 0 °C while it is melting.

Energy is still being transferred to the ice cube while it is melting, but does not cause a temperature rise. Instead, this energy breaks the bonds between the particles in the solid. This bond-breaking energy is called the **latent heat**. When water freezes, the latent heat is given out again. There are also transfers of latent heat during evaporation and condensation.

2 Explain why a cold drink taken from the fridge will warm up.

How the temperature of water changes as it cools down

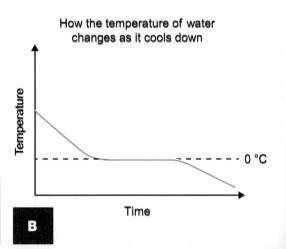

0 °C

Time

B

3 Graph B shows the temperature of water in a puddle as the water cools on a freezing cold night. Explain the shape of the graph. Include the words 'latent heat' in your answer.

C | Hurricanes are huge storms, but they die out quickly once they are over land. The energy to keep them going comes from the latent heat that is released as water vapour from the sea condenses again to form clouds.

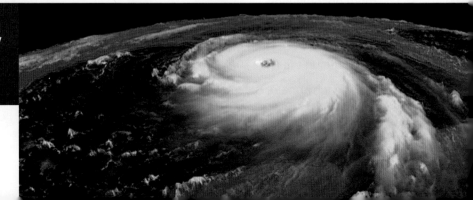

Density and pressure differences

Changes in temperature cause materials to expand or contract. When fluids (liquids or gases) warm up they expand and become less dense. If parts of a fluid have different densities, the less dense part will rise. These density changes can cause **convection currents** to form.

The Earth is warmed by energy from the Sun during the day, and cools down at night. But the temperature of the land increases more than the temperature of the sea for the same amount of energy transferred. The energy needed to raise the temperature of 1 kg of a substance by 1 °C is its **specific heat capacity**. Water has a higher specific heat capacity than soil or rock. The resulting difference in temperature causes light winds that flow from the sea towards the land during the day.

Substances with high specific heat capacities also cool down more slowly than substances with low specific heat capacities. This can cause 'land breezes' during the night.

> The air above the sea is cooler and so more dense than the air above the land.
>
> The air above the land warms up more than the air above the sea. It becomes less dense and rises. The air pressure drops where the air is rising.
>
> The air pressure is higher than the air above the land, so a breeze blows from the sea to the land.
>
> The sea has a higher specific heat capacity than the land, so it does not warm up as much.
>
> Land has a lower specific heat capacity than the sea, so it gets hotter more quickly than the sea.

D | Light winds called 'sea breezes' occur during the day because differences in temperature cause differences in density. The density differences cause convection currents.

FACT

The highest wind speeds occur in tornados, but are very difficult to measure accurately. The official record for wind speed is **113 m/s (over 400 km/h)**, recorded in Australia in **1996**.

E

---

4 Joyah heats up some water in a beaker, and heats the same mass of soil in another beaker.

a| Which one will be the hotter after 10 minutes? Explain your answer.

b| If she also heated up the same mass of wet soil in the same way, what would its temperature be compared to the other two substances? Explain your answer.

5 Explain how land breezes occur, in as much detail as you can.

6 Explain the difference between 'latent heat' and 'specific heat capacity'.

I can ...

- describe how temperature differences can cause convection currents
- state the meanings of latent heat and specific heat capacity.

9Kb FIELDS

HOW IS THE IDEA OF A FIELD USED IN PHYSICS?

In physics, a **force field** is a volume where a non-contact force has an effect. The three non-contact forces that produce fields are magnetism, static electricity and gravity.

Storing energy in fields

Gravitational potential energy is the name for energy stored because of an object's position in a **gravitational field**. If an object is moved away from the Earth it stores energy. The raised object can transfer this energy when it is allowed to fall.

Hailstones are small lumps of ice that form inside large clouds. As they fall, their gravitational potential energy is transferred to kinetic energy.

A | The energy transferred by falling hailstones can damage cars, buildings and crops.

FACT

The largest hailstone recorded had a mass of nearly 1 kg. This would store 10 kJ of gravitational potential energy if it were 1000 m above the ground.

B | The skydiver has a store of gravitational potential energy.

1. Look at photo B.

   a | How did the gravitational potential energy become stored in the skydiver?

   b | How will this store of energy be transferred as he falls?

The amount of gravitational potential energy stored in an object depends on its mass, how high it has been raised, and on the gravitational field strength (approximately 10 N/kg on Earth). The formula is:

gravitational = mass × height × gravitational
potential energy   (kg)   (m)   field strength
(J)   (N/kg)

2 a| Calculate the energy stored in a skydiver with a mass of 80 kg at a height of 1500 m.

b| Explain how your answer to part a will compare to the energy of an astronaut with a mass of 80 kg at a height of 1500 m above the Moon.

Example

A 65 kg skydiver is at a height of 2000 m. How much gravitational potential energy does the skydiver store?

gravitational potential energy = 65 kg × 2000 m × 10 N/kg
= 1 300 000 J

Energy can also be stored in **electric fields** and **magnetic fields**. You need to use a force to pull two magnets apart. The work done by moving the magnets stores the same amount of energy in the separated magnets. If you let them go, the stored energy is released as they move back together.

Modelling fields

Diagram C shows how the gravitational field of the Earth can be represented. It shows the direction in which a small mass will move if it is released in the Earth's gravitational field.

All the lines in diagram C point towards the centre of the Earth. The Earth's gravitational field is strongest close to the Earth, and this is where the lines are closer together.

Field diagrams such as this:

- are two-dimensional representations of three-dimensional fields

- indicate (by the closeness of the lines) qualitatively where the field is strongest

- have lines that do not cross.

We can draw similar diagrams for electric fields and magnetic fields. The arrows on these fields show which way a positive charge or a north pole would move.

C | A model of the Earth's gravitational field.

3 Look at diagram C. Write down:

a| two things that the diagram tells you about the Earth's gravitational field

b| one thing that it does not tell you.

field lines

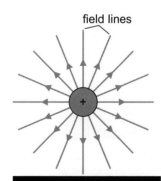

D | the electric field around a positive charge

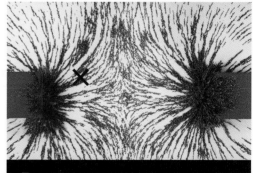

E | Iron filings show the shape of the magnetic field between the north poles of two bar magnets.

4 Explain why diagram D above is different from diagram F on page 153.

5 a| Sketch the magnetic field of a bar magnet. (*Hint:* page 150, diagram B may help.)

b| Describe two differences between your sketch and diagram D.

6 Use photo E to help you to describe how a north pole would move if it was placed in position X.

I can ...

- use the formula for gravitational potential energy
- model force fields using diagrams and interpret them.

HOW ARE CAUSES LINKED TO EFFECTS?

Many people ask themselves what causes the changes they observe around them. Many myths and legends are about explaining things around us.

Scientists also think up explanations (causes) for the changes (effects) they see around them, but then they test the explanations. In this way, science tries to find the best explanations for why things happen.

A | Some cultures explained that winds were caused when powerful beings blew. Our modern explanation is that winds are caused by temperature differences between different places on the Earth.

B

> Stones fall because their natural place is in the Earth. Light objects fall slower than heavy ones because their natural place is above the heavy ones.

> My experiments show that lighter and heavier objects of the same size and shape fall at the same speed.

> There is a force between masses that acts to pull them together.

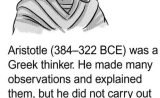

Aristotle (384–322 BCE) was a Greek thinker. He made many observations and explained them, but he did not carry out experiments to test his ideas.

Galileo Galilei (1564–1642) was an Italian scientist who carried out experiments in many different areas of physics.

Sir Isaac Newton (1642–1726) was an English scientist and mathematician who used experimental evidence to suggest laws and equations that described how objects move and fall.

Correlation and causation

A **correlation** is when two things happen together, or when two sets of data appear to be linked. Sometimes this shows that a change in one factor causes the other, such as the length of a spring increasing when you pull it harder. But the fact that things happen together does not necessarily mean that one thing causes the other. Sometimes there may be a third factor that affects both, or there may be no connection between them at all.

1
a | Aristotle is sometimes called a scientist. Explain whether or not this is a good description of him.

b | Explain why Galileo and Newton can be described as scientists.

2
Newton described how forces affect the motion of objects. Describe what causes a car to:

a | accelerate (speed up)

b | change direction.

3 The average world temperature is increasing, and the number of pirates is going down. Do you think that the change in one of the variables causes the change in the other? Explain your answer.

4 Look at graph C. Suggest why there is a correlation between the two variables. (*Hint*: there is another factor that affects both variables.)

If scientists think that changes in one variable cause changes in another, they try to find out *how* this happens. It is only once they have found out why one thing affects the other that they accept that the cause and effect go together.

Spotting the effects

Many causes and effects are obvious, but some are not so clear. For example, you know that when you drop a ball the force of gravity makes it accelerate downwards. But there is also a force from the ball that pulls the Earth upwards, towards the ball. This idea that forces are always in pairs is called Newton's Third Law.

Some materials are radioactive. This means they emit particles or waves that can ionise atoms and molecules. We can detect this radiation using photographic film or a Geiger-Müller detector. Scientists have worked out that this ionising radiation is caused by changes within the radioactive atoms.

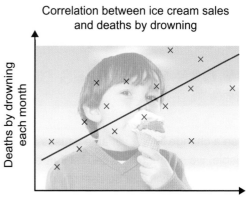
Correlation between ice cream sales and deaths by drowning

Deaths by drowning each month

Ice cream sales each month

C | The number of deaths by drowning increases when sales of ice cream increase.

FACT

The Earth's gravity keeps the Moon in its orbit. The Moon's gravity also affects the Earth, causing the tides.

5 When a soccer player kicks a ball, their foot exerts a force on the ball. What is the other force in this pair?

6 Diagram E shows a mass attached to a spring. The spring has stretched and the mass is now not moving.

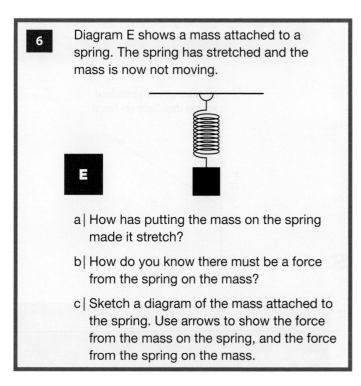

E

a| How has putting the mass on the spring made it stretch?

b| How do you know there must be a force from the spring on the mass?

c| Sketch a diagram of the mass attached to the spring. Use arrows to show the force from the mass on the spring, and the force from the spring on the mass.

D | The parkour athlete attracts the Earth with the same force as the Earth attracts him.

I can ...

- describe some examples of cause and effect in science
- describe the difference between correlation and cause.

LINKS BETWEEN VARIABLES

HOW CAN VARIABLES BE RELATED MATHEMATICALLY?

When a change in one variable causes a change in another variable, we say there is a **causal link** between the variables. Sometimes the link can be described using a mathematical formula.

Graph B shows how the temperature and pressure of the air change with height. There are causal links, because air pressure depends on the height of air above a particular point, and temperature depends on several different variables, including height. However, the relationship between height and temperature or pressure cannot be described using a simple formula.

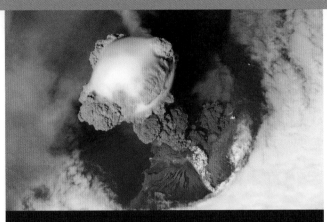

A | A change in the altitude of the volcano plume causes a change in temperature, which causes water vapour in the plume to condense.

FACT

The boiling point of water gets lower as air pressure gets less. At an altitude of about 19 000 metres the boiling point of water is about the same as the temperature of the human body. At this height, tears, saliva and the liquid inside the lungs will boil. Humans cannot survive more than a few minutes at this altitude without a pressure suit.

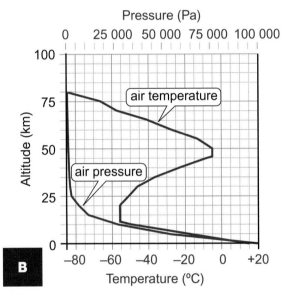

B

> **1** Look at graph B. Describe in words how:
> a | air pressure changes with height
> b | air temperature changes with height.

Proportional and linear relationships

Graph C shows how the length of a spring changes when the force on it changes. This is a **linear relationship**, because the points on the graph fall on a straight line, but the line does not go through the (0,0) point on the graph.

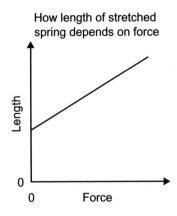

How length of stretched spring depends on force

C | The stretched length of the spring can be worked out using this formula:
stretched length = original length
+ (spring factor (a constant) × force)

Graph D shows how water pressure changes with depth. The graph is a straight line that goes through the origin (0,0). This shows that the pressure is **directly proportional** to depth, and the relationship can be described by the equation shown in the caption.

For two variables in direct proportion:

- if one variable is zero the other is also zero

- if the value of one variable doubles, the other also doubles.

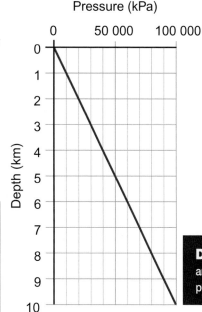

Pressure (kPa)

D | the relationship between pressure and depth can be described by:
pressure = depth × density of fluid × g

> **2** Explain why the relationship shown in graph C is not showing direct proportion.
>
> **3** The weight of an object is directly proportional to its mass. Sketch a graph of weight against mass that shows this.

Inverse proportion

The current in a wire depends on how much charge flows in a given time. For a fixed amount of charge, if the time doubles, the current halves. This is an **inversely proportional** relationship. Graph E shows an example of an inversely proportional relationship.

> **4** Look at graphs B and E.
>
> a| Compare the shape of the graph for air pressure to the graph for current.
>
> b| Air pressure is not inversely proportional to height. Suggest why it is easier to spot a directly proportional relationship using a graph than to spot an inversely proportional one.
>
> **5** Class 11 measured the amount of rain that fell in one day. Each student used a container of a different size. Table F shows their results.
>
> | Cross-sectional area of container opening (cm²) | Volume of water collected (cm³) | **F** |
> |---|---|---|
> | 10 | 90 | |
> | 30 | 270 | |
> | 80 | 720 | |
> | 150 | 1350 | |
> | 300 | 2700 | |
>
> a| Plot a graph of these results on graph paper. Cross-sectional area of the container should be on the horizontal axis.
>
> b| Explain what kind of relationship is shown on your graph.

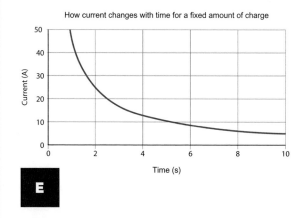

How current changes with time for a fixed amount of charge

E

I can ...

- identify linear and proportional relationships from graphs.

9Kd INFORMATION FROM GRAPHS

WHAT KIND OF INFORMATION CAN WE OBTAIN FROM GRAPHS?

Equations for graphs

Lines on graphs can often be described using an equation. Straight lines on graphs can be described using equations of the form:

$$y = mx + c$$

Using a graph to work out the values of m and c can tell us about the relationship shown by the graph.

When a gas is heated the particles move faster. If the gas is inside a sealed container the particles hit the walls harder and more often, so the pressure increases. If the pressure increases enough it can cause an explosion.

Graph B shows that there is a linear relationship between the pressure inside a container of gas and its temperature.

A | This gas cylinder exploded because the gas pressure inside it increased as it was heated.

B

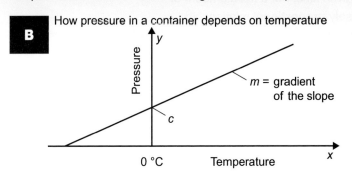

How pressure in a container depends on temperature

Pressure

m = gradient of the slope

c

0 °C   Temperature

For graph B:

y is the pressure

m is the gradient of the line, so it tells you how much the pressure increases for each 1 °C increase in temperature

$$y = mx + c$$

x is the temperature

c is the point at which the line crosses the vertical axis, so it tells you what the pressure is at 0 °C

1 Look at graph C on page 172.

a | What kind of relationship is shown in this graph?

b | The line on the graph can be described in the form $y = mx + c$. Explain what the values of m and c in this equation tell us about the spring.

Graphs for motion

Graph C is a **distance–time graph** for a journey. The gradient of each part of the line shows how fast the car was going for each part of its journey – the steeper the line, the faster the speed. A horizontal line shows the car was stationary.

2 Look at graph C. At what speed is the car travelling for the first hour of its journey?

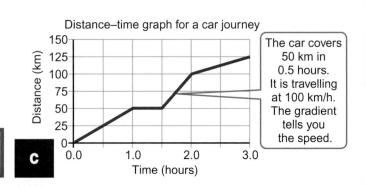

Distance–time graph for a car journey

The car covers 50 km in 0.5 hours. It is travelling at 100 km/h. The gradient tells you the speed.

C

A journey can also be shown on a **speed–time graph**. Graph D shows a different car journey. Horizontal lines show the car travelling at constant speeds, and sloping lines show when the car is accelerating.

Acceleration is a way of saying how quickly a moving object is speeding up or slowing down. The units for acceleration are metres per second per second (m/s^2). An acceleration of 5 m/s^2 means that the object is going 5 m/s faster every second. The steeper the line on a speed–time graph, the faster the car is accelerating. The acceleration can be found from the gradient of the line.

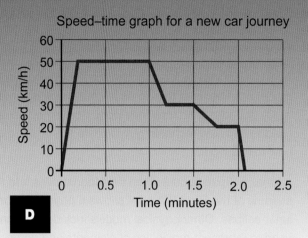

Speed–time graph for a new car journey

D

 3

Look at graph D.

a| What was the top speed of the car during this journey?

b| When was the car slowing down fastest?

c| Sketch a speed–time graph that shows a car accelerating for 1 minute to 90 km/h, travelling at a constant speed for 5 minutes, then accelerating for 1 minute to 110 km/h.

The formula relating speed, distance and time can be used to work out how far a vehicle has travelled:

distance = speed × time

Look at graph E. Between 10 and 20 seconds the vehicle was travelling at 15 m/s.

distance = 15 m/s × 10 s
= 150 m

This is the same value you would get from working out the area of the orange rectangle on the graph.

For the first 10 seconds of the journey the vehicle is accelerating. The distance it covers during this time is the area of the yellow triangle on the graph.

area of triangle = ½ × base × height
= ½ × 10 s × 15 m/s
= 75 m

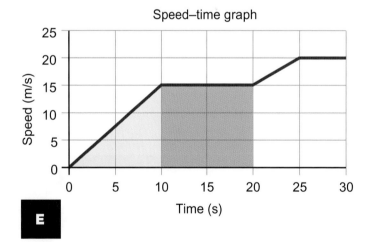

Speed–time graph

E

4 Calculate how far the vehicle in graph E travelled between 25 seconds and 30 seconds.

5 The distance travelled between 20 and 25 seconds can be calculated by splitting the area under the graph into a rectangle and a triangle. How far did the vehicle travel in this time?

I can ...

- use the formula for a straight line to help interpret graphs
- use gradients to interpret distance–time and speed–time graphs
- calculate distances from the area under a speed–time graph.

9Ke MODELS

HOW ARE MODELS USED IN SCIENCE?

A model is a way of representing something. In science, models can be used to help us to describe things more easily or understand how they work. Some models can be used to test new technology, or to help scientists to discover how things work.

A **lunar eclipse** occurs when the Moon moves into the shadow of the Earth. Photo A shows a **physical model** of a lunar eclipse. Other physical models include balls and sticks used to represent molecules of elements and compounds.

Abstract models are models that exist in computers or in your imagination. Diagram B is an abstract model showing what happens during a **solar eclipse**. People standing in the shadow of the Moon see a **total eclipse**. If the Sun is only partly blocked, they would see a **partial eclipse**.

> **1** Draw a diagram similar to B to show what is happening in the lunar eclipse modelled in photo A.

Mathematical formulae, graphs and chemical equations are also abstract models. Computer models must be checked by using them to make predictions and then testing the predictions.

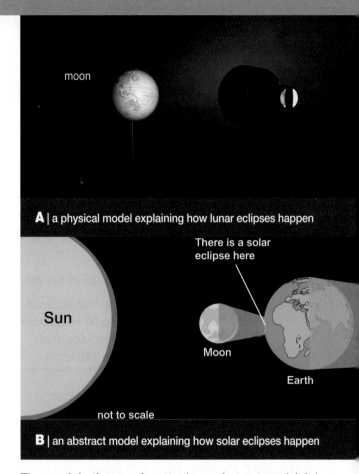

A | a physical model explaining how lunar eclipses happen

There is a solar eclipse here

Sun

Moon

Earth

not to scale

B | an abstract model explaining how solar eclipses happen

The **particle theory** of matter is an abstract model. It is also an **analogy**, because it is comparing the particles that make up everything to small balls that are stuck to each other or moving around and bouncing off things.

> **2** Describe one other analogy you have used in lessons. (*Hint*: analogies are often used to describe how electrical circuits work.)
>
> **3** Describe four different kinds of model mentioned in this Unit and say whether each is a physical or abstract model.

It is important to remember that a model is usually simpler than the thing it is describing. Sometimes scientists use different models for the same thing, depending on what they are trying to understand. Diagram D shows some different models that scientists use to represent atoms.

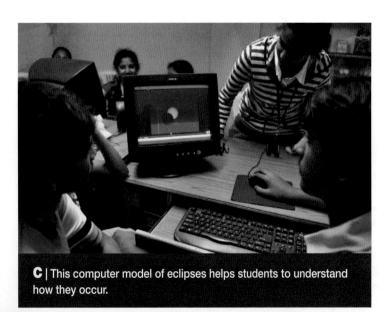

C | This computer model of eclipses helps students to understand how they occur.

solid ball
(particle theory)

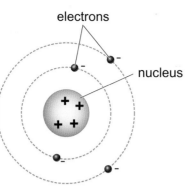

electrons

nucleus

nucleus surrounded by
electrons (used when
learning about static
electricity)

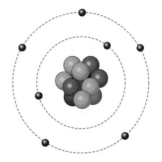

nucleus contains protons and neutrons,
with electrons at different distances from
the nucleus (used when learning how
chemical bonds form)

protons and neutrons
made of even smaller
particles (used when
explaining radioactivity)

D | how the abstract model of an atom changes as you learn more science

Wave models

Waves transfer energy without transferring matter. We can see waves on the surface of water, and we can see how they are reflected and refracted.

We cannot see sound being reflected, but we *can* hear echoes. We can carry out experiments to show that sound is also refracted. We use a wave model to help us to think about how sound travels. Light can also be reflected and refracted. We can explain many of the properties of light by thinking of it travelling as a wave, but the wave model does not explain *all* of the properties of light.

E | When water is disturbed, waves transfer energy outwards.

FACT

The largest wave ever recorded was a local tsunami wave that caused damage over 500 metres above sea level in Lituya Bay in Alaska, in 1958.

The tsunami stripped all the trees and soil off this land.

4
a| Describe what happens to the particles in air as a sound wave passes through.

b| Describe two differences between a sound wave and the water waves shown in photo E.

5 Describe two differences between the wave model of sound and the wave model of light.

6 Why is it not correct to say that light is a wave?

I can ...

- explain the difference between physical and abstract models
- describe some ways in which models are used in science.

HOW ARE COMPUTER GAMES DEVELOPED?

Around the world, about two billion people play computer games. Games can be exciting, such as car racing games, or they can let players build their own worlds, or go on simulated adventures.

Games are developed by a large team of people with different skills. Most developers need to study at college or university, learning skills such as computer art, computer science, programming or mathematics. Some universities offer courses in game design.

Game designers need a good imagination to design characters, stories and the worlds in which they happen. Both game designers and game programmers need problem solving skills. Everyone needs to be able to work well in a team, and must have good communication skills.

Virtual reality

The simulator in photo B allows people to experience the thrills of racing without the risk of crashing. Games such as this are based on simulators developed to train racing drivers. The game includes a computer model of how cars behave in the real world.

4   Suggest why the designer of a car simulator needs to study physics.

Some simulations use virtual reality (VR) visors (headsets) instead of computer screens. The person can move around to look at different parts of the imaginary world. Sensors detect the position of the visor and the direction it is pointing.

A | playing a computer game

1   Game designers invent characters for adventure games. Suggest two other things they need to invent or design.

2   Explain why some developers study computer art.

3   Sound is a key part of many games. Suggest two things to consider when creating sound for a game.

B | The wide screen in this driving game helps the player to feel as if they are in the real world.

Some VR games include the sense of touch as well as sight and sound. Sensors on the player's body allow the computer to detect hand positions, and small motors or other devices allow the user to feel forces or vibration.

C | The computer screen on the top left of the photos shows what the player is seeing through his headset.

D | These gloves/sensors add the sense of touch to the game.

> **5** Explain why the computer running a VR game needs to know the direction the VR visor is pointing.

> **6** Suggest two ways in which the sense of touch can be used in a VR game.

New games

Designers need to be inventive to come up with new ideas, or help to develop new technology to make a game more exciting or realistic.

It costs a lot of money to develop a computer game. This means that the games company needs to be confident they can make money by selling the finished game. They must evaluate the game, using opinions from gamers.

> **7** Games companies usually evaluate the idea for a game, as well as the finished game. Suggest why they do this.

ACTIVITY

Your company is developing an adventure game set 1000 years ago in your country. Your team must evaluate the new game by doing a survey of gamers. The evaluation is in three stages:

- concept (initial idea, storyline and artwork for some scenes and characters)

- partly developed (a partly working game, including the scenes and actions)

- final test (fully developed game).

Draw up an evaluation form for each stage of the testing. Analysing the results is easier if you ask people to rate different statements from 1 to 5, so you can add up the scores from different people. The form should include what you will show to the gamers, and the statements you will ask them to rate.

Show: artwork for opening scene (5 = completely agree, 1 = completely disagree)				
Question	Gamer 1	Gamer 2	Gamer 3	Gamer 4
This scene really makes me want to play the game.				

E | Your evaluation form could look like this.

WHAT IS BEING RESEARCHED IN PHYSICS?

Research in physics can be classified into different types:

- applied research is often aimed at improving a particular technology, such as designing materials that are more efficient at converting sunlight into electricity

- basic research is investigating things that may not have an application, but that scientists are interested in.

All scientific research needs money to pay for equipment and to pay the scientists. Applied research is often funded by technology companies. Basic research is usually funded by governments.

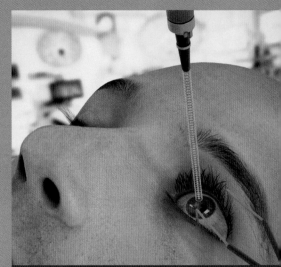

A | When lasers were invented, the scientists did not have any applications in mind. But this 'basic research' turned out to have many different applications, from welding and surgery to communications.

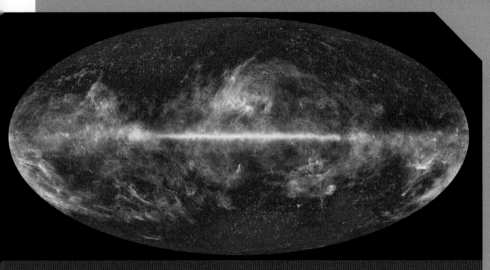

B | This map of the sky was made using a satellite. The pattern of radiation coming from the sky can help scientists develop theories about what happened just after the beginning of the Universe.

1 Once the first laser had been invented, many scientists investigated ways of making more powerful lasers.

a | Explain what kind of research this is.

b | How is this kind of research different from the kind of research illustrated by photo B?

2 Scientists studying hurricanes fly aeroplanes through them to gather information, including how much rain there is inside the clouds.

a | Why do scientists need to collect data in real hurricanes when they have computer models?

b | The scientists hypothesise that the more rain there is, the more energy is being transferred to the hurricane. Why does the formation of raindrops release energy?

c | The lift provided by an aeroplane's wing is proportional to the density of the air through which it is flying. Explain what proportional means.

HAVE YOUR SAY

Do you think it is right that in many countries taxpayers' money is spent on research that may never be useful?

WORKING 9L AS A TEAM

Most research is done by teams of scientists. Before starting, the team members agree on what they are going to do. Each team member has time to explain their own ideas and listens carefully to others. Some of the things that they will need to discuss are shown in panel A.

1 Suggest one advantage and one disadvantage of having a confident speaker making the presentation.

For complicated investigations with many stages, the team members decide how long to spend on each stage. Someone is in charge of making sure the group sticks to the timetable.

At the end of a teamwork task, it is important to evaluate the whole task. Each team member has time to explain what they think went well, and what could be improved. The team then decides on recommendations for how to do the project better. The methods, results and conclusions of scientific experiments are checked by **peer review**.

You can do peer review in school by showing your report to another group. You should get feedback on:

- which parts the reviewers thought were done well
- which parts were confusing or unclear
- if they think any more information is needed.

2 Write down two questions you should ask when you evaluate a teamwork task.

3 Suggest two differences between a scientist having their work peer reviewed, and you showing your report to another group at school.

A team needs to make decisions about the project, such as:

- what question they are going to answer
- what additional research is needed

how to carry out the investigation.

The team also decides who will carry out the different tasks, taking into account people's different skills. For example, who:

- does different parts of the additional research
- sets up the apparatus
- changes the independent variable
- measures the dependent variable
- records the results
- evaluates the results
- designs the presentation or writes the report
- gives the presentation.

A | some things a team must discuss before starting a project

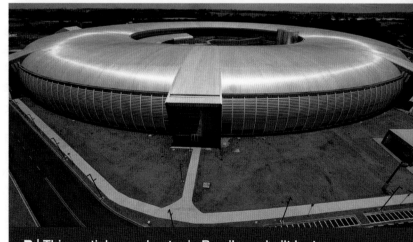

B | This particle accelerator in Brazil was built by teams of scientists and engineers. Teams from all over the world can use it to study the structure of materials and biological molecules, and how materials behave at very high temperatures and pressures.

9L1 EARS AND EYES

Bionic ears and eyes

Today hundreds of thousands of people have cochlear implants. A tiny microphone in the patient's ear transmits signals to a receiver implanted in their head. The receiver converts the signals to impulses in the patient's auditory nerve. A cochlear implant can give some people who are completely deaf the ability to hear. Inventions such as cochlear implants involve combining ideas and knowledge from engineering and medicine.

A | A person with a 'bionic eye' might see a face like this.

B

Bionic eyes are more difficult. A microphone can be hidden inside or behind the ear, but the cameras needed for a bionic eye must be built into a pair of glasses (photo B). The patient has to have a receiver implanted into their skull, with a tiny wire leading to an implant in their retina.

1 The story above is from an online news site. Use your communications skills to write answers to readers' questions explaining the science. Here are two of the questions:

a| Do microphones and ears hear sounds in the same way?

b| Are eyes and cameras the same thing but just one is electronic?

2 There are many different ways in which eyes can fail or be damaged. Sometimes people cannot see clearly because they cannot focus on objects at different distances. Collect information to help you to explain how 'short sight' and 'long sight' are caused, how they affect people, and how lenses can be used to help people with these conditions to see clearly. Communicate your findings in two concise paragraphs.

3 Find out more about cochlear implants. Write a story of 350 words for an online newspaper, describing what cochlear implants are, how they work and the kinds of people who can be helped by them. Make a list that records all the sources of information you used.

> Think about how you are going to structure your answer before you start to write. You could describe how each one works and then point out similarities and differences, or you could make a table to help you to compare the two. Make sure you use language that your audience will understand.

9L2 GOING FASTER

INVESTIGATION

Unbalanced forces on an object can make it change speed. Acceleration is the change in speed over a particular time.

Planning

You are going work in a team to plan and carry out an investigation to find out how different variables affect the acceleration of an object. Here are some questions you could investigate.

- How does the steepness of a ramp affect the time it takes for a toy car to run down it?

- Does the mass of a toy car affect how long it takes to run down a ramp?

- You can pull a toy car along a flat surface. Does the mass of the toy car affect how fast it accelerates?

- How does the size of the force affect the acceleration of a toy car?

- The force of gravity accelerates objects downwards. Does the acceleration caused by gravity depend on the mass of the object? Does it depend on its size?

A | This ski jumper is accelerating down a ramp. Does the steepness of the ramp affect their acceleration? What other variables might affect their acceleration?

FACT

Acceleration is important for animals as well. The cheetah is the world's fastest accelerating animal. This helps it to catch its prey.

B | Drag racers use a short, straight track. The winning car is usually the one with the best acceleration. What variables affect the acceleration of the car?

Results and conclusion

- Present your results in a way that helps you to reach a conclusion. Other people should be able to look at your results and see why you reached that conclusion.

- Write a conclusion based on the data you have gathered.

Evaluation

- Have you gathered enough data to reach a conclusion?

- Is your data good enough to give you confidence in your conclusion?

9L3 SPEED LIMITS

COMMUNICATING WITH THE PUBLIC

Speed limits are lower in towns than on open roads because vehicles are more likely to need to stop quickly in towns, to avoid hitting other traffic or pedestrians. Also, if a car does hit someone, the person's injuries are usually not as severe if the car is going more slowly.

The distance a car travels from the time the driver notices an obstacle to when they press the brakes is the thinking distance. The distance the car travels while the brakes are slowing it to a stop is the braking distance. The stopping distance is the sum of these two distances.

The distances in the chart are typical distances. The thinking distances will be longer if the driver is tired. The stopping distances will be longer if the road is wet, or the car's tyres or brakes are not in good condition.

A | some typical UK speed limits	
Type of road	**Speed limit (km/h)**
Highways	110
Roads in the countryside	100
Roads in towns	50
Some roads near schools or housing developments	20

1 A road safety organisation wants leaflets to be given out with new cars, to encourage drivers to stick to the speed limits. Design and write a leaflet, using information from this page and from further research. You need to include:

- what the speed limits are

- why the speed limits are different on different roads

- when drivers should stick to speeds *below* the speed limits.

2 The thinking distance depends on the driver's reaction time. Find out how reaction times are measured and what typical reaction times are. You could also find out how much longer reaction times are when people are tired. Use the information you find to write a script for a one minute TV advert with the slogan 'Think before you drive'.

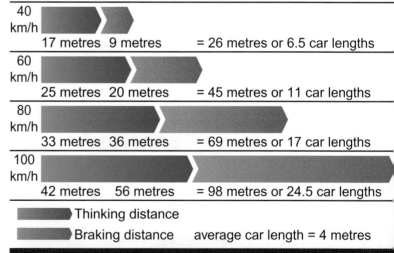

Typical stopping distances

40 km/h — 17 metres 9 metres = 26 metres or 6.5 car lengths

60 km/h — 25 metres 20 metres = 45 metres or 11 car lengths

80 km/h — 33 metres 36 metres = 69 metres or 17 car lengths

100 km/h — 42 metres 56 metres = 98 metres or 24.5 car lengths

Thinking distance

Braking distance   average car length = 4 metres

B \| typical stopping distances

HAVE YOUR SAY

A road safety organisation is campaigning to have the speed limit set at 30 km/h in all towns. Research and prepare an argument either in favour of this change, or against it.

GLOSSARY

Pronunciation note: A capital 'O' is said as in 'so'

absorb	To 'soak up' or 'take in'.
abstract model	A model that only exists in your thoughts or as a computer program, formula or diagrams (such as ray diagrams).
accelerate	To change speed.
accuracy	A measure of how close a value is to its real value.
accurate (*ak*-yer-it)	A measurement that is close to the true value.
across (physics)	When one component is connected in parallel to another.
aim	What you are trying to find out or do.
air resistance	A force that tries to slow objects down that are moving through air. It is caused by friction and by the objects pushing the air out of the way.
ammeter	A piece of equipment that measures how much electricity is flowing around a circuit.
ampere (A) (*am*-peir)	The unit for measuring current.
amplify	To make bigger.
amplitude	The size of vibrations or the distance a particle vibrates when a wave passes.
analogy (an-al-O-*jee*)	A model that compares something complicated to something that is easier to understand.
angle of incidence	The angle between an incoming light ray and the normal.
angle of reflection	The angle between the normal and the ray of light leaving a mirror.
angle of refraction	The angle between the normal and a ray of light that has been refracted.
anomalous (uh-*nom*-uh-luh s)	Something that does not fit a pattern. When talking about water, this means that water does not behave in the same way as other liquids when it freezes.
aperture	A hole in a camera that controls how much light goes to the sensor.
apparatus	Pieces of equipment.
appliance	A machine, usually powered by electricity, and used at home.
artificial satellite	A satellite made by humans.
atomic energy	A name used to describe energy when it is stored inside materials. Another name for nuclear energy.
attract	Two things pulling towards each other are said to attract.
auditory nerve (*ord*-it-orry)	The nerve that carries impulses from an ear to the brain.
auditory range (*ord*-it-orry)	The range of frequencies that an animal can hear.
balanced diet	Eating a variety of foods to provide all the things the body needs.
balanced forces	When two forces on an object are the same strength but in opposite directions.
biofuel	A fuel made from plants or animal droppings.
boiling	When there is a liquid turning into a gas in all parts of a liquid, creating bubbles of gas in the liquid.
boiling point	The temperature at which a liquid boils.

Brownian motion (*mO*-shun)	An erratic movement of small bits of matter caused by being hit by the moving particles that make up liquids or gases.
carbon dioxide	A waste gas produced by respiration.
causal link	When a change in one variable causes a change in another (this is not the same as correlation).
cell	A source of electricity with a low 'energy' (low voltage). Cells push electrons round a circuit.
change of state	When a substance changes from one state of matter (solid, liquid or gas) into another.
charges	Tiny particles that flow around a circuit.
chemical change	A change that forms one or more new substances.
chemical energy	A name used to describe energy when it is stored in chemicals. Food, fuel and batteries all store chemical energy.
circuit breaker	A safety device that switches off the electricity supply if the current is too big.
climate change	Changes that will happen to the weather as a result of global warming.
coal	A fossil fuel made from the remains of plants.
cochlea (*cok*-lee-a)	The part of the ear that changes vibrations into electrical impulses.
comet	A ball of dirty ice that has a very elliptical orbit around the Sun.
communication	The transfer of information.
compass	A magnetised piece of metal that can swing around. One end always points north.
component (com-*po*-nent)	Something in a circuit, such as a bulb, switch or motor.
compress	To squeeze into a smaller volume.
conclusion (con-*cloo*-shun)	An explanation of how or why something happens, which is backed up by evidence. You use evidence to 'draw' a conclusion.
condense	When a gas turns into a liquid.
conduction	The way energy is transferred through solids by heating.
conductor	A substance that allows something to pass through it (e.g. heat, electricity).
cone cell	A cell in the retina that detects different colours of light.
constellation	A pattern of stars. The stars in a constellation are not usually close together, they only appear to be close when seen from the Earth.
contact force	A force where there needs to be contact between objects before the force can have an effect (e.g. friction).
contract	To get smaller.
convection	The way energy is transferred by heating in fluids.
convection current (con-*veck*-shun)	A flow of liquid or gas caused by part of it being heated or cooled more than the rest.
convention	A standard way of doing something or representing something, so that everyone understands what is meant.
converging lens	A lens that makes rays of light come together.
cornea	The transparent front part of the eye, which covers the iris and pupil.

correlation	A relationship between two variables. If an increase in one appears to cause an increase in the other it is 'positive'. An increase in one linked with a decrease in the other is 'negative'.
cubic centimetre (cm³)	A unit used for measuring volume.
current	The flow of electricity around a circuit.
data	Observations or measurements collected in investigations.
decibel (dB) (*dess-i-bell*)	A unit for measuring the loudness of a sound.
decimal place	The position of a digit to the right of the decimal point in a number. The number of decimal places in a number is the number of digits after the decimal point.
deform	Change shape.
degrees Celsius (°C)	A unit for measuring temperature.
density	The amount of mass that one cubic centimetre of a substance has. Often measured in grams per cubic centimetre (g/cm³).
diaphragm (*dye-a-fram*)	A thin sheet of flexible material.
diet	The food that you eat.
diffuse reflection (*di-fuse*)	Reflection from a rough surface, where the reflected light is scattered in all directions.
diffusion (*diff-you-zshun*)	When particles spread and mix with each other without anything moving them.
digital camera	A camera that uses electronics to record an image.
direct proportion	A relationship between two variables where one variable doubles when the other doubles. The graph is a straight line through (0,0). We say that one variable is directly proportional to the other.
dispersion	The separating of the colours in light, for example when white light passes through a prism.
displaced	To push out of the way.
displacement	The distance in a straight line between an object and its starting point.
dissipate	Spread out.
distance multiplier	A lever or other machine where the load moves further than the effort.
distance–time graph	A graph that shows how far and how fast something travels during a journey. Steeper lines on the graph show faster speeds.
drag	Another name for air resistance or water resistance.
ductile	A ductile material can be pulled into a wire, without breaking.
ear canal	The tube in the head that leads to the eardrum.
eardrum	A thin membrane inside the ear that vibrates when sound reaches it.
ear protection	Ear plugs or covers that prevent damage from loud sounds.
Earth	The planet we live on.
earth wire	The green and yellow wire in a cable or plug. It is there for safety.
echo (*ek-O*)	We hear a sound again when it reflects off a surface. The reflected sound is called an echo.
echolocation (*ek-O-low-kay-shun*)	Finding prey or obstacles by emitting sounds and listening for the echoes.
efficiency (*e-fish-en-see*)	A way of saying how much energy something wastes.
effort	The force put on something, especially a lever or other simple machine.
elastic	An elastic material changes shape when there is a force on it but returns to its original shape when the force is removed.
elastic limit	If you stretch a spring beyond its elastic limit it will be permanently stretched. It is no longer elastic.

elastic potential energy (*po-ten-shall*)	A name used to describe energy when it is stored in stretched or squashed things that can change back to their original shapes. Another name for strain energy.
electric current	A flow of electrons around a circuit.
electric field	The space around an object with a charge of static electricity where it can affect other objects.
electricity	A way of transferring energy through wires.
electric motor	A machine consisting of a coil of wire in a magnetic field. The coil spins when a current flows through it.
electromagnet	A coil of wire with electricity flowing in it. An electromagnet has a magnetic field like a bar magnet.
electron	A sub-atomic particle found outside the nucleus of an atom. It has an electrical charge of −1.
elliptical (*e-lip-tick-al*)	Shaped like an oval.
emit	To give out.
energy	Something that is needed to make things happen or change.
energy resource	A store of energy that we can use for heating, transport, and to keep our bodies working.
environment	The conditions in a habitat caused by physical environmental factors.
Equator (*ee-kwate-er*)	An imaginary line around the middle of the Earth.
equilibrium (*ek-will-ib-bree-um*)	When things are balanced and not changing, they are 'in equilibrium'.
evaluate	Looking at the good and bad points about something, in order to reach an overall decision.
evaporate	When a liquid turns into a gas.
evidence	Data used to support an idea or show that it is wrong.
expand	To get bigger.
extension (*ex-ten-shun*)	The amount by which a spring or other stretchy material has stretched. It is the stretched length minus the original length.
fair test	An experiment in which all the control variables are controlled and only changes in the independent variable cause changes in the dependent variable.
field	The volume around something where a non-contact force can affect things (e.g. magnetic and gravitational fields).
field line	A line drawn to show which way a magnetic field act.
filament	The thin piece of wire inside a light bulb that glows when the bulb is on.
filter	Something that only lets certain colours through and absorbs the rest.
fluid	A gas or a liquid.
focal length	The distance between the centre of the lens and the focal point.
focal point	The place where parallel rays of light are brought together by a converging lens.
force	A push, pull or twist.
force field	The volume around something where a non-contact force can affect things. Examples are electric, magnetic and gravitational fields.
force meter	A piece of equipment containing a spring, used to measure forces.
force multiplier	A lever or other machine where the load is bigger than the effort.
fossil fuel	A fuel formed from the dead remains of organisms over millions of years (e.g. coal, oil or natural gas).
freeze	When a liquid turns into a solid.
freezing point	The temperature at which a liquid turns into a solid. It is the same temperature as the melting point of the substance.
frequency (*free-kwen-see*)	The number of vibrations (or the number of waves) per second. Different frequencies of light have different colours.

friction	A force between two objects that are touching. It usually acts to slow things down or prevent movement.
fuel	A substance that contains a store of chemical or nuclear energy that can easily be transferred.
fulcrum	A point about which something turns. Another name for a pivot.
fuse (*fewz*)	A piece of wire that melts if too much electricity flows through it.
galaxy	Millions of stars grouped together.
gas	One of the states of matter. Does not have a fixed shape or a fixed volume and is easy to squash.
generate	To produce electricity.
geothermal power (*jee-O-therm-al*)	Electricity generated using heat from rocks underground.
gradient	A way of describing the steepness of a line on a graph in numbers. It is calculated by taking the vertical distance between two points and dividing by the horizontal distance between the same two points.
gram (g)	A unit for measuring mass.
gravitational field	The space around any object with mass where its gravity attracts other masses.
gravitational field strength	The force with which a gravitational field pulls on each kilogram of mass. The gravitational field strength (g) on Earth is approximately 10 newtons per kilogram (N/kg).
gravitational potential energy (*grav-it-ay-shon-al*) (*po-ten-shall*)	A name used to describe energy when it is stored in objects in high places that can fall down.
gravity	The force of attraction between any two objects. The Earth is very big and so has strong gravity that pulls everything down towards it.
hazard	Something that could cause harm.
heating	A way of transferring energy from hot substances to cooler ones.
hemisphere (*hem-ee-sfear*)	Half of a sphere: the shape you would get if you cut a solid ball in half.
hertz (Hz) (*hurts*)	The unit for measuring frequency.
Hooke's Law	The law that says that the extension of a spring is proportional to the force on it.
hydroelectric power (*hy-drO-el-eck-trick*)	Electricity generated by moving water (usually falling from a reservoir) turning turbines and generators.
hydrogen	A gas that burns. It is an element.
hypothesis (*hy-poth-uh-sis*)	An idea about how something works that can be tested using experiments. Plural = hypotheses.
image	A picture that forms in a mirror or on a screen, or is made by a lens. You see an image when looking down a microscope.
incident ray	A ray of light going towards the mirror or other object.
infrared radiation (*ray-dee-ay-shun*)	A way of transferring energy by heating that does not need a medium (material). Infrared radiation can travel through transparent things and a vacuum (empty space).
infrasound	Sound waves with frequencies below 20 Hz, the lower limit of human hearing.
insulating	A material that does not allow something to pass through it is an insulator or insulating material.
insulator	A material that does not allow something to pass through it (e.g. heat, electricity).
intensity	The loudness or volume of a sound.
interface	The boundary between two materials.
internal energy	The energy stored in the movement of particles. Sometimes called thermal energy.
inverse proportion	A relationship between two variables where one variable doubles when the other halves. We say that one variable is inversely proportional to the other.
iris	The coloured part of the eye.
joule (J) (*jool*)	A unit for measuring energy.
kilogram (kg)	A unit for measuring mass. There are 1000 grams (g) in 1 kg.
kilojoule (kJ)	A unit for measuring energy. There are 1000 joules (J) in 1 kJ.
kilometres per hour (km/h)	Unit for speed when the distance is measured in kilometres and the time is measured in hours.
kilowatt (kW)	A unit for measuring power. There are 1000 watts (W) in 1 kilowatt (kW).
kilowatt-hour (kWh)	The amount of energy used by a 1 kilowatt (kW) appliance in one hour. It is equal to 3600 kilojoules (kJ).
kinetic energy (*kin-et-tick*)	A name used to describe energy when it is stored in moving things.
latent heat	The energy needed to break the bonds between particles in melting or evaporating, or the energy released when these bonds form in condensing or freezing.
law of conservation of energy	The idea that energy can never by created or destroyed, only transferred from one store to another.
law of reflection	The angle of incidence is equal to the angle of reflection.
lens	A curved piece of glass or other transparent material that can change the direction of rays of light.
lever	A simple machine that consists of a long bar and a pivot. It can increase the size of a force or increase the distance the force moves.
light	A way of transferring energy waves. Light waves can travel through transparent materials and through empty space.
light year	The distance that light travels in one year.
limit of proportionality (*prO-por-shun-al-it-ee*)	The extension of a spring is proportional to the force on it, up to a certain point called the limit of proportionality. If you apply more force the extension is no longer proportional to the force.
linear relationship	A relationship between variables that produces a straight line when plotted on a scatter graph. The line does not have to go through the (0,0) point.
line graph	A graph that shows how one variable changes when another changes (usually time). The points are joined with straight lines.
line of best fit	A line drawn on a scatter graph that goes through the middle of the points, so that about half the points are above the line and about half of them are below the line.
liquid (*li-kwid*)	One of the states of matter. Has a fixed volume but not a fixed shape.
live wire	The brown wire in a cable or plug.
load	The weight or force on something. For a machine, the load is the weight that is being moved.
longitudinal wave (*long-it-tyood-in-al*)	A wave in which the vibrations (e.g. of particles) are in the same direction as the direction of the wave.
lubricant (*loo-brick-ant*)	A substance (usually a liquid) used to reduce friction.
lubrication (*loo-brick-ay-shun*)	Adding a lubricant to something.
machine	A device, such as a lever or ramp, which makes it easier to move something by multiplying a force or a distance.
magnetic	A material, such as iron, that is attracted to a magnet.
magnetic field	The space around a magnet where it can affect magnetic materials or other magnets.
magnetism	A force that attracts objects made of iron or other magnetic materials.
mass	The amount of matter that something is made from. Mass is measured in grams (g) and kilograms (kg). Your mass does not change if you go into space or to another planet.
mean	An average calculated by adding up the values of a set of measurements and dividing by the number of measurements.

mean speed	The total distance something travels divided by the total time taken is the mean (or average) speed for a journey.
medium	Any substance through which something travels.
melt	When a solid turns into a liquid.
melting point	The temperature at which a solid turns into a liquid.
memory card	Part of a digital camera that stores the images.
metal	An element that is shiny when polished, conducts heat and electricity well, is malleable and flexible, and often has a high melting point.
method	A description of how an experiment is carried out, written in simple, well-organised steps.
metres per second (mps)	A unit for speed. Someone travelling at 1 m/s covers a distance of one metre every second.
microphone	A machine for converting sound waves into changes in electrical current or voltage.
miles per hour (mph)	A unit for speed. Someone travelling at 1 mph covers a distance of one mile every hour.
Milky Way	The galaxy that our Solar System is in.
mixture	Two or more substances jumbled together but not joined to each other. The substances in a mixture can often be separated from each other.
model	An example of something happening which can be used to explain how a scientific idea should be understood.
moment	The turning effect of a force. It is calculated by multiplying the force by the perpendicular distance of the force from the pivot.
Moon	The Moon (with a capital M) is the moon that orbits the Earth.
moon	A natural satellite of a planet.
motor effect	The force produced when a wire carrying a current is placed in a magnetic field.
natural gas	A fossil fuel formed from the remains of microscopic dead plants and animals that lived in the sea.
natural satellite	A satellite that has not been made by humans. The Moon is a natural satellite of the Earth.
negative charge	The type of electric charge on electrons.
neutral wire	The blue wire in a cable or plug.
neutron	A sub-atomic particle found in an atom's nucleus. It has no electrical charge.
newton (N)	The unit for measuring force.
newton metre (N m)	The unit for the moment of a force.
non-contact force	A force that can affect something from a distance (e.g. gravity).
non-renewable	Any energy resource that will run out because we cannot renew our supplies of it (e.g. oil).
normal	An imaginary line at right angles to the surface of a mirror or other object where a ray of light hits it.
northern hemisphere	The half of the Earth with the North Pole in it. Most of Asia is in the northern hemisphere.
north pole (north-seeking pole)	The name for one end of a magnet – the north pole of a magnet will point to the Earth's north magnetic pole if the magnet is allowed to swing freely.
nuclear energy	A name used to describe energy when it is stored inside materials.
nuclear fuel	A radioactive metal such as uranium. Nuclear fuels are used in nuclear power stations to generate electricity.
nucleus (*new*-clee-us)	The central part of an atom, where protons and neutrons are found.
nutrients (*new*-tree-ents)	Substances needed in the diet.
ohm (Ω)	The unit for measuring resistance.

oil	A fossil fuel formed from the remains of microscopic dead plants and animals that lived in the sea.
opaque (*O*-payk)	Material that does not let light through. It is not possible to see through an opaque substance.
optic nerve	The nerve that takes impulses from the retina to the brain.
orbit	The path that one body in space takes around another.
organism	A living thing.
oscilloscope (oss-*ill*-O-skope)	An instrument that shows a picture of a sound wave on a screen.
parallel circuit	A circuit with branches that split apart and join up again.
particle (*part*-ick-al)	A tiny piece of matter that everything is made out of.
particle model	Another term for particle theory.
particle theory (*part*-ick-al)	A theory used to explain the different properties and observations of solids, liquids and gases.
pascal (Pa) (*pas*-kal)	A unit for measuring pressure. 1 Pa = 1 newton per square metre (N/m2).
payback time	The time it takes to get back (in energy savings) the money you spent on making an energy-saving change.
peer review	An evaluation of the quality of a scientific paper carried out by other scientists who work in the same area of science.
percentage	'Per cent' means 'out of 100'. A percentage compares part of something with the whole, where the whole has a value of 100.
phases of the Moon	The different shapes the Moon seems to have at different times.
photosynthesis (fO-tow-*sinth*-e-sis)	A process that plants use to make their own food. It needs light to work.
physical change	A change in which no new substances are formed (e.g. changes of state).
physical model (*fizi*-kal)	A model that you can touch or a model that you could build.
pinhole camera	A piece of apparatus that forms an image of an object on a screen when light rays travel through a tiny hole in the front.
pitch	How high or low a note sounds.
pivot	A point about which something turns. Another name for fulcrum.
plane mirror	A smooth, flat mirror.
planet	A large body in space that orbits a star. The Earth is a planet.
plastic	A plastic material changes shape when there is a lot of force on it but does not return to its original shape when the force is removed.
positive charge	The type of electric charge on the nucleus of atoms.
potential difference (po-*ten*-shall)	A way of saying how much energy is transferred by electricity. Energy will only be transferred if there is enough difference between the charges in two places to make the charges move from one place to the other as a current. Another term for 'voltage'.
potential energy	The scientific word for stored energy.
power	The amount of energy (in joules, J) transferred every second. It is measured in watts (W).
power pack	A source of electricity with low voltage, which is safe to use.
power rating	The number of joules of energy an appliance uses every second.
precaution (pre-*cor*-tion)	An action taken to reduce the risk of a hazard causing harm (e.g. wearing eye protection when handling an acid to prevent it splashing in your eyes).
precise	Measurements that are close to one another.
prediction	What you think will happen in an experiment.
prefix (*pree*-fix)	Something added to the beginning of a word to change its meaning. In 'kilometre', 'kilo' is the prefix.

pressure	The amount of force pushing on a certain area. A way of saying how spread out a force is. Often measured in newtons per square metre (N/m²) or pascals (Pa).
pressure wave	Waves like sound waves, where the vibration of particles transfers energy.
prey	An animal that is caught and eaten by another animal.
primary colour	One of three colours detected by the cone cells in our eyes. The primary colours are red, green and blue.
prism	A block of clear, colourless glass or plastic. Usually triangular.
proportional (*prO-por-shun-al*)	A relationship between two variables where one doubles if the other doubles. A graph of the two variables would be a straight line through the origin.
proton	A sub-atomic particle found in an atom's nucleus. It has an electrical charge of +1.
pulley	A simple machine consisting of a wheel that can turn on an axis with a rope running around it. Using more than one pulley with a rope allows a force to be multiplied.
pupil	The hole in the front of the eye that light can pass through.
pure	A single substance that does not have anything else in it.
quantitative	Data that is described in numbers.
radiation (*ray-dee-ay-shun*)	A way of transferring energy by heating. Also known as infrared radiation. Infrared radiation can travel through transparent things and a vacuum (empty space).
ramp	A sloping surface. A ramp is a force multiplier: it needs less force to pull something up a ramp than it does to lift it directly.
random	When there is an equal chance for one event occurring as there is for any other events in the same set.
random error	An error that can be different for every reading.
rating (fuse)	The largest current a fuse can conduct without melting.
ratio	A way of comparing two different quantities. Two numbers separated with a colon (:).
ray	A narrow beam of light, or an arrow on a diagram representing the path of light and the direction in which it is travelling.
ray box	A piece of equipment that produces a narrow beam of light.
ray diagram	A diagram that represents the path of light using arrows.
ray tracing	A method of investigating what happens to light by marking the path of a light ray.
receptor cells (*re-sep-tor*)	Cells that detect stimuli, such as cells in the eye that detect changes in light.
reflect	To bounce off a surface instead of passing through it or being absorbed.
reflected ray	A ray of light bouncing off a mirror.
refracted	A light ray that has changed direction as it passed from one medium to another.
refracted ray	A ray of light that has changed direction on moving from one material to another.
refraction	The change in direction when light goes from one transparent material to another.
relationship	A link between two variables, so that when one thing changes so does the other. Best seen by using a scatter graph. Also called a correlation.
relative (speed)	The speed of one object compared to another – both objects could be moving.
relay	A switch that is turned on and off without a person touching it. One type of relay uses a small current to make an electromagnet close the contacts in a circuit that carries a much larger current.
renewable resource	An energy resource that will never run out (e.g. solar power).
repel	To push away.
resistance	A way of saying how difficult it is for electricity to flow through something.

resistor	A component that makes it difficult for electricity to flow. Resistors are used to reduce the size of the current in a circuit.
result	A measurement or observation from an experiment.
resultant (force)	The difference between forces in two opposite directions.
retina	The part at the back of the eye that changes energy transferred by light into nerve impulses.
ring main	A type of parallel circuit used in house wiring.
risk	The chance that a hazard will cause harm.
rod cell	A cell in the retina that detects low levels of light. It cannot detect different colours.
Sankey diagram	A diagram showing energy transfers, where the width of each arrow is proportional to the amount of energy it represents.
satellite	Anything that orbits a planet or a moon.
scatter	When something is scattered, parts of it go off in many different directions.
scatter graph	A graph in which data for two variables is plotted as points. This allows you to see whether there is a relationship between the two variables. Lines (or curves) of best fit are often drawn through the points.
scientific method	Any way of testing that involves collecting information in order to show whether an idea is right or wrong. This is often done by developing a hypothesis that is tested by using it to make a prediction. The prediction is then tested using experiments.
secondary colour	A colour made when two primary colours mix. The secondary colours are magenta, cyan and yellow.
sensor	An instrument that detects something. In a digital camera, the sensors detect light and change it to electrical signals.
series circuit	A circuit in which there is only one loop of wire.
shadow	A place where light cannot get to, because an opaque object is blocking the light.
shutter	A device that shields and protects the sensor in a digital camera. It opens when the picture is taken.
significant figure	The first significant figure in a number is the digit with the highest place value, the second significant figure has the second highest place value and so on.
SI unit	A standard international unit used by scientists. 'SI' stands for 'Système International d'Unités'.
solar cell	Flat panels that use energy transferred by light to produce electricity.
solar energy	Energy from the Sun.
solar panel	Flat plates that use energy from the Sun to heat water.
solar power	Generating electricity using energy from the Sun.
solar power station	A large power station that uses the Sun to heat water to make steam. The steam is used to make electricity in a similar way to fossil fuel or nuclear power stations.
solar system	A solar system is a star and the bodies that orbit it. The Solar System (with capitals) is Sun and the bodies that orbit it.
solid	One of the states of matter. Has a fixed shape and fixed volume.
sonar (*sO-nar*)	A machine for finding the depth of the sea or finding fish by sending sound waves and listening for the echoes.
sound	Vibrations in a solid, liquid or gas that are passed on as a wave.
sound intensity meter	A meter that measures the loudness of a sound.
sound wave	A wave is a way of transferring energy. A sound wave is vibrations in particles of a solid, liquid or gas, which are detected by our ears and 'heard' as sounds.
source	Where a sound or other wave begins.
south (-seeking) pole	The end of a magnet that points south if the magnet can move freely. Often just called the south pole.

specific heat capacity	The energy needed to raise the temperature of 1 kg of a substance by 1 °C.
spectrum	The seven colours that make up white light.
specular reflection (*speck*-you-lar)	When light is reflected evenly, so that all reflected light goes off in the same direction. Mirrors produce specular reflection.
speed	How fast something is moving. Often measured in metres per second (m/s), miles per hour (mph) or kilometres per hour (km/h).
speed–time graph	A graph that shows the speed at different times during a journey. Horizontal lines show constant speeds, and sloping lines show accelerations.
spring	A coil of wire that can be stretched or compressed.
star	A huge ball of gas that gives out energy. We see some of the energy as light.
states of matter	There are three different forms that a substance can be in: solid, liquid or gas. These are the three states of matter.
static electricity	A positive or negative charge on an insulating material caused when rubbing transfers electrons from one material to another.
stationary (*stay*-shun-arry)	Not moving.
strain energy	A name used to describe energy when it is stored in stretched or squashed things that can change back to their original shapes. Another name for elastic potential energy.
streamlined	Something that has a smooth shape to reduce the air resistance or water resistance.
stretch	To pull something to make it longer.
sublime	When a solid turns into a gas, without becoming a liquid.
Sun	The star that the Earth orbits.
superposition (*soup*-er-poz-**ish**-un)	When two waves meet and their effects add up or cancel out.
systematic error (sis-tem-**at**-ick)	An error that is the same for all readings, such as when forgetting to zero a balance before using it to measure a series of masses.
table	An organisation of data into rows and columns.
temperature	How hot something is, usually measured in degrees Celsius.
terminal velocity	The maximum speed of an object. Usually only applies to falling objects when the downward force is balanced by drag.
theory (*thear*-ree)	A hypothesis (or set of hypotheses) that explains how and why something happens. The predictions made using a theory should have been tested on several occasions and always found to work.
thermal conductor	A material that allows internal (thermal) energy to be transferred through it easily.
thermal energy	A name used to describe energy when it is stored in hot objects. The hotter something is the more thermal energy it has. Another term for internal energy.
thermal imager	A device like a camera that makes images by detecting infrared radiation.
thermal insulator	A material that does not allow internal (thermal) energy to be transferred through it easily.
thermometer	Any device used to measure temperature.
trace	The line on an oscilloscope screen that represents a sound wave.
transfer	When energy is moved from one store into another or from one place to another, we say it is transferred.
translucent (*trans*-**loo**-sent)	Material that lets light through but scatters it. You cannot see things clearly through translucent materials.
transmit	To pass through a substance.
transparent	Clear, can be seen through. A material that light can travel through without scattering. (Note: transparent substances may be coloured or colourless.)

transverse wave	A wave in which the vibrations (e.g. of particles) are at right angles to the direction the wave is travelling.
truth table	A table that shows all the possible combinations of switch positions in a circuit, and what happens to the other components in the circuit.
ultrasound	Sound waves with frequencies above 20 000 Hz, the upper limit of human hearing.
unbalanced forces	When two forces working in opposite directions on an object are not the same strength. Unbalanced forces change the motion of objects.
Universe	All the galaxies and the space between them.
upthrust	A force that pushes things up in liquids and gases.
uranium (*you*-**rain**-ee-um)	A radioactive metal that can be used as a nuclear fuel.
vacuum (*vak*-yoom)	A completely empty space, containing no particles.
valid	Something is valid if it is doing what it is supposed to do. A measurement is valid if it measures what it is supposed to measure. A valid conclusion is drawn only from the data that the conclusion is supposed to be drawn from.
variable (*vair*-ee-ab-el)	Anything that can change and be measured.
variable resistor	A resistor whose resistance can be changed.
vibrate (*vibe*-**rayt**)	To move backwards and forwards.
vocal folds (*vO*-kal)	Flaps of skin in our throats that vibrate to make the sound when we speak.
volt (V)	The unit for measuring voltage.
voltage	A way of saying how much energy is transferred by electricity.
voltmeter	A piece of equipment that measures how much energy is being transferred by a current.
volume (*vol*-yoom) (matter)	The amount of room something takes up. Often measured in cubic centimetres (cm3).
volume (*vol*-yoom) (sound)	The loudness of a sound.
water resistance	A force on objects moving through water. A force that slows things down that are moving through water. It is caused by friction and by the object pushing the water out of the way.
water vapour	Water as a gas. Also called steam.
watt (W)	A unit for measuring power, 1 watt (W) is 1 joule (J) per second.
weight	The amount of force with which gravity pulls things. It is measured in newtons (N). Your weight would change if you went into space or to another planet.
white light	Normal daylight, or the light from light bulbs, is white light.
windpipe	An organ in the shape of a tube that takes air to and from your lungs. Also called the 'trachea'.
wind turbine	A kind of windmill that generates electricity using energy transferred by the wind.
work	The energy transferred when a force moves an object. It is calculated using the size of the force and the distance moved by the force. The unit for work is the joule (J).

STEM skills

The STEM pages in each unit focus on key STEM skills. These skills are listed and described below.

STEM skill	STEM skill description	STEM pages developing skill
Numeracy and use of maths	Using maths	7I, 7K
Generation and analysis of data	Design ways of collecting and analysing data to reach answers.	7L 8J, 8K
Critical analysis and evaluation	Give reasons why data (or proposed solutions) are or are not good enough (e.g. to answer questions, solve problems).	9I, 9K
Application of knowledge	Apply knowledge to unfamiliar contexts to reach answers. Understanding of the principles of science and mathematics	8L
Communication	Use language and maths to communicate ideas effectively.	7L 8I, 8J
Problem-solving	Use reasoning and systematic approaches to reach answers.	7I, 7J 9J

INDEX

Photographs

(Key: T-top; B-bottom; C-Centre; L-left; R-right)

123RF: Ginasanders 005b, Jennifer Barrow 006t, Olga Sapegina 006b, Jennifer Hogan 007tr, Andrii Vergeles 007l, Alan Davidson 007b, Sergey Jarochkin 008bl/A, Midosemsem 008br/A, 06photo 014r, Elizaveta Galitckaia 021l, Andreypopov 025bl, Weerapat kiatdumrong 034t, Peter Hermes Furian 035c, Natalya Aksenova 036bc, Rostislav Ageev 039tr, Barsik 044br, Ian Iankovskii 045tl, Vitalii Nesterchuk 045tr, Konstantin Zaikov 045r, Laures 047, Vasiliy Vishnevskiy 054t, Song Qiuju 060br, Christian Mueller 062t, Ollirg 067t, Gary Webber 068l, Maximkostenko 102tr, Andriy Popov 107tl, Manit Larpluechai 107bl, Sergey Kostrykin 108cl, Nico Smit 134bl, Ivan Sizov 137, Sergej Razvodovskij 139tl, Gala98 141bl, Andriy Popov 144br, Ekaterina Kondratova 155, Khunaspix 182tr; **Alamy Stock Photo:** Jason O. Watson (USA: Alaska photographs)/Alamy Stock Photo 128tr, Martin Bache/Alamy Stock Photo147cr/E, Dave Reede/All Canada Photos 004b, Marmaduke St. John 004b, Richard Wayman 004t, Sentinel3001 010l, Greg Balfour Evans 011bl, Imran Ahmed 014l, Ian Shaw 015, Kaiser/Agencja Fotograficzna Caro 016br, Martin Bond 019tr/C, Chris Howes/Wild Places Photography 019bl/C, Laurent Davoust 019b, Losevsky Pavel 020tr, Clive Streeter/DK, Courtesy of The Science Museum, London/Dorling Kindersley ltd 022r, Boris Roessler/ dpa picture alliance/Alamy Live News 032tr, NASA/ JPL-Caltech/AB Forces News Collection 032tl, Richard Watkins 035, Chronicle 036br, Photo Researchers/ Science History Images 039b, Stephen Chung 040t, 041tl, Realimage 042l, George S de Blonsky 042r, Gerhard Zwerger-Schoner/imageBroker 045l, NASA Image Collection 046c, Van der Meer Marica/Arterra Picture Library 048l, Stevenson, Bill/SuperStock 052t, Tim Matsui 052b, Wladimir Polak/Lebrecht Music & Arts 054b, Sciencephotos 058, Blickwinkel/McPhoto/ Nbt 060tl, Avalon/Construction Photography 064b, Xinhua 070, WorldFoto 074, Phil Degginger 075bl, Rapt.Tv 077tr, David Lomax/Robertharding 078tr, QAI Publishing/Universal Images Group North America LLC 080br, Dpa picture alliance 081tr, Richard Wayman 082tr, Dpa picture alliance 082br, EDB Image Archive 084tl, Cindy Hopkins 101tr, Ton koene 101cl, Günter Lenz/ImageBroker 101br, Jan Wlodarczyk 104tr, Frilet Patrick/Hemis.fr 110tr, David Snyder/Zuma Press, Inc 111bl, Joe Sohm/Visions of America, LLC 113tr. Filip Jedraszak 112tr , Trappe/ Agencja Fotograficzna Caro 112bl , Mirrorpix/Trinity Mirror 113cr, Tim M133, Nature and Science133, AF archive 136tr, Kevin Britland 136br, Rieger Bertrand/ Hemis.fr 138tr, Stephen Barnes/Military 138br, Zakir Hossain Chowdhury/ZUMA Press, Ltd 141cl, Ingram Publishing 148b, Moviestore collection Ltd 150tr, Photo Researchers/Science History Images 150tr, Tom Tracy Photography 156tr, Chris Warham 158cr, Photo Researchers/Science History Images 160, NASA Image Collection 161, James King-Holmes 165tr, Oliver Furrer 168bl, Brian Maudsley 169, Firephoto 174, John D.Ivanko 179tl, Sebastiao Moreira/EFE News Agency 181; **AP Images:** Reiri Kurihara 103tr; **EESA:** S.Corvaya/European Space Agency 164cr; **DK Images:** Steve Gorton 035tr, 035bl Gerard Brown 042r, 153tr, Trish Gant 176bl; **Dr. Eric WM Stienen:** 018; **Edwin van der Heide:** Edwin van der Heide/Courtesy of the Inventors dr.ir. Bas Gravendeel 038r; **Getty Images:** Solarseven/iStock 010r, Brooks Kraft LLC/Corbis 016tr, Bettmann 021bl, Science & Society Picture Library/ SSPL 029, London Stereoscopic Company/Hulton Archive 036tl, Andy McCandlish/Barcroft Media 037b, Michael Durham/Minden Pictures 053tl, Ken Hively/ Los Angeles Times, Ulianna/iStock 066, Mike D Kock/ Gallo Images 068r, Katherine Frey/The Washington Post, Ilbusca/DigitalVision Vectors 076bl, Kevin Winter/ Getty Images Entertainment 086bl, Fritz Goro/The Life Picture Collection 095tl, Sajjad Hussain/AFP 113br , Raveendran/AFP 113tr, Hulton Archive 135, John Macdougall/AFP 139bl, Science & Society Picture Library/SSPL 148t, Thomas Koehler/Photothek 156cl, Piccell/Photographer's Choice 157, Noah Seelam/ AFP 176bl, Hero Images 179tr, Michael Kappeler/DDP 183tr; **Mary Evans Picture Library:** Unnamed artist in allers familj journal (swedish) 8 march 1927(No.11) P1 146t; **NASA:** 017, JPL-Caltech 033tr, 039l, 039r, 056, 069bl, Sdo/Aia 130c, Hubble Heritage Team, ESA 131bl, 132bl, Esa/K.Retherford/Swri 132cl, 093tr, MODIS Ocean Group, NASA GSFC, and the University of Miami 105bl, 149tr, 149cl, 149bl, 150br, 154, 158tr, 162, 164tr, 165cl, 172, Esa, hfi & lfi consortia 2010 180cl; **NOAA:** 166bl; **Minden Pictures:** Flip Nicklin 055tl, **Pearson Education Ltd:** Jon Barlow 007tr, Jules Selmes 007tr, Trevor Clifford 008bl/B, Martyn F Chillmaid 021br,022tl,022bl,023r,025tr,028tl,028tr ,072tc,088bl,088br,093br,106bl,109bl,109bl, Trevor Clifford 030, 031t, 031c,040b, Gareth Boden 031t, Jules Selmes 046t, 072tr, 072c, 072c, 072cl, 072cl, 085cl, 159, Jim Reed/Robert Harding World Imagery/Digital Vision 16; **Penny Johnson:** 077bl, 077br; **Reuters:** VLtdent West 051b, Brendan McDermid 082tl, Will Burgess WB086tr, Edgar Su 100br; **Rex Features:** Photofusion 038b; **Science Photo Library:** British Antarctic Survey 069cl, Michael Pitts/Nature Picture Library 076tr, Claus Lunau 076br, Andrew Lambert Photography 078br, Loren Winters/Visuals Unlimited 095bl, David R. Frazier 105br, Pascal Goetgheluck 106br, Martyn F. Chillmaid 110br, Ted Kisman 153cr; **Shutterstock:** StanislavBeloglazov 004b, Pablo77 004t, Antonio Guillem 007tr, Nuttapong 008tl/A, Galayko Sergey 008tc/A, Valentyn Volkov 008tr/A, Redko Evgeniya 008bc/A, Arthid Whungupdolloh 011tr, Pablo77 012tr, StanislavBeloglazov 013l, Raulbaenacasado 016bl, VH-studio 019tl/C, Patryk Kosmider 019br/C, Wavebreakmedia 020tl, Jacob Lund 020b, Pikselstock 020cl, Guillermo Pis Gonzalez 023l, Sonpichit Salangsing 025br, Srisakorn wonglakorn 034b, Jason Salmon 036bl, Greg Epperson 038l, 037t, Maxim Petrichuk 043t, Abdul Razak Latif 043l, Action Sports Photography 043b, Grogl 044t, Victor Maschek 044bl, Ventura 048r, LeoBrogioni 049, Mohamad Zaidi Photography 050t, Quang nguyen vinh 050c, 051t, Nata Kotliar 051c, Evgeniya Uvarova 053b, Sergey Uryadnikov 053tr, Tanya Puntti 055b, Tom Reichner 055tr, Praisaeng 062b, Solent News 063, Kiev.Victor 064c, EQRoy 065, Koolyphoto 067c, Keystone/Zuma/ REX 069tr, Dora Zett 071l, Natursports 071bl, Gary yim 075r, Hank Shiffman 079tr, Everett Historical 079bl, Andrea Danti 080bl, Gaie Uchel 081bl, Leonard Zhukovsky 084br, Albert Barr 130bl, Tobkatrina 130br, Vector FX 130tr, Gleb Moiseev 131tr, Stephen Girimont 132tr, MarcelClemens 085cr, Happystock 085tr, Patrick Foto 088t, Pisaphotography 090, Abc7 092, Loskutnikov 094, Image Point Fr 095br, Dragon Images 096tr, Arztsamui 096cl, Dezay 097, Olga Kot Photo 098tr, Mopic 098bc, Corepics VOF 098br, Alexandru Axon 100tl, Ekkapan Poddamrong8 100cl, Jose Ignacio Soto 103bl, Yiargo 102bl, Sydeen 104bl, Evgeniya Uvarova 105cl, Ushi 106tr, Makuromi 108tr, ThomasLenne 111tr, Esbobeldijk 114, Bill Cross/ Associated Newspapers 133, Everett Historical 134tr, Alexander Tihonov 134l, Ingo Wagner/EPA 139r, Cyo bo 140, Syaheir Azizan 142, Serpeblu 143, Xristoforov 144bl, Cp dc Press 146b, Algol 152, Syda Productions 156br, Minerva Studio 165br, Thitinun Lerdkijsakul 166tr, Swa182 168cr, Christian Delbert 168tr, Olga Rutko 170, OneLtdhpunch 171br, Markus Mainka 171tr, EpicStockMedia 177cr, Mikhail Leonov 178bl, Amirraizat 178tr, Cigdem 180tr, Paul Cooper 182cl, Digital Storm 183bl; Pearson Education: 041tr; **USGS:** 177bl.